Riding the Subway with Heidi:

A Father's Journey of Grieving

Charles Schmidtke

© 2012 Charles Schmidtke
All Rights Reserved.

No part of this publication may be reproduced, stored in a retrieval system, or transmitted, in any form or by any means, electronic, mechanical, photocopying, recording, or otherwise, without the written permission of the author.

First published by Dog Ear Publishing
4010 W. 86th Street, Ste H
Indianapolis, IN 46268
www.dogearpublishing.net

ISBN: 978-1-4575-1622-1

This book is printed on acid-free paper.

Printed in the United States of America

Dedication

To Diane: my love, my soul mate, my critic, my joy - the woman who has given my life meaning, depth and purpose.

To the other women who have inspired me more than they will ever know:

Tara: whose word crafting has brought life to the pages of this journey.

Kristen: whose smile, energy and long talks breathe life into my ideas and heart.

Katie:: whose spirit continues to amuse me and whose style reorders my way of looking at life.

Heidi: whose journey has become the most unwanted gift and blessing I have ever received.

To these mothers and to our rosebud: please know that you have made love in my life much more than a word, an ideal, or even a dream.

Table of Contents

Prologue: August 18, 2000. The Beginning vii
    Setting the Stage x

I.   February 7, 2003. The Final Visit......................1
    Grieving Is Individualistic...7

II.   August 23, 2000. The Diagnosis 11
    Riding the Subway 15

III.   April 5, 2001. First Transplant 21
    The Gift 26

IV.   March 2 and 3, 2001. Mister Hyde's Visit 34
    Context Spheres 39

V.   October 30, 2001. Relapse................................48
    American Values 50

VI.   May 2, 2002. Second Transplant 60
    A Prism and a Rainbow 66

VII.   Heidi's Childhood: Vacation Experiences 73
    Thoughts that Matter 79

VIII.   July 19, 2002. The Moon Party 91
    Coping with Temporal Flow.......................................94

IX.   December 23, 2002. The Enigma Is a Paradox............105
    The Social Dimension of Faith 109

X.   February 6, 2003. Her Reflection 117
    Touching Consciousness..120

XI.	February 10, 2003. Transforming	129
	Death's Singularity	133
XII.	February 15, 2003. Saying Good Night	138
	Attitude's Power	143
XIII.	January, 1989. The Show Must Go On	161
	Signs	162
XIV.	February 6, 2004. Celebrating Her Life	185
	So You Have Cancer	188

Prologue

AUGUST 18, 2000.

The Beginning

On a warm Friday night in mid-August, I sat with Heidi, my 18-year-old daughter, in the emergency room waiting area of our small, local hospital. Although it was hot outside, the air conditioning blew relentlessly inside and Heidi shivered. She was always cold, it seemed, especially that summer.

Earlier that day, Heidi had returned from her summer job hostessing at a pancake house and collapsed on her bed. "What's the matter, Sweetie?" Diane, my wife, asked.

"My back really hurts," she cried, tears dotting her face.

"It's probably because you're not used to standing and walking for long periods of time," I said. "It'll get better with some rest." Since I had dealt with lower back pain in the past, I thought I knew what she was experiencing.

"No, Dad," she said. "This is different. It <u>really</u> hurts."

Since Heidi was not one to complain about her job and what it required her to do, we decided a trip to the ER was in order. As always my attitude was: here is another problem that we shall readily resolve. She didn't walk in the contorted position that I do when the spasms pay me a visit; and it didn't register at the time that her pain was from a world we'd never expect.

As Heidi filled out the paperwork, I found myself staring at her delicate hands, with the long fingers that exuded gentleness. Hands were important to her; as a burgeoning actress whose goal was to return dignity to the theater, Heidi felt that a person's hands were an important tool to provide insight into her character. When I ventured into Community

Theater productions, she taught me how to use my hands effectively. "They provide a wonderful focus," she said, "as long as the gestures or actions are not faked or forced." Heidi herself had a conscious habit of raising her hand with a twisting flourish that always demanded attention. When I portrayed C. S. Lewis in "Shadowlands," I used Heidi's advice, and my hands became nervous beacons of ineptitude when facing both the prospects of falling in love and confronting the cancer that befell the woman who had stolen my character's heart.

It was not just her hands that Heidi focused upon; she had also carefully developed her posture, gait, and deportment. Her voice was trained, though not affected or unnatural. Her expressions were practiced to achieve an effect. She used her entire face to convey what she was thinking, feeling, or imagining. In fact, everything that Heidi was and trained herself to do was with one dream in mind: to act ... and to restore Audrey Hepburn's class to the stage. Heidi carried her slender frame with a grace and elegance that she had cultivated throughout the years. Her gait was always natural, but slow and sometimes measured. It seemed almost impossible to get her to move quickly. "Look at me," her bearing seemed to shout. "Stop. Slow down. Savor each moment. Life is precious."

Only her eyes gave Heidi away. Those blue arrows spoke so much, or so little, depending on the situation and context. Her eyes could easily dance or darken into steel. As guarded as her temper often was, her eyes spoke the truth. They could readily open to others or close for privacy; they could praise, and they could rip through any plastic way of speaking or acting. For those who knew her well, a glance into her eyes would reveal the thoughts within. All of her discipline and practice regarding her other assets never were quite enough to control her eyes (and, then, again, maybe that was exactly her intent).

Heidi was our youngest of four daughters. Her three sisters, Tara, Kristen, and Katie, were between seven and ten years older than she, which caused Heidi to complain that she had four mothers instead of three sisters. She took not-so-secret delight in the fact that she grew to be several inches taller than any of them. Her blonde short hair accented her cheekbones and gave her a maturity beyond her years. To look at her sleek body and long legs, you might think she could glide on any track. However, part of the enigma that was Heidi was her lack of athletic prowess, despite her knowledge and exposure to sports. She had returned from her first year of college even thinner than usual with tired eyes and a sharp tongue. I remember dancing with her at Katie's wedding, just a few months before this visit to the emergency room. Her body felt frail, but her will was so strong, I never thought of her as fragile.

After the paperwork was complete, Heidi and I eavesdropped on the other waiting patients. There was a man sitting next to us holding his towel-wrapped hand in the air. The woman with him kept sighing as they discussed whose fault this work-related cut was.

After a while, Heidi suddenly turned to me. "We might as well talk," she said. I laughed, and we started discussing her desire to drop out of college and pursue pure theater – not the academic variety. "C.W. Post is just not the place for me," she said. She paused. "I don't know if any college is."

"I know. Mom and I don't want you to be unhappy, and we certainly don't want to crush your dreams. My concern is do you really want to spend so many years as a waitress?" We both smiled as she shook her head at my pat answer. I really didn't know how she would make enough money to afford her dreams.

"Look, all my sisters went to college. Yes, I know a college degree is important if acting doesn't work out. But, Dad," her voice softened (in the practiced tone all of my daughters had learned to use on me) until it was almost pleading, "what if acting **does** work out? Acting is all I've ever wanted to do. You know that. And CW Post is not for me at all. In fact, it's holding me back." She took a deep breath. "I've thought a lot about this and I **am** planning on going back this fall to be in "Rocky Horror", but after December I want to move on."

She sat back in the hard green chair and stared at me, clearly waiting for my response.

"Okay," I said, after a pause. "Are you still thinking about the program at North Carolina?."

"Actually, I just want to try auditioning in New York first – you know, really give it a go." She grimaced a bit and I couldn't tell whether it was her back or the strain of standing up for her own future that hurt.

"If that's want you want, we'll figure something out."

Surprised, Heidi smiled at me. "Thanks, Dad," she sighed.

Little did I realize just how irrelevant that discussion would become in the days, weeks and months ahead.

As to be expected, we waited for about an hour before being led into a small, curtained corner of the treatment area. A nurse came and asked a series of questions and said that the doctor would be available shortly.

When the doctor finally entered, he took one look at Heidi, sitting pale and somewhat gaunt on the table, and said, "Looks like you're anemic. Go to your primary care physician as soon as possible and get blood testing authorized." The irony was Heidi had just been to the primary care physician two weeks earlier and he had not mentioned her anemic look. In fact, he had told Heidi that she should watch what she ate and needed to exercise more. Diane and I had exchanged stunned looks when Heidi told us that's what he had said, especially since Heidi's thinness was approaching gauntness and she had been struggling with eating issues. "How arrogant," Diane had said. "He obviously knows nothing about Heidi or even female patients in general!"

Now, I could sense Heidi's relief that she was being taken seriously. She actually relaxed as I wheeled her to radiology to get x-rays. I remember thinking that pushing her in a wheelchair felt strange because she was so self-assured and cherished her independence. That night, though, she seemed to accept the attention she was getting. How little did we realize the extent that wheelchairs would play in our future? The emergency room doctor came in later and said that the x-rays were negative. We left the hospital feeling better but confused, never imagining that the blood tests that were taken on the following Monday would change all of our lives forever.

Setting the Stage

I now see that evening as just one memory in a mosaic of my life. This book is about Heidi's journey through illness and death and my journey of grieving, which includes what I've learned along the way. It is a composite of my reflections, observations, feelings, discussions and experiences. I also am giving voice to my daughter's life and what her legacy means to her family, friends, and to me. Grieving, I believe, necessitates that we tell the story about our loved one to any and all who are willing to listen. Writing has always been an outlet for me to express myself; thus, I am trying to capture a few of my memories and some of my feelings and reflections about Heidi's life and what it has meant and continues to mean. Although the primary focus is my personal grieving journey with Heidi, I hope that my reflections go beyond just my own feelings and experience. Although each person grieves in a very individualistic way, there are shared human feelings, values, and attitudes that relate to any grief experience. I hope that my reflections touch any one of you who is dealing with any type of grief in your life. Also, I hope Heidi's life story proves as inspiring to you as it has to those who knew her and saw her courage and heroism.

My journey of grieving is an on-going conflict between the emotional impact of my daughter's death and my intellectual struggles to make sense out of her illness and dying. This book is my attempt to reconcile the spiritual dynamics of these experiences and my intellectual understanding of the issues involved. In a sense it is an attempt to find the meaning and harmony between what I am feeling and how I reflect upon those emotions. Finding meaningfulness within the fabric of pain and suffering makes more sense to me than trying to return to some type of normalcy that may have existed before we began to deal with my daughter's illness. Instead of trying to move on or find closure in my grief, I am trying to find meaning, harmony, and a healthy attitude to grieving and living. Meaning is both personal and shared. We are unique, and, thus, we have a personal meaning in life that is dynamic and ever-changing. We are also social and heavily influenced by the cultural and other social forces in our lives. Dealing with the ever-changing nature of our meaning in life can be a real challenge as we try to balance all these dimensions, forces, and influences we experience. In a sense we may want time to stop for a while, and sometimes we may really want a break from the demands of adjusting and redefining who we are and who we may "be-coming".

Health is far more than just absence of illness. In fact, health is far more than just physical well-being; it is personal well-being. The health I am trying to achieve in my grieving is a balance of the mind, the heart, the soul, and the body. I am not looking at a particular state of "being" because I do not see grieving as arriving at some end-point or state of completion. Grieving remains an on-going part of who I am. In this regard I do not accept the mantra of so many therapists who seem to follow Freud's notion that grieving people should "move on."

Structuring grief into phases or stages and trying to move patients to some end state may be a way to claim some type of "cure rate," but that approach misses the reality of grief's ebbs and flows. I see grieving as an on-going process of growing, becoming healthy, and continually developing who I am.

Although this book is primarily about Heidi, the reality is that it is a journey about our entire, immediate family. My journey of grieving is inextricably interwoven into the on-going fabric of all of them. Heidi's journey through her illness and death has become an integral part of each one of our lives. I do not presume to speak for them or for their feelings and reflections, but I must include how I perceive their presence in my journey. They have taught me how to live, feel, and grow as a person.

Heidi was our youngest daughter, born on Oct. 3, 1981. She was diagnosed with Acute Lymphoblastic Leukemia on Aug. 23, 2000. She underwent many treatments (chemotherapy and radiation) leading to a bone marrow transplant in 2001. She relapsed within five months of the transplant and went through a second round of treatments leading to a stem cell transplant. After that transplant, she encountered a wide variety of problems that ultimately led to her death on Feb. 10, 2003.

My wife, Diane, and I were married on August 24, 1968 after having met at a wedding the previous November. We started dating in December; I asked her to marry me at the end of January; and on Valentine's Day she accepted. For practical reasons we waited until August to be married. (Thankfully none of our daughters were as brash and foolish as we were!) We had just completed our undergraduate studies in Buffalo, New York, and I was going to attend graduate school at Tulane University in New Orleans.

Our oldest daughter, Tara, was born in 1971 while I was still in graduate school and my wife was a primary school teacher. Tara married Joe Reyda in 1997. They were high school English teachers in Mayville, New York, during Heidi's illness. Tara was Heidi's second donor for her stem cell transplant in May 2002.

Kristen was our middle child of the three oldest. She was born two years after Tara and was married to Bill Barry in 1999. They moved to Rochester, Minnesota, after Heidi's first transplant. Kristen was Heidi's first donor when Heidi had the experimental bone marrow transplant in April 2001. Both Tara and Kristen were perfect matches for Heidi.

Heidi's third sister, Katie, was one year younger than Kristen ; she married Anthony Marino in 2000. Katie was an oncology nurse at Memorial Sloan Kettering throughout Heidi's illness and was the family's medical expert and advisor. Katie and Anthony live in Ho-Ho-Kus, New Jersey.

I was an Associate Professor at a Jesuit college in Western New York. I served in various administrative positions for 18 years and was a full-time faculty member for 17 years. My position was unique because I taught in a wide variety of disciplines (Anthropology, Communication Studies, English, Gerontology, Psychology, Philosophy, Sociology and Women's Studies). My PhD is in Philosophy, but my teaching and research is thoroughly interdisciplinary. In the spring semester of 2006, I was on sabbatical and had outlined four projects that I really wanted to address. They had been delayed by the events of the previous six years. As I started my sabbatical, I could muster no motivation to begin any of the projects that I had said were important to me. Inside, I felt very strongly that now was the time to listen to my heart and share the lessons I had been learning. Now was the time to write about grieving; the projects could wait. Once started, I knew I was doing something that was important for my healing process. I have an overwhelming need to share Heidi's story and what I have learned from her and the rest of my family. Maybe I am just subconsciously addressing my feelings of helplessness. Getting this material published is not my primary goal. I have learned that the journey is far more important than any end-product. However, giving voice to the pain of a father's grief is something I believe is very important to share. So whether Heidi is pushing or inspiring me or whether my intuitive self has sensed that for whatever reason this is the right time, I decided to scrap all the other projects and focus on giving voice to my ride with Heidi on the subway. In June 2008 I retired and am now a Professor Emeritus.

I.

FEBRUARY 7, 2003.

The Final Visit

The Bone Marrow Transplant unit at Roswell Park Cancer Institute (Buffalo, New York) is situated on the fifth floor. On our final, although we did not know it at the time, visit, Heidi quietly allowed me to push her wheelchair to the unit. We had her portable oxygen tank along, since she needed it almost continually now. Her graft vs. host disease (GVHD) was becoming critical. GVHD is a condition that occurs after a bone marrow or stem cell transplant when the patient's immune system rejects her own organs or parts of the body. Heidi had to have two transplants, one an experimental bone marrow transplant, the other a stem cell transplant. For each one she had to go through a series of chemotherapy and radiation treatments that were designed to "kill" the leukemia, put her into remission, and eliminate her own immune system. The donor's stem cells or bone marrow became the source for a new immune system for her. Generally speaking, a patient's new immune system may start rejecting organs or parts of the patient's own body because it is reacting to "foreign material." After her first transplant, the Roswell team controlled the GVHD and Heidi seemed to be a wonderful success story. After her second transplant, the team had to allow some GVHD activity to occur in order to destroy her very virulent strain of leukemia. The graft vs. host started with her eyes, which stopped tearing; then, the skin on her fingers became very sensitive. She had joint pain on and off throughout her entire struggle, but now her joints were very painful, and slowly she lost her ability to walk with the grace and deportment she had so carefully developed. By October her lungs became affected, and we had to provide oxygen for her. Graft vs. host becomes a terminal condition when it attacks the respiratory system.

The previous Friday, January 31, Heidi and I had been to Roswell for a number of reasons. She was experiencing considerable chest pain. They needed to draw blood from her that day. Drawing blood is usually a routine procedure for most patients, but, for Heidi, it was becoming increasingly problematic because her small veins were starting to collapse. After the painful draw, Heidi was sent for another EKG. The results showed that she had irregularities in the blood flow pattern as compared with tests taken the previous November. Her physician was worried, yet hopeful that these irregularities were the source of her GVHD problem. He knew that he and others could treat a heart condition. Heidi's nurse practitioner, Pam, came into the room to talk to us about having a PIC line or some other access means installed since Heidi's veins were so compromised. "We could try it on your hand, although the neck would be the most effective," she said.

"Heidi had one in her neck the first time she was admitted," I nervously commented.

"I really don't think I can handle one in my neck right now." Heidi said, a slight bit of trepidation creeping into her voice. "Do we really have to have one?" Tears welled in her eyes.

"Well, the decision is yours. We just thought the PIC would be the best solution now," said Pam, gently patting Heidi's knee. Heidi bent her head and started crying softly. Pam left the room to give her some time to decide. When she left Heidi cried even harder. I knew this decision was difficult for many reasons. It was an obvious signal that she was regressing and not improving. Also, the consultations with Memorial Sloan Kettering and Johns Hopkins were not fruitful. Finally, the pain of putting in a line had always been intense for her.

Again, I was feeling helpless, but leaned forward in my chair and touched Heidi's hand. "I know this isn't what you wanted to hear, but isn't it better than going through the poking in phlebotomy? I know Leon is great, but he's not always there." Heidi's tears were starting to slow, so I quietly sat back in my chair and stared blankly into space. She needed my presence, not my advice.

A couple of minutes later, she calmly raised her head. "I'm getting tired," she finally said. She swallowed and I could actually see the lump in her throat. "I'm not going to have a neck IV. I wish they would just put in a port. The pic line is a real pain." We sat in silence for awhile.

When her tears had dried and her face lost the panicked look, I told her I had to go to the bathroom, which was a common enough occurrence. My real intent was to talk to Pam and her nurse.

I saw them at the nurses' station. They were talking quietly and reviewing someone's file, but looked up with caring eyes as I approached.

"Pam, I think you need to know a couple of things," I said deliberately keeping my voice matter of fact, my eyes dry. "Heidi is quite fragile right now. She's 'tired' and afraid of going through these procedures again. Her long-term boyfriend left for Kuwait today. She's becoming overwhelmed and is really struggling to be the 'perfect patient.'" *I paused. Pam and the nurse nodded reassuringly. They understood.*

I continued, "She does not want anyone here to see her 'sick' or selfish or depressed. She wants you to only see her with a smile. To see the obedient patient who does whatever she is asked to do. This may surprise you, but she's concerned that the staff might 'yell' at her because she was doing something wrong."

Pam and the nurse shook their heads and smiled as if to say, "of course that's what Heidi would think - our dear, sweet girl." *When Pam returned to the room, she took Heidi's hand.* "Listen, Heidi, if anyone, and I mean anyone, yells at you for any reason, I'm going to slap that person silly. You are the hero here. Our job is to take care of you – you don't have to worry about us." *The smile on Heidi's face was priceless.*

Later, a cardiologist came in to check on her condition. He was kind and gentle with her (even though he had been quite arrogant on previous occasions). He told her that she had not had a heart attack and did not have heart disease. I thought how strange it is to hear this news and be terribly disappointed. The irregularity was caused by the chamber of the heart that leads to the lungs. It was working extra hard and had become thicker and more muscular than the other chamber.

Dr. Wetzler, her attending physician throughout her struggles, then came in and told Heidi that there was an experimental regimen that had been used at Johns Hopkins for kidney transplant patients. "As strange as it may seem," *he said,* "it might be helpful. You need to know that the drug is very dangerous and we'll have to monitor your condition carefully," *Dr. Wetzler glanced my way, but quickly turned his gentle eyes on Heidi.* "We can administer the drug today."

Heidi's eyebrows shot up. "Today?" *The relief that there was something to be done echoed in that simple word.*

Dr. Wetzler nodded. "You'll have to come back on Monday so we can monitor the progress and you'll have to also return next Friday so we can test the results." *Heidi and I were at Roswell for over six hours that day. Most of the time, we played games: card games, Yahtzee, an occasional crossword puzzle. For 2 ½ years we had been holding competitions, keeping records, and crowning* "Castle" *champions periodically. I still have many of the sheets we used to keep score. Sometimes being close to someone does not require words and does not involve profound experiences. Simple activities and quiet moments themselves can be meaningful and memorable.*

The following Monday, February 3, we were back to the hospital. Heidi had decided to bake cookies to take to her friends at the hospital (David, the Monday volunteer at the front door, the friendly and competent "vampires" in phlebotomy, and the nurses). Katie had made contact with the doctor at Memorial Sloan Kettering who had not been returning the calls to Pam. We all knew that Heidi was far too compromised to travel, but we were hoping that a second opinion would be helpful. It was not. All the doctor could say was that she agreed that the staff at Roswell was doing all that could be done. There really was nothing else to do. It was on that Monday that Heidi stopped being able to lift herself up from the toilet seat. Pam ordered the portable potty and my lifting her became another routine part of her life.

So it was on Friday, February 7th that Heidi and I were heading to Roswell yet again. She sat beside me in the car, oxygen canula in her nose, eyes fixed straight ahead. "Hey, Heid, look, the Mega jackpot is now at $28 mil – do we need the money or should we let someone else have it?" She smiled as we carried on some of our usual banter to the hospital.

"It's amazing how every time we go to Roswell, something unexpected happens. Who would have predicted last Friday, for example," I remarked.

"That's what makes life so interesting, isn't it? It's fun to enjoy those unexpected blessings," Heidi replied.

How little did we realize how prescient that conversation was? We thought we were going to the unit to get the results of the tests from the previous week and to attend to the bed sore that had been developing. Pam saw me in the hallway and said that Dr. Wetzler wanted to see me privately. My stomach clenched – he never had met with me alone before. "Something's wrong," I thought, but I willed the positive. I would not let the reality of what was going to emerge come into consciousness. Although in the recesses of my mind I knew that respiratory GVHD was fatal, we had spent 2½ years living positively. We approached life with Heidi's will and determination serving as our guide. She and Diane looked for the blessings in each day. We had organized two prayer vigils and had remained faithful and active in our church. Heidi never spent a night alone at the hospital and we had learned how to change her dressings, set up IVs, administer a wide variety of shots and had an oncology nurse only a phone call away, when Katie wasn't visiting and helping us directly. The entire family had done everything "correctly". And still ... I couldn't finish the thought.

One of Heidi's favorite nurses was working that day, and she and I devised a plan for me to meet with Dr. Wetzler without Heidi knowing that something unusual was happening. When he was available, Bobbie, the nurse, came into our room and said, "I need to talk to Heidi, why don't you wait outside?" When I entered Pam's room, my heart sank. Pam and Dr. Wetzler were glum, and the sadness they felt pervaded the room. Pam was quiet and leaning forward in her swivel chair, while Dr. Wetzler sat with his head slightly bowed, hands folded in his lap. He almost looked small in that little round chair. When I entered he slowly raised his head and looked at me with strangely blank eyes. I inched to the cushioned chair that was strategically placed for this terrible moment. I touched it before sitting, just to make sure I didn't fall and shatter a silence that needed to be kept dangling. He knew me well – how I had read all the material he had provided and had researched Heidi's illness from other resources also – how I had kept daily journals and tracked each of the treatments – how I always had questions and would ask them if Heidi hadn't already done so. In that context he started with a brief description of how the tests from the previous week had come back with negative results.

"Could it just be too early to tell?" I asked, grasping onto any hope.

He shook his head. "No," he said. "There should have been immediate, positive effects. We should have seen some signs of improvement by Monday. The best we can do now is treat the symptoms for a **very brief** period of time." He paused a moment and looked down at his hands. His emphasis on "very brief" struck me with a jolting force. His eyes came back to mine with an empathy and sadness. He quietly dropped the bomb: "It's time to call her sisters home. Is Diane available to come to the hospital today?"

The end was near and all of our hopes and dreams for Heidi came crashing down on me. We agreed that I would call Diane, then her sisters. He wanted to know the status of Heidi's DNR and health care proxy, and he wanted to tell Heidi and Diane what he had just told me. When I called Diane, I gave her some lame excuse about bringing a lunch up for Heidi. I did not want to tell her what was happening over the phone. It was clear that I wasn't very convincing that that was the real purpose of my call, but Diane didn't push the matter – mothers just know things, don't they? I also met with the friendly social worker who had been liaison for us on a number of occasions. She was handling the paperwork for Heidi. "Charlie, we're all so sad – the whole staff has been grieving since Monday when Pam informed us of her condition," she gently said.

The walls of the family rest room seemed to shrink and the desk just melted away – somehow the world was becoming just a little bit smaller.

When Diane arrived, I pretended that the lunch was really important. Later that afternoon Dr. Wetzler walked into the room. Heidi was in a wheelchair while Diane and I were sitting on chairs at different angles to her. She had been in the bed but when she had gone to the bathroom, I suggested she sit in the wheelchair rather than go back to bed. She thought that was a good idea. As he walked in he grabbed the other available chair and slipped it into position to face Heidi directly. He looked directly into her eyes and calmly said, "We need to discuss your condition." He hesitated. I can only imagine the difficulty he had getting the next words out. "The treatments aren't working. Your condition will not improve. You need to make sure that your advanced directive expresses exactly what you want." He could not bring himself to utter what was obvious to him.

Diane and Heidi were a bit startled. Heidi's eyes widened and she looked at each one of us in rapid succession. Diane closed her eyes as if she had been punched in the solar plexus.

"What does this mean?" Heidi asked.

Dr. Wetzler did not answer her directly; rather he explained that if she wanted to be resuscitated, "we would induce a coma and it is highly unlikely that you would ever regain consciousness." No one could utter the dreaded words of death or dying – their inevitability was now near. None of us wanted to give them any opportunity to become real. Was it denial? Maybe. Was it a conscious decision to avoid those words? Not really. For 2 ½ years we did not allow their possibility to shape the contour of our journey; we may all have considered them from time to time, but we weren't going to let them take root and color our thoughts or actions.

Heidi's heavy eyes sought ours. "What do you think I should do?" she whispered.

"Whatever you want, Heid," I said immediately.

Diane tried to smile reassuringly, but it looked painful. "Don't think about us," she said. "Do whatever you want for yourself."

Dr. Wetzler then said there was one other experimental drug they could give her, but she would have to come back the following Monday as a part of the treatment.

"Okay," Heidi said. "I want to continue to fight."

The nurses hung the medication that would prove to be useless. It was the last treatment she ever received from anyone at Roswell.

Grieving Is Individualistic

Images from those final days are emblazoned in my consciousness, even though I walked through that time in a fog and in a daze. I did go to the nearby shopping mall to purchase charms (the Daoist symbol of Yin Yang) for all of my girls for Valentine's Day. I wanted to make sure that Heidi received my present. Ever since they were children, I would take my daughters out on "dates", and every Valentine's Day I would buy them a gift and make a card – usually writing something that reflected my sense of who they were and how important they were to me. My initial reaction to the impending tragedy was to "DO" something – to cling on to the world I had cherished and loved. I keep Heidi's charm in my pocket today as a physical presence that I can still touch and see. Sometimes I catch myself playing with it the way some men play with the change in their pockets.

As the days and months after Heidi's death continued to roll, I became aware that each person who was close to Heidi had been grieving in different ways. Each person's death is a singular event, and each person's grieving is an individualistic process. One of the many blessings our family has discovered during our journey is that we respect the different paths that each one of us takes. We also revel in those moments when our paths converge and we can share tears and laughter together. By the time we had placed Heidi's body into the grave, the center of my life had changed forever; at the center of my very being was a sphere of grieving that had become the core of my existence.

It is impossible to describe this sphere or core of grieving. As with so many important elements in life, the reality transcends any attempt to verbalize its breadth and depth. At times the sphere feels like a bottomless pit that consumes everything I say or do. My mind and heart can spin and swirl with the slightest provocation: a picture – a song – a playbill – a word – a smell – a penny. At first I thought my grief was a black hole that would suck all life and enjoyment into its fearsome grasp. But Heidi's spirit – her smile – her legacy - prevented this cosmic feeling from overpowering me. I don't want to release the grieving because I don't want to relinquish my connection with Heidi. This connection is now one of pain. There is an unreal feeling about her death, but the immense sense of this pain prevents me from deluding myself for too long; she won't be walking in our front door ever again.

The absolute character of death sustains the core of grieving. Grieving is a very individualistic process because the context and meaning of our pain is so unique; however, there are dimensions and feelings of that grief that we can share with others. One of the tragic elements in American culture is the idea that grief needs to be placed within a compartment or timeframe. "It is OK to go through the stages of grief, but once those stages have been completed, it's time for us to move on." This compartmentalization of grief is destructive and unhealthy. For those who want to "move on" and get back to normal living, they have missed the immensity of pain that attends to anyone's death. In addition, those who respond to grief by keeping it locked inside as if it is in some protective vault are missing the "gift" that grieving is giving to us. Getting rid of the grieving process or being incapable of wrestling free from the clutches of grief's despair are both unhealthy attitudes towards death and grieving.

The sphere of grieving is not the only one that now exists for me. I also have a performance sphere and a functional sphere. These areas are my presentation of myself to the world. In the days and months after Heidi died, I found myself often dancing in the performance sphere. Although it is tethered to my sphere of grieving, I have been able to console others in their grief for Heidi or in their grief for their own loved ones. I was able to teach (beginning four days after she was buried), serve as liturgical and preaching deacon, and even preside at a church-member's funeral. To the world I may have appeared strong and blessed by God. Inside I felt that grace was working through me, and Heidi's strength fortified me. I could venture into the performance sphere and play the roles that were expected of me. It still feels as if I am two separate people: the one who yearns to live in grief and strives to keep Heidi's legacy alive; and the other, a type of entertainer, who meets the needs of situations that call for "performances." Smile – the show must go on – this was Heidi's theme that we recognized even when she was a young girl.

There is also another sphere: a functional one. This level interpenetrates with my core of grieving and, sometimes, tiptoes into the performance sphere. At the functional level I have an incessant need to do projects, accomplish tasks, and fully engage in a wide range of activities (including addressing my "bucket list" in retirement). I can point to a long list of "things" that are done and a competent demeanor in my professional and social life. Those who know me can see Heidi's handiwork etching itself in all that I do. Maybe this is my way of overcoming the feelings of helplessness and the frustration that comes to a father who cannot protect his child and make life "right." These functional and/or performance spheres are necessary as we continue to engage in life. There are a number of mistakes that others may make when they see me "getting back to normal." I've talked to other grieving parents and they all concur. Yes, we can continue to function. We return to our jobs – we attend social functions – we "celebrate" holidays – eventually we even may go to parties, etc. But in all situations we are now different. Life has changed so dramatically for us that the motivations and meaning of all of our experiences have a different hue and flavor to them. Others may not notice this change. After 9/11 America decided to go back to business as usual because it did not have the patience or the insight to see that the center of our lives should have shifted. Americans accept the fact that life is constantly changing. However, they want to control the change and keep it within the compartments of their own world that tend to avoid pain and remain on the "surface" of life.

Another important sphere that remains in my life relates to my roles as husband, father, and grandfather. At times I feel so diminished in these roles as the other spheres exert their time and control upon my consciousness. But my love for my wife has always been the foundation for my life and for our family. My best gift to my daughters has been my love for Diane. A genuine tragedy after Heidi's death would have been for our bond of love to dissipate or dissolve. This sphere is coated with a sense of pain but also contains the faith and hope that makes life meaningful. My daughters and their families provide me with a renewed sense of purpose and belonging without which life would be bleak and oppressive. Although the journey of grieving is ultimately a solitary trek, the respite of love that I find with them makes life appear whole and purposeful. Surrounding and touching this sphere are so many friends whose care and support make it easier to face each sunrise. Recently, grandchildren have come into our lives. They have changed the contours of our world in magnificent ways.

My daughter Kristen expressed her feelings about these spheres in the following way: "I too find myself operating on all different spheres, but I panic when I remain in one too long. What if I become too functional, or too good at performing and therefore estranged from my inner grief, or too consumed with grief that I lose the ability to tap into the other spheres? And you're right - at the base, or core, of all the spheres is overwhelming and incomprehensible pain. Do you believe that there will ever be a time when all the spheres and core will intermingle peacefully, or will they forever remain a cacophony of broken chords, incapable of producing a harmony?"

As strange as it may sound, grieving is ultimately a gift. Authentic grieving requires that we strive for a healthy, meaningful life that does not surrender the core of grieving and does not ignore the reality of the pain that grieving encompasses. For me the challenge in grieving is to find balance in my life. It is okay to feel the pain; in fact, it is essential in grieving to work on and "go to the pain" at times. The truth of the matter is that the pain will come to us whether we are looking for it or not. Being able to live in that pain is important – learning how to adjust myself to those moments of pain are essential for health. On the other hand, it is important to avoid the pitfalls of turning the experiences of pain into torture. The limits and experiences of pain and torture vary from individual to individual. Some people need to go to the cemetery daily; others cannot. When do we clean out a room or go through a loved one's clothes or get rid of some possessions? The answers are as varied as there are people who grieve. Anyone who attempts to set a timeframe or norm for such behaviors and actions on someone else is acting cruelly and is misunderstanding what the grieving parent really needs. If people allow themselves to be driven by some schedule imposed by any force or person, they need to reconsider the reality and the dynamics of healthy grieving.

Each person needs to find balance in his life. This balance provides meaning and purpose for living. There is not, or should not be, a goal or end to authentic grieving. Those who espouse such a view are trapped in the American model that all life should be governed by goals and tasks that can be accomplished and evaluated. We become judged by what we do. We make our lists and like to add lines to our resumes. For the person who is grieving, such goals and activities become rather trivial. In fact, it is common for grieving parents to express the feeling of impatience with people who find the trivial things of life to be so important. Thus, the balance I'm trying to sustain in my life is not a goal or task; it is an attitude about life. This attitude seems to be at the heart of healthy grieving (and, quite possibly, at the heart of healthy living). We must learn to live with the loneliness that grief creates and try to convert it to a solitude that is character building, rather than personally destructive. Each of us will continue to cry, but we retain the capacity for laughter. We will feel alone, but our loved ones are still in touch in strange and miraculous ways – if we but stay open to their presence and signs.

II.

AUGUST 23, 2000.

The Diagnosis

*D*iane and I were waiting for our friends to go "Buffalo hunting." The four of us have done some rather unusual things over the years, but this day was actually going to be rather normal. Decorated buffaloes were located all around town. Many cities had adopted animals of some sort, and the bison was an obvious choice for Buffalo, New York. The project was sponsored by Roswell Park Cancer Institute. Little did we know that our connection with the hospital that day would be very different from our intentions that morning! We had a map with the locations and wanted to see the various designs and clever renditions that had been created. We were somewhat limited in what we could do because Diane had broken a bone in her foot a couple of weeks earlier and was rather immobile. She was using crutches and was becoming adept with them, but could not go long distances.

Looking back, this day was filled with what would become ironic moments - signs were everywhere. The previous night our dog, Vragil, had slept with Heidi. He had never done so before because he always slept on our bed. Shi Tzu's are a bit arrogant and tend to bond with the first one who holds them. Diane was the benefactor of Vragil's attentions when he was a puppy. Later on, he also became attached to me, but never to Heidi. In fact, he actively ignored Heidi, even refusing to sit on her lap, despite her repeated pleas, cajoles, and bribes over the years. But that night, he jumped off our bed while we were reading and ran downstairs. I thought he had to go outside again, and went down to help him out. Instead, he went to Heidi's bed and stood there. She too was reading. "Hey, Vrag, do you want to come up?" she asked. He looked back and forth between Heidi and me and gave a short bark, so I put him up on her bed. Heidi and I looked at each other quizzically, then shrugged our shoulders; she smiled. I figured he would be back up the stairs later, bothering me to pull him up on our bed, since he was no longer able to jump up. However, the next morning, as we came down for our intended safari, we found him curled up on Heidi's bed, contentedly snoring. "He spent the whole night here," Heidi said, delightedly, softly patting his head. "Maybe he does like me after all!"

Later that day, while we were getting ready to go around town, Diane shared a dream she had had the night before. "I was being stung by bees," she said. "It was so realistic." We learned the significance of this dream later that night. Another strange occurrence for us had happened two days earlier when I was grocery shopping with Diane – a very rare experience, since I avoid any type of shopping. While we were going to the checkout lane, I saw a stand of composite notebooks. I pointed and said that we needed one of those. Diane asked me why. My reply, "I don't know, but we have to buy it." Diane humored my impulse, so we bought it. That day we thought we were going to use it to record the buffalos; instead it became the first daily journal that we kept for Heidi – a journal that eventually expanded to two volumes.

As we waited for our friends to arrive, the phone rang. I have never liked the phone. From the late 1960s until 1973 when my father died, I had had terrible phone calls about his health. By the 1980s the calls were about my mother. Then on Christmas Eve 1986 we were at Diane's sisters for our usual Christmas Eve celebrations when we received the call that my mother had died (she was suffering from a rare form of Parkinson's). I had spent the afternoon with her and we were going to take our children to be with her on Christmas day. Not only did we never have that opportunity, but my mother's second husband had her immediately cremated so I never got to say good-bye. Thus, a ringing phone unsettles me. (Of course, having four teenage daughters did not endear me to the telephone either.)

This day the two calls we received were devastating. The first was from Heidi's doctor's office saying that they had to see Heidi immediately about the blood test results. Since she was 18, they would not tell us why she needed to come in. A little while later one of the nurses who was a friend of ours called and said, "Don't tell anyone I said anything because I could lose my job, but the tests indicate Heidi has leukemia. She has to get in here as soon as possible." Panic began to engulf us. Heidi had gone shopping at a mall with her boyfriend just a little while earlier. They had no cell phone; we weren't even sure which mall. Furthermore, we had told Heidi that we were going to be gone all afternoon. She did not have to work that evening, so she and her boyfriend were planning to have dinner together, and we had no idea where that might be. Our friends came; we told them the news; they stayed with us as we paced and fretted until Heidi called.

She didn't know why she called us. It was so out of the ordinary for her to do so, especially given the plans of the day. But she did.

"Hi. How's everything?" she asked. What do you say to such a question, knowing that the answer was going to change all of our lives forever? Diane just told Heidi that the doctor needed to see her right away and that we would meet her at the doctor's office. Strangely, she didn't ask any questions. (We've come to believe that she probably already knew what she was going to hear – not the particulars – just the challenge that she would now be facing.) We were taken into the doctor's office as soon as Heidi arrived. Another doctor in the practice came into the office and simply said that the blood tests indicated that Heidi may have leukemia and that a room had been reserved for her at Roswell; we should go there immediately. His cold and nervous demeanor didn't help our level of anxiety. Heidi quickly left the room and stood outside of the office complex crying. She didn't cry for long, and we didn't say very much. I remember giving her a gentle hug as a way of trying to reassure it. Besides, what was there to say?

The drive to the hospital was long (despite only taking 20 minutes), and sadly would become all too familiar. The admission process and the initial stages were a whirlwind of activity. Nurses and aides came in and out of the room. Heidi was questioned with us; and, for a short period we were asked to leave while they asked some personal questions. A very gentle, kind looking doctor came to the room and introduced himself. He said that he was going to perform a bone marrow biopsy in order to determine exactly what type of leukemia we were confronting. We began our learning curve about leukemia that night. We continued to learn far more than we ever wanted to know about the disease, the complications, the treatments, and so much more. The physician said that we could stay for the procedure and that he would have results back as soon as possible. When he started he told Heidi that the needle would sting like a bee. Diane's head jerked up. "My dream," she whispered. As the doctor began to "pound" on the needle, I became nauseous and feverish. How could her slender body take such a beating? I left the room without trying to be noticed. A resident came to check on me, and I realized how weak men can be at times. God was clever to give birthing solely to women; I'm not sure the species would have survived if men were responsible for delivering babies.

After the biopsy, the doctor implanted three lines in Heidi's neck. They needed ready access to draw blood on a daily basis and needed separate lines for administering drugs and chemo. Much of the rest of the evening was blurry and confusing. The one clear moment in my memory is listening later that night to the diagnosis: Acute Lymphoblastic Leukemia. It is usually found in children and has a very high success rate. Heidi, at age 18, almost 19, was not considered a child, so the treatments and success rates were different. Further complicating the treatments were her genetic markers.

Heidi amazed us all those first couple of days. During the summer she had become rather self-centered and annoying. There were times when her sisters wanted to pitch her out the window. But, from the moment of her diagnosis, Heidi's demeanor was incredibly remarkable. She said, "You know, I've never done anything to cause this illness. So, I'm going to do everything I'm supposed to do to beat this thing."

Her first stay in the hospital lasted over three weeks. She received chemotherapy and went into remission rather quickly. During her stay she had two rules for anyone who came to visit: absolutely no one could cry in her presence and everyone had to draw a picture to hang in her room. No one dared cry. The pictures slowly began to multiply as so many family, friends, and neighbors came to see her. The pictures became reflections of those who visited and helped Heidi to remain connected to those who loved her. Some of the drawings were simple, others complex; some were humorous; others were thought provoking.

Each of Heidi's sisters learned about the diagnosis in very different ways. Kristen lived close to us, and we left a cryptic message for her. When she called our house, we had already left for the doctor's office. When she could not get in touch with any one of us, she drove to the local hospital where Heidi and I had gone the previous Friday. When she could not find our car in the parking lot, she ended up calling the doctor's office. They told her that we had gone to Roswell, and she began to panic. The name Roswell means cancer. She was there from the very beginning.

Katie was working at Sloan Kettering on the day we heard the news, and we did not have a pager number for her. We called her apartment and Anthony answered. He wrote the word "Roswell" on a sheet of paper by the phone. When she arrived home and saw the name, her heart sank. We talked to her and she flew home the next morning.

Tara was vacationing in North Carolina and did not leave us with a phone number. We concocted a number of strategies to get in touch with her, and finally were able to get a number by the next morning (August 24). I called Tara from the airport just as we were picking up Katie. She was surprised and thought we were being sweet and calling her on her birthday. Needless to say her mood changed drastically when I explained the situation. She and her husband drove home immediately.

All of Heidi's sisters readily volunteered to be tested to see if she was a match for Heidi, in the event Heidi needed a transplant. Their commitment to her recovery was a tremendous source of strength for all of us. In essence they were all newlyweds, yet each one sacrificed a great deal in order to share each moment they could with her, and support us throughout the entire journey

Riding the Subway

After Heidi's death a number of people encouraged us to join a grief support group. We hesitated for a variety of reasons – all of which were excuses. We didn't have the energy to go into a group of strangers and share our inner pain. We felt that our family and friends had been so supportive throughout Heidi's illness and death that we would be able to heal and continue living without having to extend ourselves to a new group of people. As I reflect back upon those feelings, I can see a subtle form of denial and "male pathology" working. Male pathology refers to the unhealthy cultural and biological forces that prevent men from healing emotionally, sharing meaning with others, and restoring a genuine sense of harmony in their lives. Our testosterone and "macho" characteristics really do get in the way.

I have two brothers and no sisters, which led to a very male dominant household growing up. As my brothers and I grew older, we treated our mom as one of us, and she encouraged this type of behavior. Having four daughters was a genuine cultural adjustment for me. In a sense this book is a reflection of what all of the women of my life have taught me, not just what I've learned from Heidi. My family upbringing and American culture created mandates in my life. I was responsible for my family and was supposed to fix anything that was broken, solve any problem that arose, or answer any question that was asked. (Diane still rolls her eyes when she utters a rhetorical question and I unwittingly provide an unwanted answer.) While Americans tend to objectify and compartmentalize the world, American men try to handle emotional issues just like any other problem or broken object. Men become uncomfortable, even incompetent, when we find ourselves in helpless or vulnerable situations. Additionally, Americans tend to want to remain in control of themselves and of situations. We clearly realize that power and control define human relationships and inter-group dynamics. It would be a mistake to reject these forces and label them as "wrong." America culture is not a failure, nor should it be demonized; doing so is an over-reaction and too simplistic an attitude. The drive for controlling situations, for always having to be correct, for solving all problems, for ignoring any vulnerability and for showing no weakness, however, needs to find a countervailing force in each person's life. If we understand the forces and power of culture, then we have a better way to grieve in a more meaningful and healthy fashion. This understanding can help us find the balance in our lives that is so necessary for healing and personal fulfillment.

Feeling helpless is a painful experience for me; however, that helplessness does not strip me of my purpose in life. It does not diminish me as a person. In fact, like any adversity, it can become another piece in the strange puzzle of character building that is a life-long task for each one of us. Diane and I did begin attending a grief group at Roswell because the psychologists who were coordinating the sessions knew Heidi. They shared their feelings about her during the group sessions. Their testimony affirmed her place as well-known and well-loved at the institute. We were the only people in the group who were grieving the death of a child, and felt as if we were treated with special respect. There seemed to be an unspoken sentiment that the death of a child was particularly painful and unfair. Diane and I have now discovered that participating in groups who share the experience of the death of a child is crucial for our healing and personal growth. A colleague of mine at the college encouraged me to meet a friend of hers whose daughter was killed in a car accident just before Christmas in 2002. Diane encouraged me to meet him; she is insightful and completely cognizant of my male pathology. Jim and I met and he encouraged me to join with him in the grief support groups that have helped him so much. We did.

Most of the participants in the groups we now attend are women. I believe that is because as a whole, women are better "trained" for dealing with emotions and seeking personal health. Women tend to meet to "just talk" or share feelings or experiences more than men. My wife has a number of groups she consistently attends. Her friends from college are "club" and they have met monthly for over almost 40 years. One of them died of ovarian cancer when she was in her 30s. These women know how to care and support one another. Diane also has a group of neighborhood women who have shared each other's lives for over 35 years. It started with them sharing the raising of their children, progressed to "craft club," continued through "tea group," morphed into "book club" and is now known as "bookless" club.

I am quite different and believe that I am quite typical of males. Men tend to need a reason to get together. We need to have some activity that can be the focus for our attention. At a recent grief group meeting, a man said that he had been grieving "the wrong way" for nine years. He had tried to do it on his own and not show any sign that he needed others. He was coming to the group now realizing that he wanted to do "it right." I believe he meant that he wanted to find some healing in his life and wanted to work on the pain that was at the core of his life. He was finally admitting that men DO need help, care, and other people. I believe that the female ability to share their stories, emotions, and lives help them achieve a healthy balance between their heads and their hearts. This capacity certainly is a crucial factor in women living longer than men.

Diane and I attend three grief groups, all of which are interrelated. They are sponsored by the area's Children's Hospital. There is one group that meets once per month in the evening. This group is usually large: 15-35 people. Some are just beginning their journey, while others have been anywhere from one to fifteen years "out" from their child's death. The composition of the group changes monthly. A second group meets twice a month on a Tuesday morning. This group is smaller so the discussions are more intimate and generally tend to address spiritual experiences more fully than the larger group. And for the past few years a number of couples have started meeting monthly to address the different dimensions of grieving that occur for those whose child has been dead for two or more years. The rawness of the pain for those new to the journey is very different from the ongoing pain that the "veterans" experience. The woman who runs the groups is a skilled, sensitive professional whose son died over 30 years ago. She speaks with an understanding that is not just intellectual or learned. Each year she and others from the hospital organize a Remembrance Service for all of the people in Western New York who are mourning for a dead child. The coordinator asked me to speak at the service in 2005. As I prepared my comments I realized what an honor it was to stand in front of hundreds of people who belong to a "fraternity" that no one wishes to join. I was given the opportunity to share my child's story, while trying to share some insight into what this horrible journey of grieving might mean. One of the issues I raised that evening was the analogy of our journey being like a subway.

I feel as if I am on a subway, and I cannot leave this underground system. The tracks and train follow predetermined routes, and, thus, I often feel as if I am being swept along in life by forces over which I have no control. There are times when I will cry or will be returned to my grieving instantaneously with just the tiniest provocation: a smell, a song, a sign, a gesture, a place. There are other times when others might expect an emotional response from me, yet the tears and feelings do not materialize. On this subway I may be able to make some choices and move from one car to another or even move to another line once in awhile. But I can never leave the subway. My core of grieving is always with me. I cannot run away from it. In fact, I do not wish to do so. A parent is a parent forever. If a child dies, the parent still feels as if he is that child's parent. Whenever I am in a situation that requires me to tell others how many children I have, my response is always four. Heidi's body may not be around anymore, but that does not mean that I am still not her father or that she is still not my child. I have not "lost" my daughter. Nonetheless, the anguish of the unfulfilled dreams, the lost opportunities and the sense of unfairness and injustice that surrounds any child's death delineates the contours of the parents' life. Those who attempt to run away from being a parent will find that their denial is a sham. They may run from the pain or try to return to the life they were living before their child died, but somewhere along that journey they will discover the folly of such attempts. This reality makes the phrase "moving on" so inappropriate.

The subway is our journey, whether we want it to be so or not. This feeling of always being a parent should not be construed as ominous or defeatist. It is a reality and with anything real we can address it as an opportunity or as a burden. In fact, the subway is not just about "grieving"; it is about living. On the subway we can read, play games, use our computers, meet with friends, and even talk with strangers. We can laugh, and we can cry. We can read the graffiti and complain about it, or we can enjoy the sayings. The core of grieving IS the subway, but we still can dance in the functional or performance spheres in our lives. The truth is that our attitude defines how we will ride the subway. The type of death we have experienced and the particular characteristics of our loved one's death will set the context for our ride. How we journey on the subway is what matters. We can do so in a way that is affirming of our loved one's life and that seeks healing and meaningful experiences. Conversely, we can turn our back on the journey and pretend that we can move on by putting the death behind us or placing it in a compartment that will save us from the feelings of pain that attend to real grieving. Another option is to go to the depths of despair and lament the journey on the subway. We can damn our fate; blame God for the ride; and make the ride miserable for everyone who comes along with us. It really is all about attitude, acceptance of grace, and seeking to find deeper meaning in life.

My wife and daughter have helped me realize the tremendous grace and blessings I have been given in life. Certainly Heidi's illness and death were completely out of the realm of possibility for us as she grew up. The irony, now, is that Heidi had told Diane that we would be on this journey. When Heidi was a young teen, Diane and she were having a "mother-daughter moment." Diane, trying to resort to a parent's ultimate weapon of guilt, said to Heidi, "You'll miss me when I'm gone." Heidi gently said, "Mom, I'm going to die before you." She made this statement as a matter of fact, and without any pretense for cruelty or matching guilt phrase with guilt phrase. Diane also recalls that there were other times during her teenage years when Heidi told her that some day she would have cancer.

I have found that there are people who can share our journey. They can ride the subway with us. It is unfair, however, to expect them to stay on the subway for too long at a time. They need to get off the train and get to their destination. They may return often or infrequently. The key element here is accepting the precious gift of their presence on the subway. It would be selfish to expect or demand that they ride with us for too long. No matter how empathetic a friend or extended family member may be, she can only touch or share our feelings – she cannot directly experience them. When Heidi wrote her advice about cancer, she said that we should embrace the friends that stay and release those who leave. Truly our life is a tapestry of people who walk in and out of our journey. This revolving parade etches profound contours in our life. The best that I can do for the rest of my life is to understand the wisdom that Heidi has been trying to instill in me: "Dad, it's ok to live. It's ok for people to be who they are. Just remember the love we shared and never give up your dreams."

I have learned how to surrender myself to the journey on the subway. At first, the lines, stops, and ride were unfamiliar and confusing, and they created differing degrees of anxiety. As time rolled over our ride, everything became more familiar – sometimes even comfortable, like a well worn coat or a favorite pair of jeans. Of course, there were repairs to the trains and seats were replaced as they wore out or got damaged. So, too, has our grieving encountered stops and starts, changes and alterations. There have even been times when an entire subway station was added or completely renovated. Some of these changes were welcomed; others just added more confusion to an already topsy-turvy world. Of course, any new routines we created were bound by the whistles and stops along our ride. They too became part of our ride that flowed with tears, laughter, sorrow, pain, and a newly defined sense of hope. These emotional responses were empowering, not debilitating.

In America we do not accept the idea of resigning or surrendering to anything. We see this response as a form of defeat, rather than as a necessary condition for understanding and healing. Resigning is empowering because it frees us from trying to be someone we cannot become. Embracing it does not mean that we are giving up on life or delving into a black hole of self-pity. I recognize that my daughter is, in fact, dead and will not walk through our front door proclaiming that we've been duped or are experiencing a terrible nightmare. This resignation allows me to free myself from the fear of death. We all know that we shall die, but that is no longer a burden. I do not fear my own death; now, it will be an opportunity to see Heidi and my other loved ones who have already transformed. I do not consider this feeling to be suicidal or depressing. I still am living with and for my loved ones with whom I continue to laugh, work, and cry. My meaning in life is generally positive and creative and is permeated with hope and blessings. It also, however, includes the resignation that I live on the subway and there will be parts of my life that others cannot completely share or understand. For me, surrendering to the truth of Heidi's death is part of the harmony that I am continuing to find in my life on the subway.

III.

APRIL 5, 2001.

First Transplant

The road that led to Heidi's first transplant was a rollercoaster with twists and turns that opened new vistas of painful experiences and gut-wrenching emotions. There were so many bumps. For example, one morning in mid-December we were at the Medicine clinic for what we thought was a "routine" procedure. However, Dr. Wetzler told us that he would have to do a biopsy because Heidi's blood results were very problematic. She was either out of remission, which would end both her treatment regimen and the experimental protocol, or her bone marrow was "tired" and it would just take longer for her white cells to replenish themselves. We hadn't expected that she would have to undergo another biopsy. This spinal tap procedure always caused her considerable pain; I never was able to stay in the room during the puncturing that had nauseated me that first night. As Dr. Wetzler explained the situation, Heidi sat with her head bowed and eyes down. This was a setback for which she was unprepared.

When he was finished, he paused before gently asking "Are you ready for the biopsy?"

Without hesitation, she lifted her head, sat up with her back straight, smiled, and said, "Okay, let's go." The biopsy turned out to be negative, and Heidi continued with the experimental protocol.

While waiting for the transplant, she also had infections and unplanned trips to the hospital. In fact, her transplant was delayed because of one bout with encephalitis which was cause for real worry.

Another concern occurred with her sister, Kristen, the donor for the first transplant. The experimental procedure called for harvesting Kristen's marrow a couple of months before the transplant was scheduled in order to culture some of the stem cells. The harvesting was supposed to be relatively routine for Kristen; however, she experienced complications afterwards, resulting in a treacherous rush back to the hospital during a snowstorm – a very unwanted birthday present for me. After days of testing and treatment, confusion and worry, the doctors determined she had been suffering from low blood pressure and dehydration.

The transplant itself had two stages. In the morning Heidi received the cultured stem cells Kristen had donated, and in the afternoon she received the actual bone marrow. All of the chemotherapy and radiation therapy leading up to this day were designed to eliminate Heidi's immune system, so Kristen's stem cells and bone marrow would become her new immune system. We had learned to be very careful about infections; Heidi's contact with people revolved around what stage of treatment she was undergoing.

Heidi wore cream colored pajamas that day. From the very beginning of her journey through leukemia, Heidi's sisters bought her stylish outfits, knowing that her flair for dressing well would not tolerate hospital garb. Her leopard outfit may have been the most entertaining for her to wear, especially when we walked around the wing for her daily exercise. Heidi was excited and nervous about the transplant and was very chatty throughout the day. She was hooked up to a monitor, and she delighted in yawning and singing in order to affect the readings. We all responded to her mood and talked about movies, theater, family stories, etc. We enjoyed hearing her sing - a lifelong passion of hers that brought me much joy. In one sense, we had a party that day: both in the morning, then again in the afternoon when the bone marrow itself was transfused. The transfusions themselves were painless. We watched as Kristen's stem cells and then bone marrow dripped into Heidi through the IV. We joked about the creamed corn smell that emanated from Heidi's body at the end of the procedures. We laughed and sang. It was a good day ... a hopeful day.

Following the transplant, Heidi's progress was storybook. The nurses, nurse practitioner, and her physician marveled at her attitude and spirit. In fact, the Bone Marrow specialist asked Heidi to write advice for other patients, so that her attitude could be an inspiration to other patients. I've included her words in the last chapter.

We were all filled with hope on April 19, the day Heidi left the hospital following that first transplant. Before she left, she visited Jeff, another patient, and gave him a sunshine balloon she had received early in her recovery. That morning, when her nurses' aide was leaving her room, he smiled at her and said, "You make the entire wing Technicolor. Everyone else is just black and white."

Although there were some glitches during her recovery period, we were all so confident in her recovery that we had a "Victory Party" on September 2 to celebrate. One hundred and sixty-five friends and family joined us. Heidi was radiant that day. Her hair had come back dark, rather than the natural blonde that she had been before, but she was just thrilled to have hair again. After everyone had been mingling and eating for a while, Heidi walked to the center of the room and called for attention. The room immediately grew silent. I watched the way she stood, so straight and tall and regal and quietly thanked God for giving me back my daughter. Heidi scanned the room for a moment, making eye contact, before saying simply, "Thank you." She paused, smiled. "Your support during the past year has meant so much. You have no idea how much it helped to know I was so loved by all of you. Your cards - the lottery tickets - the prayers - the visits - and coming here today to help me celebrate. All I can say is 'thank you.' I love you all."

Heidi felt reborn at this time. From the very beginning, she had said, "My leukemia is the best thing that ever happened to me." She told us that the leukemia took her out of herself and gave her a depth and meaning in life that she could never have had without it. "Before the diagnosis life was a 'bit vanilla' – too middle class and mediocre. This experience will give me a depth of feeling and understanding of life. It's going to make me a much better actress." She used her illness to make the world a better place.

Since we all believed that her life was just beginning anew, we relished in those days after 100 +. The medical personnel said that the first 100 days after the transplant were the most difficult. The possibility of Graft vs. Host was real, and waiting to see if Kristen's bone marrow had become Heidi's immune system was a constant worry. However, the GVHD was controlled this time and Kristen's "gift" had completely taken over! Life was good. On August 29th we were going to the Bone Marrow Clinic for what we thought was going to be our last visit. Heidi had written an article for the area newspaper and it had been published on Sunday, August 26 – one year and three days after she had been diagnosed. In the article Heidi talked about the real heroes in life. She wrote:

> **Our society is grossly devoid of heroes. ... At Roswell Park Cancer Institute, I met heroic people at every turn. The doctor, with his deft hands, soft voice and joking smile; the nurses, with their endless patience, knowledge and even love; the physician's assistant, who held my hand during**

the first bone-marrow biopsy; the ladies in the bone-marrow clinic, who made my recovery so smooth; the two women who arranged my transplant and offered so much support; the psychologist, who listened and believed in me, which made such a difference; the woman who played the harp and soothed all the worries; the physical therapist, who pushed me, but always made me want to work hard; the female aide, who called me her "pretty girl"; the male aide, who told me that I was Technicolor; the radiation technicians, who said I was pretty (even when I looked my worst); my friends, who gave me support, cards, prayers and love; and my family members, who held my hand, took my drug reactions in stride, loved me and did not let me see their worry.

The true heroes, though, went above and beyond even these strong people. They are the patients. There is the girl who is running marathons two years after her bone-marrow transplant; the great tattooed man, who smiled and taught me the perseverance of walking 33 laps around the nurses' station to get a mile; the boy who, shortly after his transplant, performed in a musical and begged to play soccer; and the man who gave me the balloon from his daughter for good luck. Then there is my personal hero – the man in the baseball cap. He had a difficult transplant. ... He was a big hockey fan, and made the hospital wing come alive during Sabres games. He made people feel special. He was never in the hallways without a smile and a greeting for everyone. He is the strongest person I have ever seen. ... According to Webster's Dictionary a hero is defined as, "A mythological or legendary figure of divine descent, endowed with great strength and ability," ... Perhaps finding heroes is not that difficult. Instead of chasing windmills and fighting in crusades, heroes exhibit courage by fighting in smaller venues. I consider myself blessed for having known all of these heroes. I am a cancer survivor. It was with the help of all my heroes that I fought to get there. Thank you.

When we arrived at the clinic we saw that her article had been posted on the board. One of her favorite nurses was reading it as we entered for the preliminary weigh in and routine check that started all of our visits. The nurse turned to Heidi and gave her a hug and kiss. The nurse practitioner said, "Jeff (the man in the baseball cap) cried with pride when he read it!"

Jeff and Heidi had become kindred spirits. Although they were from two completely different walks of life, they shared a passion for living and a will to make the world better for their presence. Jeff and I shared a love for sports and had talked about the Sabres a number of times when both he and Heidi were hospitalized at the same time. His enthusiasm was contagious, and Heidi loved his excitement when the Sabres won and made it into the playoffs. My brother-in-law and I attended one of the playoff games when both of them were in Roswell – Heidi would not let me forego the opportunity just because she was having a transplant. The Sabres won the game that night, handily, and Jeff wanted to hear the details of each goal; Heidi was just pleased that we had had such a good game to attend.

The day Heidi learned that Jeff had died was a terrible reminder of the devastation that comes from this disease. He did not have a match for his transplant, and the staff had to go to different measures to try and help him survive. He was married and had three children; they are a loving, wonderful family. Heidi, Diane, and I went to the funeral home. Before we talked with his wife, an older man approached us. "Are you Heidi?" he asked. When she said yes, he hugged her. "I'm Jeff's father," he said. "That article you wrote – it meant so much to Jeff and so much to our whole family. We even have it posted on our refrigerator so everyone can read it." Heidi's eyes glistened with tears, but she smiled. Jeff's father smiled back at her. Time seemed to stand still for just an instant. We could feel Jeff's presence. We now are sure that the two have connected in whichever way those who have died are able to relate.

Heidi received sincere thanks from other nurses for her article. The next time she saw her physician we could tell he was genuinely touched. His eyes danced as he quipped, "So, shall my deft hands perform another biopsy!" A patient who looked familiar, but with whom none of us had ever had a conversation, came up to Heidi. "I want to thank you for being an inspiration. I've seen you in the Chemo Clinic as well as in the Bone Marrow Clinic. You're so beautiful, and I am impressed with how proudly you wear your baldness." She went on to say that she had been a nurse before her cancer and was hoping to return someday. She also thanked Heidi for her article and told her that it would inspire far more people than Heidi would ever know. This experience was just one of so many blessings that we had received through this first year's journey.

The Gift

Burying one's child is "out of order." In contemporary America it seems so unnatural. Prior to the 20th century, burying a child was all too commonplace. In fact, even in the earlier part of the 20th century, it was still quite common. I know my mother's family experienced the death of a young child, and one of my father's sisters died when she was 31. In today's world, however, we do not expect to bury our children. Not only do we live in a society that is conflicted about how to deal with death and dying, but we also live in one that does not provide a healthy approach about how to journey while grieving for our children. As parents, we have given our children life. We are responsible for nourishing the child, and we should be setting the boundaries for her to learn how to participate in society (something the "helicopter generation" should start learning). Our words and actions set the context within which our child develops his own personality, values, and beliefs. Our love for our children is unconditional. Friends may come in and out of our life; we may become estranged with relatives; and the frequency of divorce illustrates the sometimes tenuous nature of marital love. On the other hand, we remain parents all of our life, regardless of what our child may do. I have come to believe, however, that since Heidi's death, **she** has given us a strange type of birth. We are different people, and in an irony that still mystifies me, we are better people. As strange as it may sound, part of the reason I am writing this book is because of the blessings I have received from Heidi – her "gift."

Young children begin asking the question "why?" My degrees are in Philosophy, and I have spent much of my professional and student life delving into and attempting to understand all of the dimensions of this question. At times I refer to this background as the "curse of the philosopher." When a child dies, the "why" question screams for a response. The context of the child's death sets the parameters and, often, the driving force to find an answer. Why did I let her drive when it was snowing? Why did that porch collapse two days before he was coming home? Why did the gun go off accidentally and kill her? Why couldn't life just have skipped that split second and saved my child? Why would he take his own life? Why couldn't she overcome her addictions? Why did that terrorist do such a thing? Why leukemia ... cancer ... brain tumor ... etc.? The why question may be one of the underlying conditions for the anger, guilt, denial, etc. that grieving parents feel. Even if someone supplies an answer, it is never good enough to take away the pain and sense of separation that we feel. In some cases (homicides, e.g.), finding out who did it and what that person's motivation may have been will provide a type of closure. An answer **may** have been given and this **may** provide some comfort. Anyone who believes that this type of closure brings the grieving to an end is sadly mistaken. In fact, this type of answer only provides an opportunity to begin a long and painful process of healing and reflection. As I have mentioned before, the refrain of "moving on" is so misplaced that it becomes insulting to most parents who have to hear it uttered, even by well-intentioned professionals, friends or family.

Very early in Heidi's illness and, again, soon after her death I decided to suspend asking the why question. I had heard the usual answers often enough to find them unsatisfactory, sometimes even irritating. "Heidi has completed her 'mission' or purpose in life" ... "She is in a better place" ... "She won't be suffering anymore." "She has fulfilled her destiny." None of these explanations are ever enough. The question is too big and the implications too overwhelming to think that any of our feeble attempts to provide an answer will ever be sufficient. Of course, finding meaning in this question has been the quest of philosophers and theologians for millennia. Their quest is usually academic and quite theoretical and abstract. For parents the questions are real, even visceral, and the pain is deep and on-going. I have chosen to not go "to the intellectual place" where this question resides. I have chosen to let it dangle in the mists of existence without any resolution. No matter what response I could ever devise, it would never be enough. There is no way that any answer could give me a sufficient meaning for her death. Instead, I have chosen to concentrate on an issue that allows me to feel the gift she has given me.

When I was 20 I was camping along Lake Ontario. One morning I went for a swim and suffered cramps in both legs. Slowly I slipped below the surface of the water and knew that the bottom was out of reach. I began to flail and struggled to find the fresh air above me. Helplessness, fear, a sense of being overwhelmed, a dread of losing everything, and a desperate attempt to return to the surface swept over me until the life guard mercifully pulled me out of certain doom. On shore I realized I had been given another chance at living. When Heidi died these feelings were just a few of the maelstrom that swept over me. I felt that I was drowning in a completely different way; this time I was plunged into depths of feelings I had never reached before and was born into a new life. And just as at birth, it was a life I did not ask to have. Over time I have come to believe that Heidi's death was a strange "gift" – a type of baptism. My old self was washed away, and I had become submerged into the depths of life, the way an anhinga submerges into the pond for a fish or robins immerse themselves in a birdbath. In a strange way this new birth gave me some freedoms: a freedom from the trivialities of life, a freedom from the worries of day-to-day routine, freedom to pursue what I knew was most important in life, and a freedom from the fear of death. As I look around me in this "new world," I see so many people who appear to be like the water bugs that skim along the surface of a pond – barely getting their feet wet. They miss out on the depth of the world that is at their feet; they just keep skimming along failing to touch the preciousness of life. Heidi's death has redefined what is important, and my pursuit of meaning and purpose has replaced any desire to seek pleasure or happiness. I have received permission to experience joyful moments again, but they are no longer a goal, just something that comes along with some experiences; they continue to be fleeting moments that shimmer and vanish so whimsically. It is strange to talk about receiving a gift with Heidi's death, but, in a real sense, she has given me a new sense of purpose. Her attitude was always so positive throughout her struggles. This gift is a call to find blessings, to do what is good for its own sake, and to honor Heidi's memory by making life better for my family and friends. Heidi's death was a strangely blessed gift; it is also the worst gift I've ever received.

We live in a Humpty Dumpty society: we compartmentalize life so much that we have taken life and put it into containers, and then, when we confront the most important questions in life, we have to try to put the pieces back together. We only delude ourselves if we really believe that we can hide the cracks and find all of the pieces. Our society is based on intellectual analysis and our culture functions by applying labels to everything so we can better control our world and environment. There is tremendous power to be found in mathematical, scientific, and analytic thinking. Sound reasoning and the scientific method have brought astounding advancements to our society and to the world. However, we are making a huge mistake when we think that our intellect or scientific thinking can provide us with all of the answers in life. As a culture we have diminished the power of our intuitive capacities which has led to significant, negative consequences.

I wrote my Master's Thesis on "The Meaning of Intuition," and my doctoral dissertation utilized a synthesis of intuition and intellectual analysis to reach my conclusions. Throughout my years as a student and as a teacher, the topic of intuition has been a key component of my thought. In a number of my courses I deal with cross cultural issues. Other cultures, particularly native, sacred, or indigenous ones, have a far more developed sense of intuitive connectedness to life, to others, and to the world than do Americans. Intuition plays a minimal role for us and certainly is not considered a standard for making judgments. Crimes must be solved by evidence, not a detective's intuition. Science may use intuition (or hunches) to begin investigations, but no one would accept intuition as an authoritative answer to any hypothesis. A mother's intuition may be respected within one's family or home, but it is not used in resolving any social conflict or community problem. We have relegated intuition to "appropriate" roles that do not impact "important" decisions or social policy. The death of my daughter has shown me how diminished we are as a society because we do not know how to integrate the power of intuition with the power of our intellects. We have trouble blending our left and right brains. We can appreciate the arts or a creative imagination for their right brain contributions, but they are not considered tools for political or social decision-making. We live in a Humpty Dumpty society whose default button is intellectual even though we know the intuitive has power.

My daughter's death has made me realize that my communication and connection with her can only be intuitive and spiritual. Instead of closure as a goal for the grieving person, I believe healing and finding meaning in life are more important. These tasks are the gift that my daughter has given to me. We live in a goal-oriented society, and we sometimes miss out on the process of living itself. The more fixated we are on the end or goal, the less attention we pay to how we are getting there. "Stop and smell the roses" is an important refrain for our society because we tend to neglect what we all know is important. We are so busy taking care of our "to do lists" that we take for granted the people that are around us and the precious gift we have been given. I knew these things before Heidi died, but now I really KNOW what they mean.

Life is a blessed gift. It becomes even more precious when we see it taken away or when a loved one dies. Intuition is a tool that we have at our disposal that needs to be cultivated and developed. Intuition connects us to ourselves, to life, to others in ways the intellect cannot. These connections are precious and can readily reveal themselves in music, poetry, or in the silence that two lovers share when they have reached the intuitive level of understanding in their relationship. Not having to fill in the "empty space" in conversations becomes a comfort to anyone in a truly loving relationship. Americans tend to talk too much. We often struggle to listen and have to concentrate to observe the non-verbal cues that other cultures use as a primary means of communicating.

These musings do not mean we should replace scientific inquiry, critical analysis, or intellectual development with an intuitive approach to life: to do so would be counterproductive and, in fact, impossible. We should never curtail our emphasis upon intellectual development in our schools. However, we must also begin to respect and learn to enhance our power of intuition. Some halting attempts do exist, usually limited to the fine or visual arts. There are pockets of such insight in other areas of study and in spiritual centers or meditation retreats, but these efforts are merely the reflection of individuals or small groups who sense the value of intuitive insights, not from any systematic cultural drive to foster this power. We are not developing ourselves as humans in a full or complete fashion. We are focusing in a way that is too limited and that continues to empower the Humpty Dumpty Syndrome.

Heidi's gift has given me the opportunity to become a whole person by finding deep meaning and purpose in my life. In a professional context, I have written about meaningfulness in life. Meaning is something that is broader in context than what the intellect can capture. We can think about and analyze any dimension in life and may gain tremendous insight; however, relationships, and the great mysteries and gifts of life (e.g. faith, hope and love), transcend what the intellect can know. Their meaning can be more fully discerned in an insight that blends intuitive insight and intellectual considerations. Within two days of Heidi's diagnosis, she was telling us that she did nothing to cause this disease because she didn't smoke, take drugs, or sunbathe. "I'm going to do whatever it takes to get better," she said, thereby giving birth to the positive attitude that would characterize her throughout her entire illness. She treated everyone with kindness and respect; she was noted for her smile and the sparkle in her eyes. The "Monday morning" volunteer who worked at Roswell greatly admired Heidi's spirit and attitude. He told Diane and me, "She has had a profound impact on my life. You know, it started with the life that I saw in her eyes. I can't tell you how much those eyes affected me."

Meaning in life becomes reflected in a person's purpose in life and the attitude that he exhibits. For those who are confused or angry, their attitude toward life may be negative, withdrawn, or even hostile. Heidi's positive attitude was genuine. In some ways her sisters, her mother, and I believe that her journey through her illness and in her death may have been her best performance. It was not an act to con people, however; it was a gift to enrich others' lives and to help us connect with her spirit, both while she was alive and now while her body is no longer here. Her attitude came out of the context and meaning in her life. Her intuitive connection to this meaning revealed itself in so many positive ways that her legacy continues to have a rippling effect, even touching people she never met and people we do not know.

Heidi was also a very reflective person, and she could be very critical as well. I remember the first time we took her to see "The Phantom of the Opera." She was 10, and the Phantom was portrayed by Colm Wilkenson. After the show I asked Heidi what she thought of it. "Colm doesn't pronounce his "s" properly when he's singing and he makes up for his weak acting abilities with a strong, powerful voice," she said matter-of-factly. During her illness we often discussed the possibility of her becoming a film or theater critic to give voice to her candid observations. As I watched my daughter journey through her illness, I was always struck by her ability to interweave an intuitive awareness of herself, others, and life with a reflective ability that was sharp and well-grounded.

An intuitive connectedness in life can provide a type of prescience – an awareness of what will happen. Science requires prediction in order to function; prediction is a driving force and a goal in the scientific method. We can judge the value of an experiment or a theory by judging how well it predicted the results. When the results diverge from the prediction, the researchers or experimenters will revise their thinking. One of the tremendous values of science is this ability to predict and then judge its efficacy. Modern science has come to realize that in all cases the predictability cannot be made in absolute terms, only in varying degrees of probability. But in so many aspects of our lives, this probability can be treated as certainty. For example, the earth will continue to rotate and today will roll into tomorrow as the earth rotates on its axis and revolves around the sun. We know intellectually that there will be an end to our world as the sun explodes or implodes, but that is so far in the future that we do not need to consider it as a possibility for us to address. Some scientific advances occur because of the mistakes, the incorrect hypotheses, and the experimental falsifications that are so necessary for intellectual verification. In like manner, intuition cannot always be counted upon for predicting what will happen; however, the power that it can play in our lives is far too important to dismiss it as irrelevant. Many of the parents who are in the grief support groups that I attend have talked about the prescience that their children had about their death. On some level they were aware of their mortality. This is not true for everyone, of course, but it is a real phenomenon for many. One powerful intuitive experience I had occurred when I was 20. I was at a girl friend's house one afternoon. We had just returned from a walk, and she went into the kitchen to make sandwiches. When she returned, she found me in a fetal position on the couch. My insides were burning. She asked me what was wrong. My response: "My grandmother just died. I have to get home." I immediately drove home. When I arrived, my father told me that my grandmother, in fact, had just died. This type of intuition is inexplicable, but real. We all are intuitively connected to one another. The problem is being open to this way of relating to others. At times we may be successful in being aware of this connectedness; most of the time we are not as astute.

One thought on this topic tends to amuse me. We make mistakes in life continually. Our thinking may be flawed in many ways and our perceptions can be deceived quite readily. We often strive to correct our mistakes, but we become frustrated when we continue to make some of the same mistakes again. Our schools foster testing to measure how much we have learned, and we accept the reality of not getting all the answers correct all of the time. Yet, if our intuition is ever mistaken or flawed, then we tend to dismiss intuition itself as unreliable. "See, I told you that you shouldn't follow your heart! Use your head, instead." We often associate intuition with emotions or the heart, while intelligence is associated with our head. Our default button remains our head, and we don't reject our head or intelligence because we make mistakes. Why, then, do we not reserve the same courtesy to intuition? Humans are forever fallible – intuitively and intellectually. This fallibility should not be a reason for dismissing either faculty or capacity in our lives. Americans are at a tremendous disadvantage in dealing with our meaning and purpose in life because we tend to address this issue in a way that leaves out too much of what life is presenting to us. We realize this narrowness when we are overwhelmed with beauty or with a profound experience of love. There is a whole world alive for us, if we but intuitively connect to it. A creative imagination can become a wonderful stepping stone to unlocking some of life's mysteries.

We can learn how to be more intuitive and can develop our connectedness to the world. American culture has not developed criteria that we can use to determine what intuitive connections are reliable, trustworthy, or "true." We cannot even agree on norms for making ethical decisions or judging what is to be considered right or wrong. We do live in an ambiguous society that perplexes us and creates considerable confusion on so many issues. The media has even created the tags of "red" states and "blue" states which imply that the standards for making judgments in those states are divided. Politicians promise consensus and nonpartisan actions, but most levels of government still operate in divisive ways that often seem to cater to special interests. It is no wonder that Americans find so much of life's decision-making confused and ambiguous. In this type of environment, it may be unrealistic to believe that intuitively based decisions can or even should become part of the social landscape. Despite the social complications, however, learning how to incorporate intuitive abilities in meaningful ways into one's own life is wise and healthy.

The writer Albert Camus once said that the first question of philosophy is whether or not we should exist. For him that first question was whether or not we should commit suicide: "To be or not to be!" I have spent a great deal of time pondering the issue of whether or not life has meaning, and if so, what that meaning might be and how might we be able to understand it. These are the rudimentary questions that create the "curse of the philosopher." All of life is a gift; there are blessings to be discovered in each and every day. Heidi's death has made my thoughts, feelings, and beliefs about such things real. I am not saying that she died so that I could write this book or come to these realizations. This book is **not** Heidi's meaning in life. Heidi's meaning in life, however, **is** one of the factors that led me to write this book. This distinction is important. Life continually evolves and changes, and meaningfulness pervades it thoroughly. Our quest in life is to discover and/or create our meaning or purpose. Heidi's gift is that her death has taken my focus and attention away from so much of the trivialities of life. Now I can immerse myself in the journey of life, into the deep waters of reality which have become my journey of grieving. For me, grieving is not always sad and not always depressing. Instead of trying to make life what it cannot be, I am learning how to live within the beauty and challenges that the world and others create. Right now I am striving to share this meaning and purpose with those who are dealing with the death of a loved one. My prayer is for everyone to discover this gift during his journey of grieving.

IV.

MARCH 2 AND 3, 2001.

Mister Hyde's Visit

"**ASK AND IT SHALL BE GIVEN TO YOU."** *So many of our friends asked what they could do to help Heidi. We often responded that prayers were (and still are) the best gift she can receive. As she underwent her bone marrow transplant and, later, when she underwent the stem cell transplant, we asked church members, neighbors, and friends to participate in a prayer vigil at our church. We asked people to sign up for a 30 minute time slot. Some stayed longer. Many prayed at their home or local church, if they were out of town. Our hope was to provide a continuous chain of prayers for the two days. We believe that God was listening and caring for her. We were requesting prayers that would help Kristen's marrow to take hold and bring Heidi back to renewed health for the first transplant and that Tara's stem cells would become Heidi's new immune system for the second transplant. That was the intent for the prayer vigils. However, the reality and the vagaries of this illness set another context for the first vigil.*

We had scheduled the vigil for the first weekend in March (Friday and Saturday), so it would occur just before her bone marrow transplant; however, the transplant had to be delayed. The complications started the previous month on Valentine's Day. We received a call from the hospital. A nurse informed us that we had to discontinue the chemotherapy treatment that Heidi was taking prior to the transplant because her white blood counts were too low. This was the fourth round of treatments that she had undergone since her initial diagnosis. She also had a round of full-body radiation. A week later she was still off the chemo treatments but began to register a very slight temperature of 100 degrees. From the very beginning, fevers were a major indicator of difficulties. If Heidi was at home, we had to call the hospital, regardless of day or time, and usually had to take her in to be checked. Sometimes the temperatures went away within hours or days; sometimes we ended up having to admit her to the hospital for treatments. We became accustomed to the phrase "fever of unknown origin," always a frustrating part of her journey. On this particular Friday, they decided to keep her overnight at the hospital. The following days were difficult and confusing for all of us.

Heidi had become very knowledgeable about her treatment and medications. So had we. We told the staff that we knew Heidi was allergic to a particular antibiotic, but there was no record of it in her portfolio (the number of binders that Heidi accumulated over the years was sad to see). During the night she began to have a rash that Diane noticed, but the doctor on call couldn't see. Later, the nurse realized Diane was correct. That doctor was one of the very few professionals we encountered who was unimpressive and uncaring. Heidi's lips were puffy and Diane wanted to know why she wasn't on an IV because her blood pressure was low. I spent the evening of Feb. 24, during which many cultures were taken and a variety of medications were administered. The cultures were negative, and they decided to give her some growth shots to stimulate the white blood counts. Headaches began to develop the next night, and her fever went up again. So far Heidi had been in the hospital for three days with continuous testing and still the verdict was fever of unknown origin. As her headaches continued to persist, the doctors prescribed Oxycodone, a narcotic that is quite powerful. On Feb. 26 a nurse confirmed what we already knew: Heidi was allergic to the med she had been given when she was first admitted. They now had found a record of the allergy, and she should never have been given the med. If they hadn't given it to her in the first place, as we had indicated, the rash would not have occurred.

The next few days turned out to be quite bizarre. The attending physician gave Heidi a spinal tap to see what was happening in her spinal fluid. They discovered that Heidi had white cells in her spinal column and brain, which indicated that she had a viral infection. Continuing the antibiotics wasn't going to help the infection, but was necessary for secondary infections that may also be occurring. We kept being reassured that this type of scenario was not uncommon and that the transplant would not be delayed too much longer. The calm confidence of the professionals was not reassuring at this time. Their idea of "common" or "normal" complications was anything but common or normal for us.

Heidi's headaches were persisting and the nurses (and I) encouraged her to take more of the Oxycodone to help alleviate the pain. Through half shut eyes, she kept saying, "I don't want this drug. I don't like the way it feels. Please don't make me take it." I now wish that I had listened to her, rather than the professionals. There are times when a patient or family members are better suited to decide what is best. Professionals should not be so ready to dismiss those who have the greatest stake in the treatments. On that evening (Feb. 28) we experienced Mr. Hyde's visit in Heidi's body. This name was an apt moniker for her. The family had affectionately used the nickname of Heid for her as she grew up. For the next couple of days we experienced a terrible behavioral change that was startling and upsetting to all of us. Heidi began to remain pleasant to the medical staff, but became nasty and belligerent to all of us in the family. Heidi was authorized to come home on March 1. I was teaching and Diane was starting a new job as the church's secretary. Kristen helped by bringing Heidi home. The nurse that day was cold and rude. The typical paperwork and delays in trying to leave contributed to Heidi's irritability. By this time I had joined Kristen to help bring Heidi home. She had been and continued to be uncommunicative, which was very atypical. After helping Kristen, I went back to school to continue teaching and received a tearful phone call from Diane. Heidi's behavior had become very nasty, caustic, and strange. She would not drink (which was a crucial necessity throughout her struggles, and something she had religiously been doing). In the mail was an autographed picture of Mandy Patinkin, one of Heidi's favorite singers and actors. When Diane handed her the picture, Heidi glanced at it, then returned to watching TV. She didn't say anything.

Heidi admired Mandy Patinkin's diverse talents and loved his singing voice. We had taken her to one of his concerts a few years earlier and she was enthralled with the experience. In fact, we also took Heidi and her boyfriend to another one of his concerts after she was recovering. After his concerts he stands in the lobby and collects donations for charitable causes, for example, "Doctors Without Borders." What I remember most about that particular evening was what happened to Heidi after the concert. She took a donation to him and said, "You've been an inspiration for me while I've been battling with leukemia." He hugged her and gave her a kiss on the cheek. "You, my dear," he said, "are the real inspiration." As we walked to the car she patted her cheek and said, "I'm never going to wash that cheek again." Thus, Heidi's indifferent response to his signed autograph in his character role in "The Princess Bride" (a real favorite for our girls) was very indicative that someone else was occupying her body.

"Mr. Hyde" became even more antagonistic to all of us, so we called the hospital. When the doctor asked to speak to Heidi, she refused to touch the phone and speak to the doctor. *"If you don't talk to this doctor, I'm taking you to the hospital,"* I said sternly.

She very reluctantly snatched the phone from me and shot me daggers. Then came the instant transformation: Dr. Jekyll emerged. *"Hello,"* she said all too sweetly. *"No, I'm doing fine,"* she replied. After a brief pause, she added, *"No, I don't need to go in."* We hadn't seen this side of her in the past two days. Heidi shoved the phone in my direction and went back to watching TV.

When I talked to the doctor, she said that it was my decision on what to do. For some unknown reason, we decided to keep Heidi at home. During the night Diane stayed with her, and Heidi continued to grit her teeth, scream at Diane, and remain defiant. Diane was beside herself with worry. Had the medication permanently altered Heidi's behavior? How could we cope with this changed "girl" in our midst? That night was a torture for Diane. The next day Heidi's anger and belligerence continued, although there was a brief period of "lucidity" and almost being pleasant. It was now the first day of her prayer vigil. Heidi yelled at me in the morning while being pleasant on the phone to her sister, Katie. Kristen came over to stay with Heidi while I went to the prayer vigil. While Kristen was in Heidi's room, Heidi turned away from the TV and glared at Kristen. *"I'm sick of seeing you around here. I hate you,"* she barked. Stunned, Kristen left the room and cried all the way to the prayer vigil. We kept wondering whether or not Heidi should be taken back to the hospital. I stayed with her until about 12:30 AM; she had been dozing on and off. I, then, went to bed, but immediately came down when she rang her bell at about 4:00 AM. Heidi rarely used the bell because she hated to inconvenience us. *"I haven't slept all night,"* she complained. *"There are bugs flying all over and the wallpaper keeps changing colors."* She then described what appeared to be a bad dream, but she insisted it was happening. She clearly was hallucinating.

We knew that the behavior change was caused by the Oxycodone that she had taken in the hospital, but the experiences of this transformed person were not typical and brought another worry to all of us. Katie had reassured us that once the effects of the med had worked through Heidi's system, she would return to her normal self. Katie's reassurance helped us through those days that seemed to drag for so long, but each of us still had lingering doubts as to whether we would ever have the real Heidi return to us. As daylight approached and the morning began to unfold on a new day, the effects of the drug finally started to disappear and our smiling, friendly daughter returned to us.

On the second day of the prayer vigil, Heidi said that she could not remember what had happened since being in the hospital. Thankfully, she had no recollection of what she had said to any of us. Weeks later when we were comfortable again, we shared some of the things she had said and done. She was embarrassed and horrified.

During this strange sequence of events, the Prayer Vigil proved to be very moving for all of us. We were surprised by the turnout and the stories that people shared with us. One friend of mine drove from Washington, DC to pray. In fact, he lay prostrate at the altar for awhile. One of our neighbors played religious music on the piano in the nave of the church. Later, some friends shared their own experiences and feelings during the vigil. Jody, our neighbor and friend who visited Heidi frequently and who still consistently talks about and remembers Heidi, came over with a little tin container. It had an angel on it with the letters: SFGTD (Something for God To Do). She gave it to Heidi and said that anyone, especially Heidi, could write a note to God and put it in the container. I know the container was full by the time Heidi died, since we all put our notes in that container periodically. I have not been able to open it and read what she and others had written. I don't know if it's because of the pain this would cause or because I believe that that should remain something personal between the petitioners and God. The friend who had organized the vigil had placed a rose on the altar and lit candles throughout the nave. We provided information sheets for those who attended. They included passages and hymns related to healing, along with specific items to pray for Heidi's transplant. Heidi had also written a poem that we laminated and made into a book mark as a thank you for everyone who attended. Here is what she wrote:

> *When faced with a dark fear,*
> *She reveled in past comforts*
> *And beauty of the future*
> *She wanted a symbol ...*
> *To focus her fear*
> *She pondered many choices.*
> *None fit.*
> *Until ....*
> *The rosebud was suggested.*
> *It was comfort.*
> *An avid rose lover,*
> *It brought together past, present ...*
> *And future for the girl.*
> *You see, her first*
> *doll was named: "Rosebud".*
> *Aptly so, with the rosebud pattern*

On her dress.
Precious remembrances
Of a simple rag doll,
A simple time.
A rosebud brings a promise.
A promise of a future.
The rosebud has an untainted beauty,
But as it grows
it will develop a unique soul,
And become a rose.
She felt the strength of its promise.
The promise of her future.
Thank you for your support,
Heidi

Context Spheres

Grief and feelings of separation occur within a social context. As human beings we are connected to others by laws, rules, norms, customs, and mores. In addition, humanity is interconnected by actions and attitudes. Each action or inaction in our life creates ripples throughout all of humanity. Everything we do shifts the cosmic sands of all life. The American belief that everyone has a right to do what she wishes as long as it does not affect anyone else is a myth. Life is continuous and that includes human existence. Like the color spectrum, we each may have our own color, but our actions (or inactions) blend, mix, and collide with the rest of the world. Whether we want to accept the fact or not, humans are social beings. We are interconnected and have a responsibility as citizens of humanity and the world to respect and care for others. The very nature of social connectedness includes (a) the conscious and unconscious forces that influence who we are, as well as who we have been and will become, (b) what we think and believe, and (c) how we respond and act in life. These forces shape the way we think and feel. In my classes I emphasize that culture means more than just our national or racial identity; it is not just customs or ethnic heritage. All the characteristics of culture help define who we are. I address the issue of cultural characteristics by using my model of "Context Spheres." Context Spheres identify the sources and areas of influence for anyone's values, attitudes, beliefs, and moral principles. These spheres are interconnected, dynamic, and overlap (that is, they are continuous). Sometimes the sources/influences are apparent; sometimes they are hidden. Many cultural beliefs, values, traits, attitudes, customs, and mores are taken for granted or assumed to be true for all people. They may only become recognized when there is conflict or when encountering differences. Context Spheres are not necessarily compatible. Sometimes they provide mixed messages, conflicted values, and confusion for individuals and/or groups. Some of the conflicts during our grief journey may be understood more clearly when we understand the characteristics of these Context Spheres:

<u>National/Dominant Culture</u> – This sphere focuses upon the dominant or primary cultural context. It includes the primary language, values, and beliefs for life within a particular society. In the United States we refer to "American" culture and can identify some generic influences that are a part of this country. For example, there is a generic form of English that is spoken, but some of the other spheres can affect our English. Not only do we have varied accents around the country, but there are also gender, generational, and work-related phrases and words that are quite distinctive. Each generation develops its own code words. Sometimes people from other generations can learn some of them. Using another generation's words can be humorous or can create discomfort in the conversation. An 80 year old man calling his friend "dude" for example seems "cute" or out of place. Wouldn't a 5 year old calling his friends "colleagues" seem a bit out of place? Are there really any 18 or 19 year old "hippies" anymore? The language of text messaging, tweeting, and cell phones is very different from the generations who used party lines or words for the beginning of their phone numbers (Butler 3-4951, for example). Of course everyone's language has been affected by computers. The level of sophistication with a computer and the frequency of use will alter the number of computer related words and phrases that become a part of the way we talk to each other. One of the tasks of feeling included in a group is learning the language (words and non-verbal cues) that are a part of that group. Children start this process when they have "secret" words for their clubs or play groups. Effective orientations for schools, jobs, churches, volunteer agencies, etc. include the words, phrases, and timing for accomplishing things. Usually, we take all of these activities for granted and do not consider the dynamics that are involved. In essence, that is one of the powers of culture at any level. We tend to take for granted or just assume that a particular way of doing something or a specific word or phrase is appropriate. I ask my students if they speak in the same fashion and use the same words and gestures with their friends, when they're in class, when they are with their parents, or when at a job. Of course, they all realize that the context changes the rules and the names or words they may use. The names we have for friends are usually not the names we would use in referring to relatives, especially parents or grandparents, for example.

Those who are grieving may find new words that affect them. Often they change the meaning of words they may have used before. For example, the word "leukemia" has a whole new meaning in my life. I had known a number of people with differing forms of the disease before Heidi. When friends and friends' children died of the disease, I thought it was terrible. Now, however, the full scale of what those people went through and the meaning of what the disease entails is completely different for me. Before I had an intellectual response to the word (connecting its sound with what little I knew). Now, my response is visceral, existential, and includes far more than I ever wanted to know. Thus, the power of language is significant in all of our lives. Sometimes language provides us with very subconscious messages that subtly reflect the attitude, values or beliefs of the dominant forces within a society. Language is only one dimension of a culture, but it is a readily recognizable example to illustrate the effects of a context sphere.

Regional/Geographic – Values differ within regional areas. This geographic context includes not only Northeast, South, etc. dimensions, but also the differences that emerge from urban, suburban, rural areas, as well as the influences that may occur with weather conditions and types of terrain (mountainous, desert, plains, "Great Lakes", etc.). Farmers, for example, from different regions of the country may have more in common with one another than their urban counterparts in their own region. We can readily identify accents as regional markers. For example, as a child I noticed a tremendous difference in the lives of my extended family, some of whom lived in Chicago, while others lived in rural, Western Kentucky. The pace of dialogues and the non-verbal dimensions of communication were quite different in the two regions. I remember my relatives in Chicago talked at the pace I was used to hearing in Niagara Falls. Talking with my uncles in Kentucky was quite different. I learned that there would be pauses, sometimes long ones. As a child I did not learn how to adapt very well, but by the time I was a teenager I began to fall into the same pace. Early in our marriage, Diane teased me about how my language changed when we would visit my relatives. I had learned how to adjust my pace of talking, to adopt different words to get my point across, and I even changed pronunciations of words when we were there. I was also struck by the diversity of concerns and values that emerged from these different regions in my life. For example, my Chicago relatives have always been avid golfers and have belonged to country clubs for most of their adult lives. They are interested in fashion and current trends in society. My Kentucky relatives, on the other hand, were interested in livestock, crops, and stretching their earnings as far as they could. I was struck by the vast difference between the daily routines. In Chicago, the big meal of the day was supper – usually around 5:00 or 6:00 PM. In Kentucky, the big meal was dinner which we ate around noontime. As a child there was a world of difference for me between spending a weekend at my northern relatives' cottage in Wisconsin as contrasted with helping to feed the chickens, cut tobacco, or run in the fields in Western Kentucky.

Local/Ethnic/Racial – The immediate physical surroundings may also influence a person's view of the world and basic values and beliefs. In this sphere we can see ethnic heritage, customs and beliefs. Sometimes ethnic groups create ghettos or highly identifiable areas. In other cases these areas are created for them. In the United States racial discrimination in housing, for example, is a reflection of local politics, attitudes, or social beliefs. In some cases, different ethnic groups may be living in close proximity. Sometimes this closeness creates conflict, because the different ethnic groups have incompatible interests, histories, or customs. For example, ethnic conflicts may define one's way of life (Israel, Somalia, etc.); or one's ethnic heritage may be self defining (many ethnic groups in the United States, e.g.); or ethnicity may have minimal influence (e.g. those who consider themselves "Americans", even though they may be from European, Asian, or African roots). In Western New York the suburbs and towns around Buffalo carry with them images of the people who live there. If you ask a local about Depew, Lackawanna, Tonawanda, or Orchard Park, he could give you a description of what people are like in those areas. For many people in the Greater Buffalo area, these locales are often associated with the school districts or the success of the sports teams that represent the high schools. One local custom that I have experienced in Western Kentucky relates to burials in the cemeteries along the Elva road on the way to Symsonia. My uncle explained it to me when we were burying his sister years ago. The family stayed at the grave side until the casket had been completely buried and the crew had left the cemetery. Years before a funeral director was caught taking the corpse out of the casket and putting the body into a wooden box, so he could resell the casket. Those buried at Wallace Cemetery knew the story and, thus, a local custom was established to stay at the gravesite. When my uncle died, and later when my aunt died, I made sure that I stayed at their gravesites until the workers were finished – that's the only place where I follow this custom.

Family/Friends – As we get older, family and friends change and the influences we may feel from them will vary. Friends come in and out of our lives. There are some friends that are significant for relatively short periods of time. Others may be absent for years, even decades, but when they reenter our lives, we may feel an instant connection. I have noticed that sometimes family traits can be noticed in the looks and mannerisms of the members. Some sons laugh like their fathers, for example. My sons-in-law and I chuckle at those times when they observe their mother-in-law saying or doing something that they have heard or seen their wives do. Our phrase for this: "Yeah, it's genetic." In fact, my daughters have even told me that sometimes they think they've married their father. We laugh, because they now realize that dad wasn't some alien creature. Lo and behold, I was a male and was doing "things" that men sometimes do.

Professional/Educational – Schools are a major influence in our lives. Some parents provide home schooling for their children because they do not like the influences in their area's schools or because they believe they can provide a better learning environment for their children. The type of school we attend and the degree to which we respond to the learning and social challenges in schools will have a lasting effect on how we think and communicate as we get older. Of course, for most schools, the goal is to promote lifelong learning; that is, schools are training students **how** to think and **how** to learn with the intent (and hope) that the skills and knowledge that their students have learned will continue to grow and develop throughout their lives. The process of learning how to learn may be even more important than the particular content of any lesson. The longer anyone participates in educational programs, the more influential that contextual sphere should be. The extent of any influence may be very difficult to discern. Educational influences often are subtle and usually become imbedded in the language that we use, the interests we have, or the mannerisms that we exhibit. It is common for people with less educational experience to have a different vocabulary and different ways of expressing themselves than those who have gone through college, for example.

There also is a difference between a person's career and her job; both will influence beliefs and values. There has been a dramatic change occurring over the past 30-40 years in the United States. It was more common years ago to work for and retire from one company or employer. Today, it is more likely for people to work for six or seven employers and maybe even move through four or five different careers. Of course, the changes in the types of jobs people have and the dramatic shifts in gender participation have produced social change that is quite unprecedented. The type of work we do and the career that we pursue will have profound impact on how we look at the world and how we relate to people. A correctional officer at the Attica prison facility, for example, will spend his days in an institution where safety and security revolve around controlling the inmates. Gates, bars, cells and rigid rules and schedules dictate daily life. For a Hospice nurse, her world revolves around comfort, empathy, and daily flexibility. Her routine may be one that cannot follow a well-defined schedule. These experiences will often spill over into the rest of a person's life.

<u>Religious/Civic</u> –There is a common myth that church and state are really completely separated in the United States. Americans tend to be very conflicted about this relationship. We are influenced by our religious upbringing (or lack thereof). We also are affected continuously by our role within the civic arena. We are either citizens or refugees or visitors. In each case, there are social expectations, influences, and behaviors that are associated with our place in society. As citizens of the Unites States, we expect to have our rights respected, and we realize that we have some duties, which we may fulfill in varying degrees. For example, some people vote in every possible election while others may have a more spotty record. The politics and the decisions of political bodies have a significant influence on our lives. Our civic self, however, goes beyond just the arena of politics. It includes the attitudes and behaviors that we consciously incorporate in our lives: freedom of speech for example. There are also subtle influences in public that may be taken for granted. For example, driving cars is risky and is totally dependent upon a remarkable level of trust for other drivers. Even if you drive very defensively and say you don't trust any other driver, you still do. You will go through a green light and expect the on-coming traffic to stop. You may look to make sure they do so, but you will still be driving through the signal when you do so. Of course, this trust becomes shattered during car accidents.

Gender/Generation – Gender differences do exist and influence one's decisions. In like manner generational experiences may have profound influences upon what people believe and how people make decisions. For example, there are significant differences in attitudes about war among the WWII, Viet Nam, and Desert Storm/Iraq/Afghan war generations. Members from different generations may agree or even disagree on whether to engage in a conflict or not, but the reasons for the agreements or disagreements may be vastly different. Of course, there are also the varied perspectives regarding the justification for war. The Iraq war has demonstrated the lack of universal agreement on what justifies going to war.

Another simple generational difference I have observed is related to fashion and hugging. Fashions change continuously and generational differences related to clothing, hair styles, etc. are readily apparent. However, I began to notice a simple difference when Heidi was alive. She and many of her female peers wore blouses or sweaters that were "too long." By "too long" I mean for my generation long-sleeves ended slightly below the wrist. Some of Heidi's long sleeve tops would extend down to her palms. I noticed that she would hold the sleeve with the tips of her fingers. Maybe this is common knowledge as a fashion style, but for someone who is as "fashion challenged" as I am, it seemed like just another change in the way people wear clothing. This difference, however, seems to extend beyond the look of the clothing and the way younger women grip their sleeves. When Heidi first came home from college during her freshman year I can vividly recall hugging her at the airport. Even now, I can feel how her hands were clenched as delicate fists on my back. That hug haunts me still – for so many reasons. Of course, first of all I wish I could hug her again. Second, I can remember how great it was to see her and how much I missed her while she was away at school. Those feelings of missing her then seem to pale compared to the feelings I have now. Third, I have looked for others who hug with their fists closed. I've seen the same type of hugging in movies and on televisions shows. In those cases it seems that younger women are the ones who will hug in this fashion (not all younger women, but more than just a random number). I do not know if this behavior is generational, personality oriented, or caused by some other cultural factor. It is not a life-changing issue, but it does illustrate that differences among the generations are real, and they can be profound or insignificant. The way others respond to these differences can be very surprising. For example, older generations may find wearing a baseball cap in the house to be an insulting form of disrespect, while the younger generation may have no clue that they are being disrespectful. In a comparable way, gender influences are profound, but sometimes very subtle. I became keenly aware of many of the differences while I was living with four daughters and my wife. Keeping the toilet seat down, for example, was an irrelevant issue when I was growing up with my brothers. My wife trained me to its importance early in our marriage. This may seem trivial, but it illustrates a more important point: that gender differences are far more complex and pervasive than we may realize.

Personal/Personality – Ultimately, how a person responds to the influences and how he organizes them will have a profound impact upon his values, attitudes, and beliefs, as well as how they are incorporated in any decision-making situation. Our personality develops as we learn to negotiate the world. Some basic personality traits can even be observed in infants, babies, and young children. Our personality shifts and emerges in varying ways throughout our life. The interaction among the other context spheres and the personality help form our dynamic character. Oftentimes our personality gets molded around the dominant influences in the different spheres in our life. Other times we may try to assert our uniqueness in very individualistic ways. Our personalities are complex webs which may include what appear to be conflicting dimensions. For example, it is not unusual for someone to demonstrate introverted and extroverted tendencies, which exhibit themselves in varying ways in different situations. Another confounding issue relates to the differing personalities within a family with more than one child. Siblings, even twins, exhibit very different traits and responses to situations. They may be living in the same family, but their personality becomes a major factor in identifying how and why they behave the way they do. When we consider a person's journey of grieving, it becomes clear that grief can have a profound effect upon personality, just as a person's personality will profoundly affect her journey of grieving.

My grieving has led me to feel conflicted with the influences these context spheres have in my life. I believe that American society has pathological tendencies that make grieving unhealthy and undermine my grieving journey. For example, there are times when I sense the "whispering": "Those are the ones who lost their daughter." This whispering may be intended to "save" our feelings while sharing information with someone else. It, however, misses the fact that the grief is always a part of my life and their attempt to spare me from the pain of saying so is foolish. I sometimes feel as if others think I have some type of secret disease from which they need to protect themselves and others. Part of my journey of grieving is working through these influences in my life and trying to understand which of them are healthy and foster a positive meaning in life and which ones are corrosive and detrimental. In essence I have come to realize that this awareness is an essential ingredient in living – it is not just a task for grieving. Trying to better understand these dynamics in my life and realizing that I need to do this type of work has enriched my life. In the following chapters I will be giving examples of the conflicts I experience with my journey of grieving and the way others think and talk about grief.

V.

OCTOBER 30, 2001.

Relapse

*D*etermined to re-engage in life outside of meds and treatments once again, but not quite sure how, Heidi decided to audit an Honors course that I was teaching. It covered Western philosophies of time and examined how different cultures perceive and organize time in different ways. Heidi enjoyed the class, especially because she was able to connect with her peers. By this time, most of her friends had drifted away. They didn't seem to know what to say or were just uncomfortable around her or had just become caught up in their own worlds. The other students appreciated Heidi's presence; she was bright, attractive, and was more than willing to argue or disagree with me, something they were hesitant to do themselves. She thrived on the intellectual stimulation and was thrilled that I did not require that she write any of the papers. She was, however, assigned to work with two groups for oral presentations.

This particular October morning, however, changed all of our lives once again. As Heidi was preparing for class, Diane and I heard her scream. Diane ran to her. "There's a lump!" she cried, pointing to her breast. The lump did not bode well and a pall settled over all of us. We each thought different things. I went to class, per Heidi's instructions. Diane called Roswell and one of our favorite nurses arranged for Heidi to go to the Breast Clinic. Heidi was assured that she did not fit the profile for having breast cancer, but she would have an ultrasound and they would biopsy to be sure. I had my own theory that I didn't share with anyone. The protocol for the experimental transplant she had received had said that the stem cells that were cultured and transfused first may create some hard masses in different parts of the body. This risk was considered minimal, but I thought that the lump may have been caused by this procedure. Later, I found out that her physician believed the same thing and was not immediately concerned that Heidi was relapsing. Besides, he had never before seen leukemia express itself as a lump in the breast.

On November 6 Diane, Heidi, her boyfriend, and I went to Roswell to meet with the specialist. Heidi and Diane met with the physician who told them that it was not breast cancer, but it may be leukemia. We all met with Dr. Wetzler a little while later. He confirmed that she had relapsed and would have to be admitted immediately and begin another protocol leading to a second transplant. This time her sister, Tara, would be the donor. We learned later that her physician had broken down and cried when he had received the report. He and Heidi had developed a special bond, and he was convinced that she was going to be one of his poster girl success stories. Heidi's response to him was firm and direct: "I'm not going to be admitted today; I'll come back sometime tomorrow."

Dr. Wetzler gave Diane and me a quizzical look and stuttered a bit: "Um, but, you, ah, probably should ..."

Heidi cut him off: "No, I'm going home now." There was no anger in her voice, just a quiet determination.

"Well, okay," he muttered.

On the way home from the hospital, Heidi suggested we stop for lunch. While eating, she looked at us intently before saying, "Since I never had the opportunity to have a party before going to the hospital the first time, I'd like to have one tonight." Seeing Diane and I exchange a look, she quickly added, "Only family, close friends, and neighbors. It won't be elaborate." She paused again. "There are only two rules: no one is going to cry and no one is going to talk about the relapse." So, we spent the afternoon calling and making arrangements, and that evening we had a house full of loving, caring friends and family. Heidi wanted everyone to play "Outburst," with the men competing against the women. The men won as we all laughed and teased one another. Heidi was beaming and everyone obeyed her rules. As usual we all followed her cues: smile, find blessings and "carpe diem."

The next day she began another very long and arduous journey. This time we all had some idea of what we could expect with the treatments and with the unexpected setbacks. The reality of what was ahead for all of us far out-shadowed any of our hopes or fears. All of us found our courage from Heidi.

When she arrived at the wing of the hospital to go into her room it was as if Dolly Levy had just returned to Harmonia Gardens. Even patients who did not know who she was, seemed to ask the nurses,

"Who's that?" "Why all the smiles?" "Isn't she being admitted?" For us the answers were obvious, "She's Heidi. You'll see!" The nurses and aides, and even the two regular floor cleaners smiled when they saw her. She lit up the hospital wing. Her smile was infectious. All of this smiling and grand entrance came at a time in Heidi's life when she should have been feeling sorry for herself and very angry with God, the world, this hospital, and everyone in it. Instead of self-pity she had a party. It seemed as if the previous night's festivities really set the tone for her: "Okay, life doesn't stop, so let's get on with this show, and let's make it grand."

American Values

Values are very dynamic, maybe even organic. As we go through life, our values change. Some of them may become more well-defined; others may slip away as less important. A crisis may help us discover what is most valuable in our life. In fact, we may reorder our values when we reemerge after any traumatic event. Grieving brings so many of our values into focus. I have strengthened my belief in some and have disregarded others that I now deem as too superficial. My journey of grieving continues to be a conflict between my heart and my mind. I continue to suffer from the "curse of the philosopher" – that incessant need to question anything, to reflect upon just about everything, and to seek answers where none may ever exist. One of the prevalent conflicts for me is between the social values that exist within the United States and what they now mean for me. The following issues are examples of a few of these conflicts. The list is not exhaustive. It is merely a sampling of issues and values that illustrate the contextual influences affecting my grieving. I would like to be clear about the intent of the following section. This section and any challenges I am making about American values or beliefs throughout this book are not intended to be taken as a condemnation of the values or beliefs within the United States. My point is to illustrate that we live within a world and society in which values are inevitably in conflict. Getting rid of the values is not an option and not desired. Identifying the reasons for the conflicts and finding a way to balance the opposing tugs on our conscience is crucial for mental and spiritual health. My intent here is to share with you how these values relate to my grieving and create dilemmas, pain, or conflict.

Democratic principles. Americans tend to believe that the majority rules. This belief becomes a subtle form for socialization. We tend to judge our health and identity with the norms that our society creates. This view often conflicts with our other fundamental belief in the development of the individual. When should we conform to general norms that society "tells" us we should follow, and when should we follow the dictates of our own beliefs, desires, or wants? This conflict is readily seen in grieving. Society seems to have a sense that grief should go through some linear stages. Once these stages are complete, the person should move on. When individuals encounter a fundamentally different experience in their grieving, they may wonder what is wrong with them. All too often "disconnects" emerge at work because other employees are getting on with life and they expect their co-worker to get back on board. Even those people who are compassionate and who try to understand may fall into this trap. Another example of this conflict relates to people who cry at wakes, funerals, and then in the months and years following a loved one's death. Society is tolerant of crying at wakes and funerals. Afterwards, people may become very uncomfortable with those who cry. I am frustrated by those who judge whether or not someone is "doing well" during a wake or funeral by observing whether or not the person is crying. This judgment totally misses the internal feelings, the cultural differences, and the variety of personality traits that are involved in crying. Not crying, may, in fact, be quite unhealthy. A third example of these social conflicts occurs with the shame or guilt that some grieving people experience. Deaths through addictions or suicide often engender feelings of shame and/or guilt for those left behind. How could a wife not know that her husband was suicidal? How could a mother not be aware of her daughter's intentions? Why can't the parents help their children with their addictions? Whether anyone in particular makes any of these judgments is irrelevant. Parents and spouses in particular are expected to know what to do and feel ashamed or responsible for what happens to their loved one. The conflicted feelings of anger, shame, guilt, forgiveness, regret, and blame can swirl uncontrollably during the grieving process. Addictions are powerful forces in anyone's life and the consequences for loved ones continue to ripple throughout their lives. The feelings that arise from social condemnation are profound. These condemnations are unjustified, but that does not diminish their effects.

Rights. Rights become very conflicted within a diverse society. For example, whose rights take precedence in any given situation?

The relationship between rights and duties are often confused and blurred. Often times as people are grieving they may lose sight of the different ways others may grieve. Don't we have a right to grieve in a way that gives us health, comfort, and meaning? When we connect our rights with the notion of social expectations, we again can see the source of real conflict within people's lives. For example, don't parents of a child who was killed in a car accident have the right to place a memorial cross, wreath, or some other reminder at the site of the crash? Some areas allow for such practices; others do not. An elementary school in our area refused to put a memorial angel in its "Memorial Garden" because the student had already graduated and his brother would be graduating in a short time. As the grief counselor said to the grieving mother, "Your family won't be remembered by future students anyhow." The cruelty may have been unintentional, but the resulting sorrow was profound.

Deserving. Diane and I were going to Hawaii (visiting three islands over a three week period). Our previous trip was a major disappointment as record rainfalls on all the islands closed beaches, highways and made some of our days there very problematic. As we prepared to go a number of our friends said, "We hope you have a good time; you deserve it!" The last group to say this to us was at a grief support group. I had been thinking about this American belief that good people deserve good outcomes (the corollary being: if you work hard, you deserve good consequences). My response to the group was that this notion of "deserving" or entitlement is a dangerous myth. Just because we are good people does not automatically entitle us to anything. Bad consequences and natural disasters occur despite good intentions or even well-planned activities. Life is not inherently fair, and God does not guarantee good outcomes for good people. Blaming God or expecting the best because it is deserved is a distortion of reality. Of course it is better to be a good person and good planning and careful decision-making are prudent ways to live. But Americans distort reality when they feel cheated because they did not receive what they had expected. Diane and I did not "deserve" a good vacation. We have had a difficult time, we have worked hard in our life, we have lived a good and ethically based life, but that does not guarantee that good things will always befall us. Our friends at the support group readily understood my message. None of them "deserved" to be on the "Subway"; none of their children "deserved" to die. Life propagates the question, "Why do bad things happen to good people?"

Information. We are living in an age when the exchange of information is central to our lifestyle and economy. This information age has shifted many social structures and is constantly influencing forms of communication and relationships. Currently this major cultural shift has ill-defined customs and ways of relating (e.g., what are the ethics of e-commerce? What is the nature of cyberspace "interpersonal" relationships on Facebook?). Our information-driven society is replacing human interrelationships with mediated relationships. Email, text messages, cell phones, twittering, Facebook, etc. seem to be the connecting link between and among people. The technology mediates the relationship. This mediation affects the nature of the relationships in obvious as well as in very subtle ways. Although these technologies are tremendously convenient, I wonder what will happen to the dynamics of interpersonal relationships and communication. Are the elementary children who relate to others through texting and cell phones becoming inadequately trained in reading another person's body language? Currently, I believe that grieving requires social interaction and interpersonal compassion. What will happen for those who may become incompetent with this form of relationship? Will interpersonal incompetence make grieving in the future even more challenging and isolating? Should "streaming" funerals so people don't have to be present become the norm?

Throw-away. A "throw-away" culture creates a context within which relationships may be jeopardized by the attitude that makes it easy to discard the unwanted, used-up, or out-of-date person. If something is too difficult, then move on to something else that is easier or more quickly achieved. Some relationships get thrown away as people follow different journeys during their grieving. The belief is that people should get rid of their grief after an acceptable amount of time. Thus, just as we need to throw away the unwanted, so also don't we need to move beyond our grief because it isn't wanted? Throw away what will drag you down or get in the way of living "normally" (that is, without pain or loss). No one wishes to be thrown away; yet, doing so to others seems acceptable. This inherent contradiction only begins to identify the pain that people impose on other people. As our interests change, how far should we go in discarding people who no longer suit our purposes? Grieving parents will have people coming in and out of their lives. It seems to be inevitable. However, the reasons for these changes may be very healthy, or they may be the result of other social forces at work.

Shifting norms and mores. Civility, customs, language, and other societal norms are continually shifting, which can lead to confusion. One of the real shifts in our culture over the past century is the pace of life and the patience people are willing to afford others. Americans are typically impatient people. We like to do things in a hurry and can become very intolerant of anything that takes too much time. Yet grieving requires a great deal of patience and time. The grieving parent, for example, **must** become patient with his own feelings and confusion. Trying to rush through any experience that relates to grieving can be quite destructive. "Isn't it time for you to get over …?" Sometimes people who are grieving may even question themselves: "shouldn't I be 'better' now?" This impatience makes it very difficult to heal. We may not be able to develop a profound sense of meaning and purpose when we are rushed by others or even by ourselves. Another area of concern relates to the shifts in gender norms which have become very confusing for everyone. These shifts lead to expectations that may be quite unfair or unrealistic. Others are very justified. For example, it is okay for men to cry and demonstrate emotions at sporting events, but in other situations they are supposed to show control. When a father cries for the death of his child, others may accept the response, but later on the others may become uncomfortable if he continues to cry. We do not know how to react or deal with a crying father. Is America trying to become a more compassionate country, or are we trying to become more in control of ourselves and our lives? Actually, we are moving in both directions, and we are experiencing conflicts and confusion in the wake of these clashing forces. The next item expands on the shifting mores related to genders.

Shifting gender roles and family structures. Gender expectations and acceptable gender behavior is shifting in ways that are often perplexing. The very structure of acceptable family relations has been profoundly altered because of a significant rise in divorces, remarriages, and homosexually-based living. What does it mean to be a man or a woman? This is not an easy or simple question anymore. In fact, maybe we need to start considering that there are not just two types of genders. Maybe there is a continuum of genders that has a wider diversity than we had ever imagined. The increasing awareness of gender dysphoria only adds to the confusion. The differences between (or among?) the genders when it comes to grieving may create unrecognized stress or even fracture relationships. For example, some couples who bury a child end up divorcing after the funeral. I do not know if the claim that 75% of grieving parents divorce is true. What I do believe is that couples who had strained relationships will find the stress of grieving overbearing and probably overwhelming. A real source of strain in a marriage may emerge from the different ways that men and women grieve. If there are communication difficulties in a relationship, these differences will only exacerbate the situation. In addition, if someone who is grieving is unaware of her own feelings of anger, depression, etc., she may take out her sense of injustice or frustration on those who are closest to her. This behavior is common practice normally in life when we find ourselves unable to vent in healthy and constructive ways. We take out our frustrations on those who are not the cause for the feelings, but they are the closest ones we can reach. This type of response seems all too common for those who are grieving. A further complication occurs when a husband or wife expects the other to agree on such things as visiting the cemetery, when to buy a headstone, cleaning out the room, or when to return to work.

An aging society. The distribution of age groups within the United States continues to change and alter the social values and structures within society. The "Baby Boom Generations" have redefined many social institutions within society. Similar types of changes are expected to continue to emerge. More people will be burying their children as 70, 80 and 90 year olds outlive their children. Is their grief any less intense than the 30 year old who experiences the death of a 5 year old to cancer? Our society has so many ageist stereotypes that older people themselves often believe these misperceptions to be true: for example, an 80 year old who is forgetful has Alzheimer's; an 85 year old is too old to learn anything; everybody ends up in a nursing home sometime and dies there; and the list goes on. We tend to believe that older people have had experience with grieving, so, they know how to cope and move on more easily than younger parents. This attitude is tragic and sad; both for the older person, as well as the people who espouse it.

Paternalism. Paternalism is found in many areas within society, most notably in law and in the way people care for others (both personally as well as professionally). The paternalistic code is: "I know what is best for you." Although self-reliance, individuality, and autonomy are important social values, paternalism still plays a crucial role in social discourse and actions. The resulting conflicts often confuse people who may not be aware of their own paternalistic beliefs or attitudes or their support of paternalistic forms of rules, regulations, or behavior. Well-intentioned friends and family members may fall into the paternalistic trap when they think they know what is best for the person who is grieving.

A couple of years ago a colleague of mine stopped me in the hallway. "Charlie," he said, "since you're an 'expert' in Gerontology, you should be able to help me. I need a nursing home for my mom."

"What's the problem?" I asked.

"Oh, she doesn't clean her place the way she used to," he replied.

"Does she have any medical problems?"

"No."

"Does she feel she needs to move?"

He gave a knowing smiled and nodded. "Not really. In fact, she's comfortable where she is, but I know what she really needs."

I shook my head and said, "She's an adult and seems quite competent. Why don't you just let her continue to make her own decisions?"

He looked puzzled for a moment, then said, "That's a novel approach."

We need a real balance between caring for another and imposing unhealthy or interfering wishes or demands. With respect to grieving, another balance needs to come from the person who is grieving. Self-pity and destructive behaviors cannot be justified because the person is grieving. Grieving is not a license to do whatever one wants whenever it suits him, regardless of the consequences to others or to one's self. Certainly, grieving is hard work. There is a real challenge in trying to find the balance between allowing grief to be expressed in meaningful ways and in wallowing in self-pity that becomes destructive.

Quantification. Americans tend to gravitate toward quantifying just about everything. We are fascinated with measurements, statistics, and competition. We award trophies and make lists of the 10 best/worst (just look at TV listings, David Letterman, the American Film Institute, or sports programming). This attitude subtly pervades our lives. "Your experience must be so much <u>better</u> or <u>worse</u> than mine." "You must be going through so much <u>more</u> than I did." "How much <u>more</u> can I take?" "How much <u>longer</u> will this last?" The list is endless. Quantification also is an integral dimension for our critical thinking and empirical analysis of anything. Financial matters are quantitative; science is predicated on mathematics; and competition is measured at every level and in every field whether it is sports, entertainment, jobs, sales, etc. Applying quantitative comparisons to grief is a real distortion of the reality. Grieving "is what it is." It is not healthy or meaningful to try to quantify or measure the amount of one's grief or the length of time for grieving. This tendency dehumanizes the experience and distorts the real meaning of grieving. There are real differences in the contexts and reasons for the death of any loved one. It is unhealthy and unfair to try and quantify which types of deaths are "worse" than other types of deaths. A father may be proud of his son who died in a military action while another is distraught at his daughter's suicide. One is not better or worse than the other. They are different because the contexts, the people, and the meaning of each one's grief are different. Difference does not need to be quantified in grief.

Justice. American culture has a deep seated sense of justice. We may disagree about the meaning of justice or how to act "justly," but there is no disagreement that whatever the meaning one may have of justice, it is a cornerstone value in America. I have noticed that many movies and television programs have as one of their themes the idea of *justifiable* revenge. Someone is unjustly accused or treated, and the story of her revenge or bringing about a just resolution underscores the primary plot. This theme often becomes visceral for Americans. I believe that our society now is very conflicted about issues of justice. There is a pervasive belief, for example, that jurisprudence in the United States is no longer really about justice. This sentiment is troublesome for people because we believe that justice should really be the centerpiece. We really want others to be held accountable for their misdeeds. A dilemma has emerged over the past few decades because more and more people (elected officials, parents, athletes, for example) are failing to be held accountable for their misconduct and tend to resort to a feeling of "what I deserve" or "what I can get away with," rather than shouldering responsibility or acting in a suitable manner as a role model. A consequence of this context is that there is a greater sense of trying to blame someone else when something goes wrong or an injustice is experienced. Within this type of environment, blaming God for bad things happening or experiencing the visceral upheaval of a traumatic injustice should be expected for anyone's grief. God is supposed to be good and just. The death of a loved one is unfair and unjust. The death of one's child goes against any idea of fairness that one could posit. Coming to terms with these feelings of injustice and unfairness are crucial for meaning and healing to occur. This sense of justice becomes enmeshed with the question of "why." It all just seems so unfair, regardless of the circumstances. Thus, either consciously or unconsciously the grieving parent must work through these very deep-seated feelings. Sometimes, however, people are quite unaware of this inner battle. There is some truth in the cliché, "Life is unfair." Death is a primary example. Trying to deal with the reality of this belief or feeling can be very confusing.

Litigious society. America has become extremely litigious. The number and types of suits are astounding, and the ambulance chasing is appalling. Litigation begins with an adversarial premise; opposing positions are established, and rules must be followed. One frustration for many people in our society is the recognition that litigation is not aimed at achieving justice; its purpose is to win. For many, it appears to be a game; yet real human lives are involved. Litigation intrudes in the grieving process in a variety of ways. When murder or a negligent death occurs, the search for justice and accountability is a necessary part of the grieving process. Although truth and justice may emerge on television and in some real-life cases, the family of victims will often feel a greater sense of injustice and pain throughout the process, and even with the final rulings. In other cases, litigation can be used to heighten someone's pain. For example, friends of ours were sued by the man who was involved in the car accident that killed their daughter. He was suing because he was having trouble sleeping. Their daughter was not at fault in the accident, but that did not stop the suit from moving forward. When it comes to money, sometimes grieving parents are merely the collateral damage. As with so many characteristics of American culture, litigation provides a very ambiguous message. The idea of justice as the goal of litigation seems to be an ideal that has long become "gone with the wind." One of the strange twists of this litigious system for grieving parents may be that it can provide a fascinating outlet for one's anger. Since anger will emerge in grief in so many strange ways, litigation can provide an identifiable culprit that helps focus the grieving person's attention. In a strange way, the source of injustice could become a means for some healing. Of course, there is the further trap of becoming caught in the grips of the litigation and not being able to readily extricate one's self from it. In this case, moving on or finding closure is absolutely essential. Unlike the grief for a child that will and should continue for the rest of one's life, litigation should not become an abiding source of pain or an on-going source for one's anger. Finding the proper balance and the appropriate amount of time and effort for such activities is part of the juggling act a grieving parent and/or spouse must endure.

Contextual influences pervade the meaning of a person's death and how loved ones will address their own grief. There is significant difference for those who experience the death of a spouse, a friend, a relative, or a child. The feelings and experiences make the context unique in each person's death (which is singular) and every person's journey of grieving (which is individualistic). Understanding the contextual elements helps people to empathize and share the person's pain. There are real differences when parents experience the death of a child who is killed in a car accident, or one that commits suicide, or one that overdoses, or one that is murdered, or one that dies after a long (or short) illness, or one that is killed while on duty in the armed forces, in law enforcement, or fighting a fire. Those who understand that it is context which makes the death and grieving unique are also equipped to share the meaning and significance of the tragedy with others. In the grief groups my wife and I attend, it is very clear that each one of us has a unique story to tell and a singular journey to live. However, we can share the meaning, the tears, and the story of our loved one because we all can relate to our own core of grief. I have told friends and family that I do not know how I would be able to live without the love of my wife and my family. The relationship that parents have with one another and with other members of the family creates the contours and the context for their journey of grieving. Part of the work of grieving is coming to terms with what these relationships mean and how they will continue to unfold in the months and years that follow a loved one's death. Context sets the conditions and significance for death, but it's the particulars, the unique character of each death that gives the context meaning. A person can transcend the context of his grief, despite the limits of culture, gender, or any other social construct. This transcendence can incorporate the particular feelings and story that the grieving person has and will allow her to share it with others. Hopefully, others will be willing to listen and try to understand the meaning of the person's journey of grieving.

VI.

MAY 2, 2002.

Second Transplant

*I*t is amazing how much difference a year can make. The complications leading to Heidi's second transplant and the experience itself were entirely different from the first time. Although she had experienced infections, setbacks, and even a bout with encephalitis before the first transplant, the medical team reassured us that none of these were out of the ordinary and that Heidi's progress was right on track. The second time around Heidi experienced conditions that were quite out of the ordinary. For example, in April 2002 she underwent a series of tests to try to determine the cause for the fluid that was around her heart. She also had a "spot" between the lining and the heart itself. Could it be a tumor? The tests were inconclusive. Furthermore, the date of the transplant had to remain flexible because of a series of other setbacks and complications.

Another factor contributing to the difference this time related to the type of transplant she was going to have. The first one entailed using Kristen's bone marrow which was extracted from her hip. It was harvested early and sent to Johns Hopkins for culturing as a part of an experimental protocol. The second transplant involved transfusions from Tara that extracted blood, which would provide the stem cells for Heidi. The choice of a stem cell transplant in lieu of a bone marrow transplant was made in order to promote a quicker recovery and to induce Graft versus Host Disease (GVHD). Heidi did not experience very much GVHD after the first transplant, and the medical staff wanted to make sure she reached level 2 GVHD in order to insure that Tara's stem cells would eliminate Kristen's immune system and destroy any resistant leukemia cells.

They expected that Tara's cells would recognize Heidi as a foreign object within a month of the transplant.

A few weeks before the transplant Heidi began to experience pain in her shoulder and chest. Of course this worried all of us. I talked to the transplant coordinator, and she indicated that Heidi's condition required that they all continue to proceed whether or not she remained in remission. At this time a spinal tap indicated that the spinal fluid and marrow was "clean"; that is, they had no leukemia cells. One of the unique wrinkles in this preparation was the fact that we kept the issue of the possible tumor from Heidi. We felt that she did not need to know about the possibilities associated with this condition until the staff had some answer as to the cause. Her physician was uncomfortable with this secrecy, but the other professional staff assured him that she would be informed if any definitive answer arose or if any decisions had to be made.

One week before the transplant we seemed to enter "the twilight zone." We were at Roswell for Heidi to have her line placed for the transplant. To do so Heidi had to have an IV started. It took three pokes (each one painful) before they could find a vein that worked. When Heidi was taken for the procedure, they determined that the line was on the wrong side because they could get no reading from the dye they were injecting. So they had to move the line to the other hand. Heidi's heart pain was becoming very problematic also. Later that day (April 25) Dr. Wetzler came up and told us that the results of the echocardiogram she had had were inconclusive. "There are a number of possibilities for the pain," he explained. He went on to detail each of them, then concluded by saying, "Heidi, it's really your decision as to whether you want to proceed with the transplant or not." His tone was professional, yet kind. We had come to respect his competent and reassuring demeanor.

Heidi paused for a few moments, staring down at her hands. What did she see in them now? She had used them so effectively in her acting, in the classroom, and in her life. I now wondered what she saw – would there be a hidden answer or source of strength for her? When she looked up, she forced a tentative smile. "I don't see any need for a biopsy or any other delay. Let's just get the show going."

Dr. Wetzler gently smiled, then pursed his lips the way we had seen him do so often before. The lips and the twinkle in his eye were sure signs that he had a pleasant surprise for Heidi. "Would you be opposed to changing the routine this time around?" he asked.

"What do you mean?" was Heidi's puzzled response.

"Would you like to go home the day after the transplant?" he asked. "We know you'll get great care at home, and besides, it's very difficult to *recover in a hospital!"* He was smiling now, knowing that he had done something to make this ordeal much more palatable for her. Although she loved most of the people in the hospital, she hated having to stay there.

Everything after this conversation and leading up to the transplant, however, seemed to be just a little "off." The drug they were using to dilute her blood had been taken off the market. Katie said that Roswell must have some left over and were using it. Heidi had some blood in her urine, which really was not a major concern – at least, not for the professional staff! Throughout the 2 1/2 years we learned many lessons. A couple of them were: institutional time is very different from patient's time, and professional perceptions of conditions were very different from the family's feelings. There were times when professional reassurance was just not satisfactory to allay our fears. Her arm was still hurting, and we brought a heating pad from home. We were told that we needed to get permission from maintenance, but we did not bother. On the Friday before the transplant, the psychologist came to the room to talk to Heidi, but instead ended up talking to me because she was too groggy to participate. The next day Heidi was more alert, so we walked with her around and around the nurses' station. Heidi placed one tentative and determined step before another, trying to minimize the effects of the chemo treatments she was receiving. Heidi learned the importance of walking from the man with the tattoos, who she mentioned in her "hero article." We never knew his name, but took his advice to heart. "Walk," he had said. "I walk 100 laps a day. It helps with the nausea. Walk. Walk. Walk." So Heidi walked as much as possible – always wearing stylish outfits and socks with treads to prevent slipping. The staff worked hard at keeping Heidi's nausea in check, too. The shoulder and chest pain continued to persist; we could see how difficult it was for her as she winced every time she would sneeze.

Tara's preparation required that she take growth shots to stimulate her immune system so the harvesting would be sufficient for the transplant. On April 30 Heidi gleefully announced, "I am officially finished with ever having another chemo treatment." The day before transplant Tara had her stem cells harvested. Although it seemed as if they had enough, the Transplant Director said that they should have more "just in case." So on transplant day Tara had to be hooked up again. This second transplant felt so surreal to all of us. We did not know how to feel. The first time, we had actually "partied" during the procedures and enjoyed each other's company. Instead of us all being together, Tara and her husband, Joe, were downstairs having the second transfusion. When Tara had to urinate during the procedure, there was a comedy routine of staff trying to hold her arms and balance her over a potty. We laugh now; she was not laughing then. The Transplant Coordinator who had been so much a part of our lives in the planning and in the execution of the first transplant was not available for the second one. A very skilled and trained nurse whom we liked very much took her place. During the day I floated between upstairs (Heidi) and downstairs (Tara) while Diane stayed with Heidi. The other girls (Kristen and Katie) decided that it was best to make this time around completely different, so they went shopping before coming up to visit Heidi after the transplant was completed. The transplant itself (the event for which so much preparation had been done) lasted about 30 minutes. Watching the bag being hung and the life-giving liquid flow through the tube was almost routine for us by then. Heidi had no immediate reaction, so everyone went home; I stayed, and Heidi and I played cards.

In a sense, transplant day is like a birthday. The patient is becoming another person. In fact, Heidi liked to joke with her sisters saying, "Okay girls what felony should I commit now? I'll make sure my DNA is left behind so you'll get blamed!" Heidi was not sure how to feel this "birthday," although she did ask me where her presents and cake were. To her surprise her sisters did have some "stuff" for her when she went home the next day. That night Katie (whom we all trusted as the most medically competent and skilled of all of us) stayed at the hospital with Heidi who did not sleep well; Tara was nauseous from her ordeal; the rest of us just seemed to wander. The next day Heidi came home and we went into the routine of meds, drips, shots, and caring for our "new baby." The following day we had to take her to the hospital for a simple check up. It actually went relatively smoothly; however, Heidi's mouth sores were getting worse, and it was very difficult for her to eat anything. That night we tried playing Trivial Pursuit. Heidi loved playing games, but that evening none of us was able to muster the enthusiasm we usually brought to game playing with Heidi. We told her that she did not have to play. Her forehead wrinkled, and she said sternly, "All of us are not together often enough! We need to seize the opportunity!" So, we all crowded into her bedroom and continued to play. She pretended to enjoy herself.

Since our out-of-town girls were home for the transplant but would be leaving soon, we celebrated Mother's Day the following day. It was a subdued affair. We grilled fish, played dominoes, laughed when we could. Tara and Joe returned to Mayville. Heidi couldn't talk very much because her mouth sores were getting worse. We thought we were going to move into a routine of home care for her with frequent trips to the hospital. I noted in my journal for that Monday that Heidi was struggling to stay awake with us; "she's so sweet and so very vulnerable."

On Tuesday, May 7, Diane and Kristen took Heidi to the hospital. They gave her a morphine sucker which seemed to help with the mouth and throat pain. She was starting to have a small rash, so our visits to the hospital were going to be longer each day. They also gave her a morphine patch which caused her to become, as she said, "loopy." At home she took a nap and woke up with a fever, a hateful sign for her: it meant that her home stay was over and she would have to return to Roswell. The subsequent stay in the hospital was consistent with the whole surreal, twilight-zone experience that we had had with the transplant itself.

Since she was admitted at night, the staff that usually took care of her were not there. The doctor was a Nurse Ratchet type who refused to treat Heidi's pain, which was contrary to any other experience we had ever had at Roswell. The nurse on duty was someone we did not know, and she was no advocate for Heidi either. Diane spent the night from hell with Heidi. I had mentioned Heidi's chest pain (which had returned) and the doctor dismissed this too believing that Heidi had a low tolerance for pain. (I guess being cute meant you couldn't be strong and couldn't endure pain. Professionals, like everyone, are not immune to the problems attendant to stereotyping.) The next morning our "friends" returned. The aide who had called Heidi Technicolor was taken aback by Heidi's pain. The nurse, then Pam, came over, and both cried when they saw her pain. I blamed the night doctor while Katie blamed the night nurse for this obvious incompetent treatment. Over the next few days, her fever rode a rollercoaster, and her feet started to turn red and become itchy. That day she told Diane, "This isn't the morphine talking, but even though I feel crappy, I feel wonderful like everything is okay." As Diane wrote in the journal, "She breaks my heart with her goodness." Heidi also told Kristen, "Don't remember me like this when you're back in Minnesota." I spent the next night with her, and she would move in and out of sleep often. Her dreams were vivid, but she could not remember them all. She did tell me that in one she could speak fluent Japanese; another time she woke up because of the phone, which she thought had been ringing.

On Thursday, May 9 Heidi's pain was most localized in her throat. She could not swallow anything, and she was coughing and spitting up mucous. She kept asking, "What am I going to do?" No one had an answer for her. She was feeling very hungry, but was unable to eat. By that afternoon the rash had spread into patches around her body. Diane asked if Heidi may be allergic to all the morphine (patch and suckers). They decided to put her on another pain control med and gave Heidi control with the use of a pump. Diane started massaging her legs – this became part of their routine thereafter. The feeling that day was that the broad antibiotics they were administering were finally taking care of the fever. The next day, instead of seeing improvement, more complications emerged. She was having trouble urinating, so they had to catheterize her. Unfortunately, they did not have the correct size "balloon" for the catheter, so she leaked. This leaking continued as they kept trying to adjust the catheter. She was spitting up more, and there was some blood now. They did not know if the sputum was coming from her lungs or stomach, but the blood was probably from sores that burst in her mouth. During rounds that day Heidi had cried because of the pain. She was upset that she had done so in front of the attending physician and the residents (Roswell has strong teaching and research components in addition to patient care). She apologized to the female physician of the team that afternoon who replied, "Heidi, you're wonderful. It's in my job description to listen to people cry. I hope that I could have 1/100th of your ability to deal with difficult things in life." On Saturday they hooked up an aspirator to help remove the sputum that Heidi was discharging. They also removed the catheter, since she was leaking so much anyhow. It took a while for her muscles to readjust and she had a few "accidents" before they started operating correctly.

Sunday, May 12th was Mother's Day. By now all of our daughters and sons-in-law had returned to their homes, and Diane and I were already missing our loving support. During rounds on this morning, Heidi was very chatty and introduced everyone to "Howard" the floppy dog Diane had brought to her for some comfort. The female physician told Heidi that they were going to have to re-catheterize her because they had to increase the "processing" of fluids. Her counts were not good and they had to relieve the burden that all the meds were having on her kidneys. This time her catheter was "leak free" for two days, then became a big problem. By that afternoon she was able to swallow a little bit, even though it still hurt. Diane spent Mother's Day sleeping with Heidi. By Monday Heidi was able to drink a glass of water. Again, we were reminded of how much we all take so much for granted until it is taken away from us. On Wednesday, Diane noticed that Heidi's arm and port were red and swollen. Despite her inability to eat and all of her pain, she was released from the hospital the next day. Katie came home for the weekend to help us settle our patient at home. Katie's reassurance and ability to put Heidi's condition into perspective was so important for all of us. Heidi depended on Katie to interpret what the medical staff said, to provide reassurance and to give advice on what to do (especially whether to call the hospital with a problem or fever). The bumps in this road became bigger.

On May 23 we took Heidi to the hospital to have a biopsy of the fluid that was in her lung. The staff did not believe it was pneumonia and asked Diane and me to wait in the room next to their procedure area. We could hear Heidi's screams and crying as they punctured her and removed a large quantity of fluid (well over a liter). Her lung partially collapsed while they were draining her. After the procedure we did not know if her lung would re-inflate on its own or whether the doctors would have to put a needle in to re-inflate it. We didn't know if the fluid was caused by chemo, by meds, by pneumonia, by leukemia, or by the possibility of the unknown infection or tumor that was posited as a possibility before the transplant. We had had to deal with uncertainty often, but Heidi was already in a very vulnerable, compromised condition. That night her doctor called to tell us that the tests indicated that it was not leukemia. Thus the worst scenario was eliminated. Since pain is so subjective, we had to experiment continually with the dosages of pain meds that she was taking. Heidi had always worked hard at knowing what she was supposed to take. In fact, one night months earlier she correctly told the nurse that the med that she was about to administer was wrong and to check the records again. Sure enough, Heidi was right and the nurse apologized. During this current session of dealing with pain, Heidi realized that she was so compromised that she had to trust us to help her. There was no book or guide, so we relied on Katie's advice over the phone and Heidi's statements of how she felt. Medicine is just as much art as science, as we learned by watching the really good artists work with Heidi in so many different venues and situations.

A Prism and a Rainbow

The more I reflect upon life, the more I think about the meaning of continuity. Each one o f us has a self, or identity, that can be understood by the idea of continuity rather than just by the labels or categories that anyone may ascribe to us. We are not the same person we were years earlier. Life, circumstances, and our response to situations and people vary over time. Underlying these changes, however, is a "self": the person we are. Despite all the changes in our lives, we can sense that there still is someone who has gone through all of these changes. This "self" emerges through life's changes and continuity. My "self" and my journey through grieving include this sense of continuity.

My journey is buffeted by the social context within which I find myself. The Context Spheres (which are essential ingredients in life's continuity) add to the confusion and conflict that I feel during my journey. The conflicts in American values are examples of this confusion in my life. In the midst of my thinking about the context of this social disharmony, I have become entranced with the vision of a prism. A prism can symbolize white light on one side and the color spectrum on the other. Is our society so fractured that the prism really represents an impenetrable wall or can it give us a focus for addressing complex social issues? We can and should move beyond the barriers that separate people and focus upon the processes that can bring about harmony within a world of differences. Even though grieving is a singular journey, should we not be able to touch one another's hearts and souls to share the meaning of what each person is feeling? Certainly many people who are grieving will refer to their loved one's death by uttering the refrain: "But that just doesn't make sense" or "That's not fair." More and more I find myself saying: "You're right" and, then, just sighing. The lack of fairness or justice extends far beyond just grieving in our society. There is widespread confusion, lack of trust, and anger that seems to be so ingrained within our social fabric. The sources for these feelings are as varied as are the issues that often divide family, friends, cities, regions, and even the country itself.

If we examine a prism, we see light entering and a spectrum bursting forth. The asymmetry is very revealing because it symbolizes the inherent differences that exist within our world. This asymmetry includes an image of homogeneity on one side and heterogeneity on the other: the classic dualism of sameness and difference or one and many. But the real essence of the analogy is that the focus is on the prism, not the light nor the spectrum. American society seems to focus either on the process or on the outcomes, but rarely seems to pay enough attention to how they relate and are interdependent. Isn't there an inherent continuity between how something emerges and the goal that is created? A prism works because there is light and because of its shape. So, too, we need our identities, our group affiliations, our habits and ordered ways of doing things. But life, like a prism, doesn't exist merely in that homogeneous world. Becoming ourselves or working towards the goals set by a particular group or a specialized way of thinking misses the real beauty of the prism's work; it misses the real essence of life: creating difference and living with change.

When a loved one dies, our order shifts. Sometimes people in our life do not share the meaning or the extent of the shifts that occur to each one of us. The social norm seems to want everyone to "go back to normal" at an appropriate time – remember the ultimate, social response to 9/11. Instead of seizing the opportunity to reevaluate our national and social priorities, our leaders urged us to go back to the ways we were living before. Thus, there is a subtle prejudice that calls us to follow a homogeneous way of doing things. "Here are the stages to go through. When you're done, it's time to move on." This attitude calls for individuals to mask their unique identity within a socially acceptable way to grieve. However, the color spectrum gives us an alternative way to view our response to crisis. Instead of falling into the trap of denying our individuality, we can focus upon the diversity that is truly essential in life. The essence of the color spectrum is that there is a continuum (connectedness) among colors, yet there is no particular demarcating line that defines the end of one color and the beginning of another. So, too, grieving may have some general traits that are shared, but there is no specific identity with particularized characteristics that defines each person's grieving. Therapists and psychologists may want a simple scheme or common set of stages so they can measure success or failure – or provide a ready way to treat "people." The truth of the matter is that they really need to heed the reality of the uniqueness and differences among individuals. That makes their studies and treatments so much more difficult to schedule and research; however, grieving is more like a prism than it is a condition to fix. It is not an ailment that can be treated and eliminated; it is a new way of living.

The prism contains the values, the strategies, and the beliefs that we hold and that we may apply in our daily activities. The prism doesn't change; it is the light that goes in and the shades of the spectrum coming out that account for the dynamic character of life. What we need to do is start finding an effective means to communicate and a way to share each other's values and beliefs. We need to respect individuality and difference. This communication and sharing should be characterized as fair and should include reciprocal respect for each person involved. I have learned this lesson by listening to other parents share their grief and their stories. Regardless of how differently they express themselves or how varied their journey, I have come to respect the validity and meaningfulness of their experiences. Furthermore, would we not be better served by treating everyone with the dignity that he ought to receive, rather than melting everyone into some gelatinous "ooze" without any distinguishing characteristics? We ought not to treat all children the same: they differ! Older people are not the same: they differ! Racial groups do not behave the same: they differ! If difference and individuality are essential characteristics in our social order, why do we persist in trying to overlay that landscape with an impossible demand for sameness?

We need to reexamine the notion that equality means sameness. People are not created the same, nor should we treat people the same. I do not have the same respect for my wife, my mother-in-law, my daughters, my neighbor, and my friends. Nonetheless, I do respect each of them. The value of respect can be found "within the prism." It is a value that relates to my life in **all** of its dimensions. Yet when it becomes a part of my experience, it becomes expressed in different ways (just as the light becomes scattered into different colors in the spectrum). Saying that there is difference does not mean that any one person is a better person than any other person. It means that some people are gifted painters, while others are not; some are gifted with singing; etc. Individual and group differences are real. Our difficulty in focusing upon the relationship between equality and fairness and interpreting them to mean sameness is rooted in our cultural eagerness for homogenizing work, time, and roles. Not only have we emphasized routine, habits, and sameness, but we have begun to narrow our vision in the face of overwhelming confusion and proliferation of information. The rate of change is getting to be too much for us to handle. Creating endless options only exacerbates the confusion that we have to confront on a daily basis.

Our real challenge is to live continually within the prism and relish in our ability to accept light (sameness) and create from it a wonderful colored spectrum (difference). Harmony and peace in the world and within our own lives require a focus upon the processes of dealing with conflict and opposites. For people who are grieving, it is important to see that balance and meaningfulness are like the white light penetrating the prism. We all need to seek these values and dimensions in our life. Doing so requires a prism that helps us see the colored contours that our journey will take: for instance, a rainbow.

As I look at a rainbow or at the light that is refracted through a prism, I can distinguish the colors as blue, green, yellow, and red. Trying to find where yellow ends and red begins is arbitrary at best. The spectrum represents the type of continuity that is necessary for achieving balance, harmony, and meaning. We can discern differences along the continuum, but the dividing lines are blurred. Yellow and red are different, yet on the spectrum they blur and blend together. In a sense, that's what I am as a person. I can look at the labels people may place on me (stubborn, teacher, father, e.g.) and identify the influences in my life (for example, those included in all the Context Spheres). The reality is that there is an overlapping of influences in our lives that creates an interconnectedness which really should not be overlooked or dismissed. For example, a common image of America is that it is a melting pot. The problem with this image is that it is neither descriptively accurate nor even a desirable goal. America is not a homogeneous grouping of people that are blended into a common mix that eradicates our differences. A stir fry represents us more accurately. We are in the same wok and may be influenced by the same sauces or spices, but we still remain separate vegetables. The strength of the United States is in the diversity of talents, interests, dreams, and lifestyles of the people. This rich tapestry is strengthened by our differences, which can be blended, especially in times of crisis or real national emergencies. Isn't this difference the very essence of the meaning of democracy? Although we live in a Republic, America still provides a country within which democratic principles are honored and respected, or at least they should be. Although each of us may be a different "color," we are connected by the influences (the spices) and contexts (the wok) within our country. The prism is a collective bond which can blend our differences, while acknowledging our basic, common humanity. Assimilating into American culture (living in the "wok") should not destroy the differences among the "vegetables" — our individualistic gifts and talents.

When we put a label on a person, we are reducing that individual to just one characteristic that he may possess. Labels may be useful indicators, but they fail miserably as defining characteristics. Any person is a mosaic of inter-lapping constellations of traits, habits, beliefs, moods, etc. A person who is grieving should never be defined by the single characteristic of grief. Saying that someone is a grieving mother gives us some information about the conditions of that person's life, but it does nothing to tell us about who that person may be. The core of grief remains at the center of my life, but it does not define who I am, and it does not determine everything that I may do. There can be a world of difference between the influences that affect a person's life and the activities, behaviors, and decisions that someone makes. There are times when the influences take over and the person follows the tide. There are other times when the person may take a different turn, or may restructure the priorities, or may choose to follow paths that seem hidden to others. Thus, it is helpful to see the labels that we associate with a person's character in the context of life's continuity. On the other hand, we should not stop at the labels as we try to understand and relate to ourselves and to others.

There are a wide variety of continua in life, for example intuition and intellectual analysis. We can blend and interconnect intuitive feelings and insights with a clearly defined intellectual analysis. In fact, "a-ha" experiences may be the result of this collision. Many times in our lives we do not bother to distinguish among the varying factors involved in the way we are dealing with an experience. We act or react often following habitual patterns of behavior that we learn to identify as the typical way to act. The reality is that the heart and head, mind and body, emotions and reasoning are interconnected. In fact, we need to start with this interconnectedness first and realize that any label or distinction we use is secondary. We create the label to help us organize our lives or our world. If we did not do so, our life would be disorganized and chaotic. The real problem occurs when we make the distinctions into realities. Like the color spectrum, the labels that we use in life only separate elements into something we can use to help us with our ordering needs. These labels do not define the person; they only give indicators that help us understand the type of behaviors a person is likely to take. For some people, this type of ordered world becomes an obsession and whenever something is out of place that person may become irritated, angry, or too distraught to function effectively.

One of my favorite biblical passages is taken from Ecclesiastes: "For everything there is a time and place under heaven." The passage then identifies the opposites that provide differing continua in our lives: hate/love, war/peace, tears/laughter, etc. Each one of these can blend into the other, depending upon circumstances and contexts. Isn't it true that we can cry when we are laughing too hard or start laughing when we cry too intensely? Love can turn into hatred when trust is broken. This sense of continuity is crucial for understanding the grieving process. Grieving may become the core of our journey through life, but we do not lose the capacity for laughter, hope, and, yes, even joy. There are times when the grieving is so overwhelming that we may lose sight of the other colors in our rainbow. However, if we realize that life is interconnected, then we can begin to believe how hope and joy can once again become a part of our life. I do not know if I have received my permission to experience **real** joy again; however, I do know that I have experienced joyous moments since Heidi's death. Our loved ones want us to regain the capacity for joy and laughter in life. This awareness may be something that we can know intellectually, and it probably is what our well-intentioned friends are trying to convey when they talk about re-engaging or moving on in life. As I have said before, I do not like the phrase *moving on* because it means that I am somehow supposed to put my grieving aside and return to normal living. That cannot and will not happen for me. I do not want to do so; nor should I. This rejection of moving on does not mean that I am trapped in a spiral of depression. Instead, I see a continuum of life with death. Learning how to understand this continuum and integrate it into my life defines the contours of my journey; it does not define me.

Human beings are ever-changing, continuous creations who balance, or who attempt to balance, a multiplicity of influences, possibilities, characteristics, and tendencies. Sometimes we clearly land on "red," and we can see our behavior as selfish and childish. Other times we cannot discern if we are "yellow" or "orange"; we're in the blended areas of the spectrum. At those times we don't seem to fit into any recognizable pattern or category. We may ask ourselves: "Who are we?" We may feel confused and others may not know how to respond to our behavior. As in all cases related to grieving, we are better served at these times to follow our intuitions and refrain from trying to force ourselves or others into artificial categories. I can vividly recall our wake for Heidi; in fact, if I think about it carefully enough I can envision many of the wakes I have attended in my life. I can picture people and situations, but I can only rarely recall anything that was specifically said. The particular words are not really all that important anyhow. It's the context — it's the sharing — it's the willingness to be a part of someone else's grieving that is so important. I have learned that there are no magic formulas, no golden words that can take away anyone's pain. The comfort and healing that one shows by caring and being present is the best gift anyone can give. A hug far supersedes any words that can be uttered.

Grieving is a continuum of interconnected feelings, thoughts, beliefs, and experiences. Healing and finding meaning in life is not resolving the component parts of the different "stages" of grief. Healing and finding meaning is weaving the dynamics of all of these thoughts and feelings into an integrated balance of the opposite forces in life. Finding this balance is difficult yet necessary to make grieving meaningful.

VII.

HEIDI'S CHILDHOOD:
Vacation experiences

*L*ooking back at this young woman who had become a hero to so many as she dealt with the ravages of her illness, I am reminded of those childhood snippets that form the mosaic of one's personality. A few examples from our family travels will illustrate Heidi's will and determination on her journey. I love to travel. Since the beginning of our marriage, Diane and I have ventured on at least one vacation together almost each year. These getaways helped us renew ourselves and spend some uninterrupted time together. Even when the children were small, Diane and I would escape for a brief time. We also vacationed with our girls. As they grew up, our trips with them became bigger events. For a long time, we owned a pop-up camper that gave us the freedom to travel the country with three, then four children. Before we owned the camper, we had rented cabins in various locations around New York State. The following snapshots are a few images of some of Heidi's experiences with these vacations over the years. These trips are a part of our family's history and collective memory.

Rocky Mountain National Park, 1983. The campsite: When Heidi was going on two, we took an extended trip out west, visiting my relatives in Kentucky on the way to the mountains and visiting Diane's relatives in Minnesota on the way back home. One afternoon we were spending some quiet time at the camp site. There was a small ridge running along the site with a grand view of the mountains and the speckled array of wild flowers. The three older girls were sitting on a log, sketchbooks on their laps, trying to replicate the breathtaking scenery with crayons and colored pencils. I looked up from my tasks to see Heidi sitting on her little lawn chair facing the camper instead of the mountain. She was sitting contentedly looking at some books that her sisters had given her. I laughed, then put on my "stern face." "Girls," I called out. "Why is Heidi facing the wrong direction?"

The girls looked nervously at one another before admitting, "You said we had to take her with us. You didn't say we had to include her."

This story has been mythologized over the years, showing so perfectly the real demarcation of our "two" families and Heidi's contention that she had four mothers.

The hail storm: On a crystal clear, blue-skied July day, we decided to drive to the top of a mountain area and hike to a secluded lake. From the lake we would hike to a path that descended the mountain and then catch a bus ride back up to the parking lot. We had two back packs: one to carry our lunch and water, while the other one was for me to carry Heidi. The sun shone brightly with thin wisps of clouds spotting the sky. We sang and chatted our way to the lake. We found an isolated spot by the lake for our lunch. Animals played nearby, the sun reflected off the lake, birds chattered, and not another person was to be seen anywhere. The hike to the ridge of the mountain was not far, but Heidi decided that a ride on my back was in order. When we reached the beginning of the path that serpentined down the face of the mountain, we felt like the von Trapp family in The Sound of Music. The valley spread out in front of us, and other mountains reached up to provide a breath-taking view. The narrow path took long sweeping curves along the side of the mountain. Just as we had started our descent, black storm clouds swept across the area. First came the heavy rain. Then the hailstones. We were drenched almost instantaneously. Since Katie was afraid of heights, Diane helped her wind her way down. Tara and Kristen (ages 11 and 9) fended for themselves. Heidi, riding in the carrier on my back, started crying with the first burst of thunder and flash of lightning. "I'm scared," she cried. And then she fell asleep. Sleeping was often her response when confronting unpleasant circumstances. When we finally stumbled to the bottom of the mountain a kind, young couple in a Volkswagen stopped and offered us a ride back to our car. That act of spontaneous good will has helped me to try to "pass it forward."

Mount Rushmore, same trip. The stairs: The sculptures of the presidents surprised all of us. The girls thought that this was just another one of Dad's vacation plans that required a stop to see some scenery or historical marker that would only bring boredom. Instead, each one of us appreciated the mastery and craftsmanship. There are an exorbitant number of steps reaching from the viewing area to a small museum and rest rooms. Not relishing the thought of carrying Heidi up and down that many, I used my reverse psychology, "Heid, there are just too many stairs for you to walk. I guess you're still so little that I'll carry you." Heidi, holding my hand, said, "I'll do it by elf" (a phrase she used whenever she was displaying her independence). She marched over to the top of the stairs with a determined look. She carefully planted one small foot on the top step, smiled, and slowly and steadily climbed down all the steps. When she got to the bottom, she turned around and gave me an "I bet that surprised you look." When we finished looking around, I said, "Well, Heid, I guess there's no way you'll make it all the way back up, too?" With a smug look on her face, she, alternately held onto my and Tara's hands, proudly ascending all the stairs by her "elf." When she reached the top, the entire family applauded. Heidi beamed.

Prince Edward Island, 1985 and 1987. My girls loved the <u>Anne of Green Gables </u>book series and campaigned vigorously to visit her "home" on Prince Edward Island. We traveled to P.E.I. twice and viewed the quaint character of the island that gave the world "Anne". Although Heidi was almost four, then almost six, for our two visits, she was enthralled with the island and grew to love the books as much as her sisters. Tara and Heidi created a special bond because Tara read all eight books in the series to her. We spent time on the island swimming, exploring, playing games, visiting sites, and attending the musical in town. The visits provided vivid experiences that brought the imagery of the books into living color. The girls saw the Lake of Shining Waters, the White Way of Delight, the Haunted Forest, and the homes that pervaded Lucie Maud Montgomery's writings. These books provided a wonderful vista into the world of imagination. It taught the girls lessons and opened their minds and hearts to the mysteries of life and the wonderment of the world of creativity. Heidi cherished the ideals and truths that were found in the pages of the series. Tara related some of them in her Eulogy.

Purmerend, 1988. The heart attack and Zubazinga: When Heidi was almost seven, we toured Scotland and England for eight days before flying to the Netherlands to stay with our friends, Peter and Tiny. We have visited them in Holland, and traveled to different parts of Europe with them (for example, our trip to Tuscany the summer after Heidi died). They have visited us a number of times also. They live in a town north of Amsterdam. Their two children are the ages of our older girls, so Heidi was still the "baby."

One adventure included the 10 of us breaking into three groups and rowing boats through the backland canals of Yisp. Heidi was in the boat with Diane and me. "I'm going to row the boat all by myself," she declared.

"Okay, sweetie, but if you get tired, we'll be happy to help out," I said.

"I'm not going to get tired. And I don't need help."

Knowing that she hated being treated as the youngest, I handed her the oars and sat back to let her row. After two minutes, she looked at Diane. "I'm having a heart attack," she said, no trace of irony in her tired voice. She then curled up in the bottom of the boat and fell asleep. Diane and I, used to her theatrics, continued rowing. When she awoke, we asked her if her heart was better.

"Yes," she said, "I'm healthy now, but rather tired from this whole ordeal."

One evening the 10 of us went to a restaurant, where we spent over two hours laughing, teasing, exchanging stories, and thoroughly enjoying one another's company. Heidi wanted a special drink so the waitress put an umbrella with a little monkey into it as a stir. Our friend, Peter, asked Heidi what she was going to name the monkey. A flurry of suggestions followed, each one encouraging louder and louder laughter. Eventually, Heidi shouted out, "Zubazinga!" We have no idea how that name came to her, but it became not only the monkey's name, but a family story there-after. In fact, when we brought our puppy home for a Christmas present that year, we told Heidi that she could name him. Zubazinga was one of her two choices. We opted for the other one, Vragil (not Virgil), because it was more "normal."

Bar Harbor, 1991. The bike ride and the restaurant: Three years after our visit to Europe, our friends came to the United States. Peter was scheduled to attend a conference in Orono, Maine, so they stayed with us for a few days, and then we drove them to Maine. We took a scenic drive and stayed in both Vermont and New Hampshire. While Peter was attending the conference, Tiny and their two children, Maaike and Wilem, Diane, Heidi, and I stayed in two adjoining cabins in Bar Harbor. After his conference we traveled to Gloucester to go whale watching then took them to Boston where they caught their flight back to Holland.

One day while we were in Bar Harbor, we rented bikes. Wilem, who was 13, was very athletic, and I was challenged to stay with him as he motored off the path and through different fields. Heidi rode with Diane, Tiny, and Maaike, who was 16. We all started riding together around a lake which had some slopes and curves. Early in the ride we encountered a gentle, descending slope. As Heidi tried to slow the bike down, her eyes widened; her knuckles turned red; and her body became quite rigid. When she managed to stop the bike Diane asked, "Can you go on?"

"I don't know," Heidi sighed. "This is real scary."

Diane thought a moment and said, "Well, we still have a long way to go. Want to try some more?"

"Okay," came the whisper of acceptance. It was clear that Heidi didn't have enough strength in her grip to brake the bike properly. I do not remember her ever feeling comfortable or enjoying that ride, yet she completed it. One evening when all of us were together we were walking through an artists' area in Gloucester. Peter and Tiny always take an afternoon "break," during which they stop whatever they're doing, relax, and have a drink. When we are with them, we love following this custom; we're not sure why we don't when we're away from them. On this particular afternoon we found a restaurant with a bar and piano. It was empty, but the proprietor was willing to serve us whatever we chose to drink. When we started to order our drinks, Heidi mumbled, "We shouldn't be here. This isn't right." Diane asked her why. "Because ..." was the only answer she could muster. Her eyes were "flinty" and she kept a scowl on her face the whole time we were there. She could not accept the fact that we would stop in a bar and have a drink during the day. As the rest of us chatted and laughed, Heidi remained glum and silent. Her looks were reproving. Since we didn't heed her desire to leave the premises immediately, she remained fidgety. To this day we really do not know what prompted this response. We serve beer and wine when people are visiting or when we are having a party, and we never witnessed such a response from her before. We knew that she had a crush on Wilem. Could she have been embarrassed for some strange reason? We will never know.

Disney World, 1994. Fireworks and The Brown Derby: Usually teens are hesitant to be seen in the company of their parents; we tend to embarrass them with our very existence. Heidi was always different in this respect. Diane, Heidi and I went to Disney World when she was 13 years old. We had been there with the whole family years before and camped at Camp Wilderness. We could not afford the upper scale accommodations, but all of us learned to accept the adventures in camping, even the June bugs that infested our camper one evening.

With Heidi it was different. When she was young she was a part of the camping scene. As her sisters proceeded into college and beyond, we found that they were no longer joining us on the vacations so we were able to upgrade our trips. There were two particular scenes at Disney World that year that give a glimpse into the development of Heidi's character. She eagerly went wherever we wanted to go but was most thrilled with the MGM exhibits and rides. She loved the waves and snorkeling at the Blue Lagoon; swimming was the one sporting activity that she not only enjoyed but displayed competence. All three of us were thrilled by the rides in the Magic Kingdom and were enthralled with the sights and sounds at Epcot. At MGM, however, she reveled in the activities. Since we were staying over the 4th of July we saw an incredible fireworks display. In addition to Mickey Mouse orchestrating the usual music and sights of the area's evening spectacular, on the 4th an additional patriotic display with the traditional music pierced the air and sky around us. I was enchanted by Heidi's almost childish delight in these sights and sounds. The three of us sat on the street (the location of the fireworks that year) and watched the dazzling display which produced a sense of carefree bliss: life was good!

The other notable experience occurred when we ate dinner at The Brown Derby restaurant. When our children were younger we tended to eat out at very modest restaurants or fast food establishments. At Disney World we decided to treat Heidi to a classy meal. Even as a youth she gravitated to the big city and the upscale lifestyle that can come with stage and screen life. At age 13 this preference was beginning to emerge as she was now turning away from the sweat pants of childhood to the more stylish clothes of adulthood. Heidi settled into the booth and soaked in the ambiance of the restaurant. The waiter came to our table and sensed that he had an audience with Heidi (maybe it was her coy, teenage smile or the lowering of her eyes when they made contact with his). With a flourish he snapped her napkin from its place and swept it onto her lap. She beamed briefly, then pursed her lips and with dignity gently tossed her hair. "Why, thank you," she said. I don't remember anything about what we ate or drank. The look of delight on Heidi's face was all the memory I needed for that experience. She almost giggled when the waiter took out his scrapper and cleaned the linen of any crumbs that had fallen. Heidi was always very attentive to details because of her sensitivity to good acting and her awareness that the "little things" separate the average from the superior.

New York City, 1995. Les Mis: The following year we decided to take Heidi to New York City for a weekend. By age 14 Heidi was enchanted with the stage and saw NYC as her Mecca. We toured and made sure she got to the Empire State building so she could experience the final scene from <u>Sleepless in Seattle</u>.

For me the true highlight of the trip was taking her to see "Les Mis" on Saturday evening. We had exposed all of our children to a variety of musical theater performances in Buffalo and Toronto. But, for Heidi, going to a performance on Broadway was the pinnacle. Again, she was not fazed that she was with her parents. She soaked in the theater; read the playbill carefully; and just sat and smiled even before the Overture began. Our entire family loves this musical. One of my characters for my *classes is Marius, the young man who I project as an arthritic old man whose life review exudes feelings of regret and survivor guilt. Part of my inspiration for that characterization came from watching Heidi during the performance that evening. The particular scene that I still vividly recall is the way the character of Eponine captivated Heidi. Eponine loves Marius, but his heart is set upon Cossette. During the attack on the barricade, Eponine steps in front of him and is fatally shot with the bullet heading for Marius. She dies in his arms and sings a beautiful song of love and surrender. Watching Heidi throughout this scene is a touching memory and wonderful gift. The tears that streamed down her face showed me that there was deep meaning in her life and that loving relationships and sensitivity to justice were an integral part of her self-worth. During her struggles, and sometimes when I watched her sleep in the hospital, this scene would pop into my consciousness. Now, I wonder if Heidi's identification with this character was even closer than I realized. Did Heidi have a sense that she would die young and that her death would be the culmination of a great performance punctuated by sacrificing so much that the ones she loved could have a life that is enriched and blessed? Was that her gift to us?*

Thoughts that Matter

As I have journeyed with my grieving, I have learned a wide variety of "pieces" of advice that make a lot of sense to me.

1. **Crying cleanses the soul.** No one should ever apologize for or feel uncomfortable about crying. I have told people who apologize for crying in front of me that I am touched and grateful that they have been willing to share their tears. It is comforting to know that others care. I have also learned the power that can come from crying. To assume that tears are a sign of weakness is to miss the truth about life. Laughter and tears are so inextricably linked that it is easy to experience tears from laughter or laughter emerging from a "soul-wrenching cry."
2. **Saying good night rather than good-bye makes sense to us now.** Good-byes are never easy, in almost any context. During Diane's journey of grieving she has found a song that makes this distinction. We like the connotation of saying good night to Heidi, knowing that we will be with her in the morning. In fact, we said good night to her when she died.

3. **"Grieving" touches me more profoundly than "grief."** "Grief" sounds too static — too easy for professionals (counselors, psychiatrists, social workers, pastoral ministers, clergy, etc.) to use as a label or category — too easy for them to identify the stage or stages that parents experience after their "loss." Stages allow them to provide steps or strategies that we can use so we can "move on" or, in their minds, hopefully find closure. These approaches undermine the density and extent of pain and sorrow that attends to our grieving. "Waves" conjure up more meaningful images; we are at sea and not in some immobile bin.

4. **In one sense many people who are grieving have gained an advantage over others when it comes to the trivialities of life.** Many of those who are grieving become impatient with trivialities. Life has changed so much for them that priorities become completely realigned. This transformation is usually good and empowering. It is important to accept the different person you may have become while grieving. The key point is to understand the changes and embrace the shift in what is important in life now. Of course, the challenge is not to get too irritated with those "water bugs" who flit through life and only attend to the most meaningless tasks.

5. **Realize that other tragedies and misfortunes in life will continue to come your way.** About three months after Heidi died, Diane and I were visiting with our daughter, Kristen, and Diane's extended family in Minnesota. Her parents were watching our dog, Vragil. We received a call that Diane's mother had fallen backwards down the basement stairs while trying to get the dog inside. She was in an ICU, her neck was broken, and the doctors had to operate and insert a steel plate. Her recovery has been long and painful. Almost six years after Heidi's death, Diane's father died. Another problem occurred when Diane had to have emergency surgery to remove her gall bladder. She had to be sedated for her surgery and it was emotionally difficult for her to watch and feel an IV line being placed into her vein. Although this experience was not life threatening or life altering, her mother's fall and recuperation and her father's death have been. These experiences have brought our grief to the surface in so many ways. Some small anecdotes will illustrate the point. When we first

went into the hospital room for her mother, Diane and I were both overwhelmed with the feelings of being in a hospital again. The seriousness of the condition intensified these feelings, and the sight of a pole with bags of saline and medicines dripping into her mother was very difficult to experience. Heidi had had so many drips and meds hung from that type of a pole. In fact, we often had one in our home during her struggle. Her father had to be put on full-time oxygen and Diane was at his side when he could no longer breathe. Other tragedies also occurred. The year after Heidi died my aunt (with whom I was very close) died; we had to put our dog of 15 1/2 years to sleep; and, we had to leave the church that had been an important part of our lives for almost 30 years. There are also the day-to-day inconveniences that just keep happening. For example, while Heidi was going through her struggle, the furnace died one evening; we had 3 inches of water one night throughout much of our basement because the sump pump stopped working; and, the water pipes in our basement burst, leading us to replace all of them in the house. Life and death continue to interweave themselves in a continual dance of joys and sorrows. Grieving does not make anyone immune from the continuing onslaughts of life.

6. **Be patient with yourself and try to do so with others.** Grieving takes time and patience. Others may not understand this lesson, so try to realize that they may be functioning from a world of ignorance or well-intentioned concern. Remember that riding on the subway makes those who grieve asynchronous from others (see Chapter VIII for details).

7. **Be willing to go to the pain in your grief, but avoid going to the torture.** This phrase has become important for me to understand. I don't want to avoid all the pain that my grieving brings to me. For those who are not grieving the way we are, this idea may seem quite alien. Americans are pre-occupied with avoiding pain at all costs. To do so in grief is quite unhealthy because it prevents healing. People have asked why we continue to attend grief support meetings, "Doesn't that just make you feel sadder?" In a sense it does exactly that, but this type of pain is cleansing and healthy because it provides an arena for understanding and

a place to grow *with* and *from* our pain. The athlete's mantra "no pain, no gain" has a strange application here.

8. **Understanding your personal limits is essential.** We all have limits in everything we do. Americans sometimes slip into the myth of invulnerability. The levels for these limits are so varied that there is no way to identify the markers or even the characteristics associated with our limits. Sometimes we may even surprise ourselves with how far some of our boundaries or limits may reach. When we exceed our limits, we will "pay" — psychologically, emotionally, physically, or spiritually (sometimes all of them). Our limits vary with time and experience. There are times and situations when we are able to tolerate what some people say or do, while at another time or in a different context we are unable to do so. Becoming attuned to ourselves and the changes that emerge and shift with our limits will help us avoid situations and people which are poisonous or tormenting. Understanding our limits will help us "go to the pain" in healthy and meaningful ways.

9. **Grieving creates a context within which we have to reconsider so many of our assumptions and the words we have used in our life.** Words that other people use can become incredibly charged and instantly change our attitude and feelings. We may find ourselves overly sensitive to what had been routine ways of speaking or acting before, for example, using the phrase, "I could shoot myself" around a parent whose child has committed suicide.

10. **It may be wise to invest time and/or money in some type of memorial.** When I was younger, I thought some of the memorials or activities I had seen were foolish or "weird." Now I know how important they are for those who are grieving, and I have learned how foolish it is to judge the way others grieve and deal with their pain.

11. **It is important to learn to be alone.** Americans tend to have a difficult time being by themselves without any distractions around (music, TV, radio, blogs, iPads, phones, etc.). The need to always have some intruding noise prevents us from finding solitude. Being alone does not necessarily cause depression, anxiety, or feelings of worthlessness. Some other factors in life are really the cause for those feelings. Solitude becomes the ability to be comfortable with being alone and learning to accept the

person you are attempting to be or become. There is a real and important distinction between being alone and feeling lonely. We can experience one without the other. We can feel lonely when we are in a crowd or even when we are with our best friends. Being alone does not necessitate that you have to be consumed with feelings of loneliness.

12. **Don't let anyone else tell you when and how you should deal with your loved one's personal effects, room, etc.** How and when you should deal with those treasures varies widely. In fact, you may find that spouses, siblings, etc. have very different time schedules or ideas about what to do. Tolerance and patience should be the guide in determining the best ways for families to heal when attending to these issues. It is very destructive for someone to try to dictate to others when and how a child's clothes, for example, should be handled. Be careful not to impose your time schedule on another family member's grief either. The person who is not ready to purge the room or the clothes should have veto power.

13. **Suicide has its own dynamics that include incredibly mixed and difficult feelings and issues.** Rational suicide involves a considered approach to taking one's life and is usually associated with severe medical issues or terminal ailments. Other suicides often lead to people blaming the victim for making a decision that is too painful to bear. "How could he do this to me?" is a common refrain. Referring back to my earlier thoughts about consciousness and life brings the conclusion that suicide is not some preordained action nor is it someone's destiny. On the other hand, the social, psychological, and personal forces within someone's life may reach a point where there is one and only one action to be taken. On the outside, others do not or cannot accept or comprehend the action. But we are not on the inside and cannot understand nor grasp the power of the forces that end in someone taking her own life. Of course, an even more complex type of suicide will haunt a loved one — when a teen, for example, dies while trying to achieve some state of ecstasy through self hanging, sexual stimulation or drug overuse. Again, the temptation to blame the person for stupidity or selfishness may miss the depth and complexity of issues that are really at work. My recommendation is to try to suspend the "why" questions

(as I did with trying to understand Heidi's death) and resign yourself to the fact that you can never truly understand why the death occurred. Isn't it healthier to resign oneself to the tragedy, realize that the death is what it is, and continue to love the person for whom he was while living?

14. **It is crucial to give your loved one's story a voice.** It is important to develop a willingness and ability to talk about your loved one's life and about your feelings about her. Too many parents, spouses, siblings, etc. are left voiceless once "normal" living is supposed to return. Other people seem to impose an unfair timetable and seem to take away the grieving person's need to talk about her loved one, or to hear his name being used. For those people who have not found their "voice" yet, I would encourage you to participate in a professionally sponsored grief group, so you will learn how to speak about your loved one's story with others who are willing to listen. For those of you who have learned to give "voice" to his story do not apologize for speaking. Of course there will be people and situations that will make telling the story difficult, if not impossible. Make sure you have friends or someone else who will truly continue to listen to the story and share in the meaning of what you have to say. This need should never cease. Be willing to listen to others' stories too. Accept the fact that there will be times when you do not feel like talking or sharing your experiences. You may feel empty or that "what else is there to say." These feelings are normal and may pass. If not, consider the possibility that you are becoming clinically depressed and need professional assistance.

15. **Invest time and effort into your child's story.** This is different from telling their story to others. We have a Heidi journal in which we have placed any experience that we or others have had that relates to continuing experiences with Heidi. Our daughters have made scrapbooks that reflect her life. It is important to spend time reflecting on your loved one's life and provide some type of recording of it.

16. **Grieving is a time to give yourself permission to follow your heart and accept the reprioritizing of your life.** Diane has been working very hard at getting me to reorient my attitude in life away from living by all the "shoulds" that seem to control what, when, and how I "ought to" behave. It's okay to cry; it's okay to relax; it's okay to do that chore

tomorrow; it's okay to do nothing. It's okay to have this attitude! It's also okay to deeply feel that anxiety that attends to the unknown. We really do not have all the answers about who our children are now becoming and what their transformed life is all about. These issues will remain a mystery for us, even as we develop theories, beliefs and explanations to try and help assuage our anxieties. It is okay to have some level of anxiety, just prevent it from becoming an overpowering dread that consumes and destroys your capacity for continuing to live and have meaning in your life.

17. **I constantly wonder about the type of person my daughter is continuing to become.** It is painful to realize that I cannot experience the changes and development that is now a part of her transformed self. I find comfort in realizing that her "core" self remains and that if I met her on the street she would not be a complete stranger. Yet the mystery surrounding her growth and development causes a sadness that gnaws at my heart. There is nothing to do about these feelings except identify and accept them.

18. **It's never too late or inappropriate to send a message of care.** When we receive cards and flowers on Heidi's birthday after she died and also on the anniversary of her death, we are touched and moved. Seven years after Heidi died, we received a wonderful gift from a girl who had acted with Heidi during her middle school stint at a Catholic High School's summer theater program. She had just heard about Heidi's illness and death, and she sent a beautiful sympathy card, along with pictures we had never seen; this blessing was priceless.

19. **The anticipation of a significant day may create more anxiety than the day itself.** There are no rules, catechism, or formula to guide someone who is grieving on what "should" be done to cope with an anniversary or birthday. Part of the work of grief is coming to terms with what is meaningful and empowering. We have dealt with these days in various fashions. No activity or lack of activity provides a definitive answer as to what is best. These days ought to be addressed intuitively, maybe more than intellectually. Often the anniversary day occurs and leaves with much less impact than the days of anticipation created.

20. **Believing that other people are ignorant of the dynamics and feelings of someone who is grieving seems to be a reasonable attitude to take.** Don't expect fellow workers, acquaintances, members of a social group or church to be attuned to your needs as a grieving parent, spouse, sibling, friend, etc. You do not need to tolerate cruelty or an abusive attitude, but expect others to want to return to the "normal" way of doing things.

21. **Expect the highs and lows of life to become less extreme over time.** Diane and I have noticed that we have reached the bottom of emotional sadness. All other sadnesses are less intense. Conversely, we also don't feel as carefree or joyous as we used to be.

22. **Expect a stumbling block with respect to interpersonal relationships during your grief journey.** As a grieving father, I am sometimes placing unfair expectations upon others. Even though I am aware of this problem, I don't believe that it will change. It is difficult to muster the energy for reaching out to others or for initiating social activities or events. I can jump into projects, respond to requests, or perform those functions that my roles in life require. My energy or interest varies, but this is true for everyone whether he is grieving or not. I have found, however, that I have become more indirect or passive with respect to interpersonal relationships. I expect others to reach out to me or to initiate activities, if they want. I don't feel overly compelled to do so myself. My sense is that there are a variety of reasons for this shift. I often do not have the energy that is required in social settings. There are many times when I just want to be alone or with Diane and not have to attend to what anyone else may require or request. I do not really like crowds or crowded situations any more. I feel that I have changed so much that there are some settings or situations that just seem too silly or too uncomfortable for me. It is almost impossible for me to ask for help or to tell someone that I need to talk or need companionship. In essence, I am expecting that those who know and/or love me will sense this need and "be there" for me. As a child, when I was hurt or angry I would get away from others and would hope that someone would come to me and take care of me. (This never happened though.) In a sense, I feel as if I may be reverting to this

type of childish behavior. What I find so fascinating about myself is that I am aware of this shift, but I have no intention of doing anything about it. This shift is a part of who I now am. I really have no compelling desire to change this part of me. It saddens me that there are friends and acquaintances who do not understand that I have changed or who do not understand the nature of this change. Frankly, I do not feel responsible for trying to fix this impediment. I'm not sure if other people feel this shift in their relationships or not. My hunch is that it may actually be more pervasive than grieving parents and their family and friends may realize.

23. **Trusting your intuition is an important step in life.** To believe that intuition is infallible is to deny the reality of the human condition. Again, the idea of balance is important. We need to seek a balanced way of trusting our intuitive powers, as well as working at trying to help them develop and grow. We can improve our intuition and we can learn when its guidance will be best for us. In order to do so, however, we have to take the process seriously and not be deterred by failures or the cynicism of others. For example, I am a touch typist, but I didn't start with this skill. I had to work at it and I had to learn to trust that my fingers knew which keys to touch. I had to trust myself not to peek to make sure I was typing the correct one. I made mistakes, but they were only part of the learning curve. Typing is so natural now that if someone asks me where a letter is located, I have to think of where my fingers go on the keyboard. My acupuncturist has told me that he has learned to feel the *Chi*. He was an accountant before going to school and learning Chinese Medicine. He now can feel the energy ebbing or flowing and can sense where the *Chi* is becoming "blocked." So, too, anyone can begin to learn how to be more intuitive and become more attuned to the inner messages in our life.

24. **There is great comfort in losing my fear of death.** That is one of the blessings that many parents experience after the rawness of their grief ebbs. It is an empowering and freeing experience: it is a gift from your child. When Diane was diagnosed with a gall bladder that had to be removed, she told me that she did not care if she died during the surgery. Losing this fear does not mean that grieving parents have a

death wish or are suicidal. It just means that death has become a part of life and there is no need to try to deny its existence or ignore its reality. Death no longer has mastery over us.

25. **Language is the survival tool that helps differentiate humans from one another and from other species.** Although all humans have language and many animals have a rudimentary form of language, the diversity of language creates ethnic difference, and the complexity of language provides us with abilities that are essential, enjoyable, and, at times, inspiring. As I think about Heidi's transformed existence, I wonder if she still has any need for language. When we think about our loved ones we keep them in a state that we remember, and we may assume their transformed life is some version of their previous existence. However, they may no longer have any need for language. Just as language differentiates us from other beings, especially trees, e.g., maybe those who have been transformed have a wholly different state of existing which does not require language. We may look upon the worm as very rudimentary and simple; maybe those who have died look upon us in a comparable way. Language may be just too rudimentary for their way of being. They may have a "meta" linguistic way of relating; maybe even communicating is too restrictive for characterizing the way they relate and connect to one another. Maybe their meta-linguistic characteristic explains the difficulty those of us left behind have in trying to communicate with them. Just as we may "talk" to our pet plants, maybe they are relating to us, and we just don't know how to relate "meta-linguistically." Legitimate psychics and authentic intuitive abilities may be an intermediate process between language and this "meta-linguistic" ability. Someday I may find out and become "meta-linguistically" proficient, and maybe then I'll become just as frustrated as Heidi as I try to relate to my loved ones who mourn my death. This thought gives me some comfort because I believe Heidi has become so much more than she was. Death is not destruction; it is transformation.

26. **Grief is not just emotional or psychological; it is also physical.** It is important to attend to your physical health. Do not hesitate to consult with a trusted physician. Exercise

and try to improve your eating habits. It will take time to begin to withdraw yourself from the comfort foods that may have become your staple diet during the first months or years of your grief journey.

27. **Invest time and/or money in some activity that you can directly associate with the healing dimension of grief.** One thing that I did very soon after Heidi's death was to burn CDs of music that connected her with me. I've named them according to our connection: "Heidi the Entertainer," "Shared Music," "Viewing Together I and II," "Just Because," "Dad's Grieving," and "Grieving Together." I play these CDs when I want to spend some time with Heidi or when I want her to be with me while I'm doing something (e.g., gardening or walking). No one else cares to listen to these CDs; Diane finds them too painful. For me, they are comforting and meaningful. Find something that provides <u>you</u> with comfort and meaning, and don't worry whether anyone else can share it or not.

28. **Above all else: respect your grief journey and the journey of anyone else you may meet.** You may need to resign yourself to the fact that so many questions will go unanswered and so many hopes will go unfulfilled. Meaningfulness is still intertwined in our lives, whether we can see or feel it or not. Accepting the "blindness" rather than concluding that life is meaningless seems to be a part of a healthy attitude toward one's grief. In essence continue to find balance in your life and respect others who are struggling in ways that may make no sense to you.

29. **Some differences in grieving may arise from gender.** It is important to recognize these gender issues. For example, a man's feeling of helplessness in the face of grief and sorrow can manifest itself in guilt or anger, and he may lash out to those who are closest to him. The social forces that underpin a "macho" approach to life can push a man toward avoidance, denial, or compartmentalizing emotions and even the grief journey itself. He will need to attend to "grief work" but others may need to tread very carefully at revealing this truth to him. Patience and understanding must blend with realism and indirect ways of showing him that he does not need to remain trapped in society's straight jacket. In some cases the male needs to be given permission to deal with his emotions and a "tender side" of life.

30. **People will often offer to do "anything that you need."** Although this offer is well-intentioned, it really isn't all that helpful. When Heidi was ill, it was too difficult to think of what people could do for us. What we appreciated and what I try to offer now is something specific: "Do you want a ride?" "I'll shovel your sidewalk whenever it snows, so don't worry about that." "I'm going to bring over dinner. How is tomorrow?" These specific offers are wonderful gestures because they don't require the person to have to think, and they demonstrate genuine care. I remember vividly how my sister-in-law and mother-in-law came over to our house and organized our linen closet and cleaned our kitchen while we were spending so much time at the hospital. Concrete actions and deliveries of food helped the most.

31. **People will also make offers that don't materialize.** The intention may be genuine, but the reality is that what they have said they would do just doesn't happen. For example, at Heidi's wake two different men I had known for years said they would call me the following spring or summer to get me out golfing. I have golfed with both of them on different occasions a number of times before. Neither one has ever called. A high school friend that I had talked with a year after Heidi died made a comparable promise. He belonged to a country club and would arrange for us to play the golf course. I still haven't heard from him. People feel as if they need to do or say something to show their concern. "Let's get together. I'll give you a call." Yet the encounter will not materialize, and the phone will remain silent. The difference for someone who is grieving is that such promises often get taken literally. I have learned to not take such promises personally, nor to judge those who make them. Many people have not learned how to turn sympathy into empathy. Being well-intentioned is the American Way.

32. **Listen to children, especially the very young.** They remain connected to life in a way that adults have lost. Their connection is more intuitive and they can capture the simplest truths and purest joys of life.

VIII.

JULY 19, 2002.

The Moon Party

*H*ope and promise began creeping into our lives again in the summer after the surreal transplant. In May Dr. Wetzler informed us, "The leukemia is gone! Your blood is clean!" We had heard these words the year before; still the news was good and welcomed. Heidi's hair slowly returned by the end of the summer; this time it was dark and straight, but "at least, it's hair," she proclaimed. Despite some fevers and setbacks, she was able to go to movies, go out to eat, shop, and re-engage in some semblance of normal living. She even flew to New Jersey to visit Katie for a few days. A friend had arranged for her to have a small part in a locally shot short film, and she was selected as a model for a hair and fashion show in September. She was delighted to show off the purple tint they had put in her spiked hair-do. A neighbor helped her secure a part-time job as a receptionist at an Import-Export company, and she quickly charmed everyone there. (Most came to the wake and/or funeral and everyone contributed to a memorial.) Of course, the elephant in the room was the Graft vs. Host Disease, but the medical staff was confident that they could control this necessary monster. Heidi again dreamed of the stage, and as in the previous summer, thoughts were drifting to her future in the new year; she just had to "get through" the summer and fall.

Heidi loved parties, whether they were well-organized or impromptu (like the one she had us host when she relapsed). Laughing, teasing, enjoying each other's company, telling stories, and playing games delighted her. Parties were a time to share the gift of love and the joy of friendship. One of Diane's "clubs" consists of women in our neighborhood who stayed home with their children and shared those growing *years with one another. As the children grew older, the women continued to meet. The husbands are brought together periodically for special events; the men never meet as a group on their own. We have shared weddings, graduations, and a wide variety of other get-togethers, including a 60s dress up bash, a St. Valentine's evening to share songs and memories, a chicken "cook off," and a Christmas gathering for "lyrics and tales." At one of our parties in spring 2002, a few of us freed our imaginations and decided that we should have a Moon Party. We did not have any real plans, except that we would have it close to a full moon in July. At the time, Heidi was still constantly looking for projects and ideas to engage her talents and energies. One idea she was floating that summer was to begin organizing party packets for a wide variety of ideas and occasions. Thus, it was an obvious choice for us to turn the planning over to our party organizer "extraordinaire." The rest of us helped in ways suitable to our talents and assignments. The party we experienced that night was and always will be a testimony to Heidi's spirit and how it can touch anyone's life with class, imagination, and ingenuity.*

As the guests arrived that evening they entered through our "portal into space." Diane and I greeted everyone with our "moon shirts" (tee shirts that Heidi had decorated). Within the portal's caverns (aka garage) were tables for the food. Everyone brought some type of "moon" dish or drink. It's amazing how a piece of paper can change the label of a large bottle of Chablis into "moonshine." Before anyone could go outside in the backyard where we held the party, he had to answer moon trivia questions that Heidi and I had gathered together. We encouraged creative answers, so later we could laugh and enjoy the twists and absurdities people wrote for unanswerable questions. A couple of our favorites were: "The moon is sometimes called a 'terrestrial planet.' Name the other four." The answer was, "John, Paul, George and Ringo." "What is a moonwort?" Answer: "What you get from a moon frog." 'What are moonseeds?" Answer: "what you need to grow a moon." The moonscape was our patio, which is covered with a tent. Around the entry to the moon, Heidi had put picture boards of Armstrong's landing. Stepping through the door was a small step for man (or woman), but a giant leap for ... (life, hope, dreams, whatever). All the tables were decorated with moon and star paper. It was the décor for the whole moon landing area that began to set the tone for an evening now filled with warm and enjoyable memories. The party started early so it was still sunny out; it was a perfect summer evening. (We have a reputation in the neighborhood for always having good weather for our parties whether they're for graduations, birthdays, engagements, or weddings.) By nightfall the moon came out and filled our party with a final dash of sparkling light.

Our backyard is encircled with gardens. It started to become a hobby for me before Heidi was diagnosed; ever since it has become a minor obsession. For the party Heidi had handmade dozens of crescent moons. We strung them on fishing wire that ran from the crab apple tree (a memorial gift in honor of my mom) to the remains of Heidi's swing set. When she was small I had made a set for her that had three support braces. When we finally took it down, I kept one side of it up so I could plant clematis and trumpet vines to climb and so there could ample room for hanging plants too. The moons were one of Heidi's clever twists. Some of them were devoted to movies, others to music. Heidi researched movies that had a moon theme; she wrote them on the crescent moon with glow pens and gave them the number of stars that critics had awarded them when they were playing in theaters. In addition to song titles, Heidi also included some book titles on these blue slivers. We had a spot light illuminating them when the sun set – the effect was much better than we could have imagined. The crescent moons glowed in the light and they seemed to be dangling in mid-air. Along the clothes line we put the American flag in the position that it had on the moon, unfurled and proud. Tara, an English teacher, helped Heidi make tag boards that included moon and star poems. They hung the boards from the clothes line. As a party favor Heidi had created a Moon CD of songs that spanned generations. One of the neighbors plays the guitar so Heidi arranged for him to bring his guitar and lyrics for some moon songs for all of us to sing, including "Moon River" and "Blue Moon."

Everyone who was there that evening had watched Heidi grow up; everyone loved (and still loves) her. We talked and joked; we sang and laughed. Heidi was thrilled with the evening. She spent much of the evening with us and was even able to sing for awhile. I made sure that I caught her singing (red bandana circling her bald head) on the video clip I took. She did not stay until the end, but went to bed while we were still going through her song sheets. Her bedroom window was next to the patio, so we all knew she was going to lie down and continue to enjoy our reverie.

Heidi's life has become a gift for all of us. Who she was, what she said, how she handled the unfairness of this illness, all of these elements contribute to her legacy. Each one of us has memories of Heidi. In some cases they are unique because we experienced moments or events alone with her. Other memories are shared. In one sense the Moon Party was an insignificant event in the history of the United States — just a summer evening when a group of friends got together to enjoy a warm, starlit sky with one another. But when I reflect upon Heidi's life, that party symbolizes more than just the evening's events. It illustrates how a person can choose to live her life. We are never in complete control. Events, accidents, illnesses, deaths will buffet us throughout our journey. There are times when each one of us will feel overwhelmed or unfairly treated. It is difficult for Americans to accept the real fact that life is inherently unfair and difficult. Heidi chose to continue to live. She sought to make other people's lives happier and more enriched. Not only do I believe she has done so; I know she is still enriching the lives of anyone willing to open themselves to her magic and wonder. Just as the Moon Party was just a simple evening for a group of friends, so this magic and wonder is not earth shattering. Heidi was not a national figure; she was not someone who had become a household name in the media. From a national perspective her life and death had little significance. However, life really is about individuals like you and me and Heidi. Much of what we do may go completely unnoticed; many of our activities may be rather ordinary and routine. But Heidi's life teaches me what I have always known: each person's life is a wonderful gift of creation. We are each blessed with opportunities and blessings. They may be simple, but they are real. We can choose to make our lives deep and rich, or we can waste them in so many different ways. We can plunge into the depths of the water of life, or we can continue to skim the surface like the water bugs. We can reach for the moon, or we can just walk in the darkness and never look up.

Coping With Temporal Flow

I have been teaching courses that deal with the question of time for almost 30 years. Americans have a concept and organization of time that is so imbedded in our consciousness that we take it for granted. In fact, it is very difficult for Americans to articulate this concept because it is so culturally ingrained in how we think and how we organize the world. I try to introduce my students to alternative views of time by telling them a story about my two oldest daughters. One day in 1976, when Tara was five and Kristen was three, I decided to try an experiment. Folk singer Judy Collins had released an album years before with the song "Who Knows Where the Time Goes." I loved the song, especially the lines: "And I am not alone while my love is near me. I know it will be so until it's time to go ... For who knows where the time goes?" I decided to play the song for my girls and then ask them what they thought it meant. When the song had finished, I turned to Tara and asked her, "Where does time go?" She paused, thought a moment, and then replied: "Well, Daddy, someday I'll get older and move away from this house. I'll probably marry someone, but I'll still love you." Bingo! I knew another philosopher was born.

I turned to Kristen. She instantly jumped up and pointed to the kitchen, "On the stove, Daddy." I laughed and realized that even at age three she was fully indoctrinated into American culture. Time for us IS the clock. Kristen was absolutely correct; time in our culture is the structure we use to organize our world by calendars, clocks, and pocket planners. Tara also was correct, because the temporal dimension in our life relates to our perceptions and the process or flow of our experiences.

In my classrooms, after I tell this story, I complete it with the next chapter. At Tara's wedding, she selected "Who Knows Where the Time Goes?" for the father-daughter dance. For me that moment of dancing with Tara was a wonderful experience. She was now a woman, a bride, leaving my home forever (just as she said she would), yet this song was a clear indication of how we would forever continue to be connected by a love that is truly amazing. Each of my older daughters has learned the power of parental love as she gave birth and now is responsible for the development and life of her own children. Kristen selected "A Bridge Over Troubled Waters" for our dance. Kristen had gone through some very traumatic experiences, which brought conflict, healing, and renewed bonds of closeness for our family. When she was a child, I had helped her through the troubles of childhood, and when she was an adult, we all came together to help her through these other crises. The song was a moment for us to celebrate her success in restoring health and harmony in her life. When Katie was born we used John Denver's version of "For Baby, For Bobby" as her birth announcement. It was a song that seemed to typify the relationship Diane and I had with her throughout her life: "I'll walk in the rain by your side/I'll cling to the warmth of your tiny hand /I'll do anything to help you understand/I'll love you more than anybody can." Katie selected this song for our father-daughter dance. Each one of my daughters had chosen music that spoke to me and touched a chord in the continuity of our relationships. Each time, the dance was a special moment for us to share our love in front of our family and friends, showing everyone the genuine enjoyment we had for each other. Heidi and I will never have that experience. The joy of that particular moment has been taken away. The reality of that loss has hit me very hard at weddings we have attended since her death.

When the daughter of one of Diane's neighborhood friends got married, we attended along with all of the club members and their spouses. The ceremony overlooked one of the Finger Lakes in New York. When the father and daughter began to dance, the music crept into me and took my wind away. With a gulp I realized once more that I would never hold Heidi in my arms again. I had to leave. Diane came with me, and for the better part of the evening, the two of us sat quietly looking out at the darkness covering the lake.

Music has always been an important part of Heidi's life. Our family has shared a wide variety of musical experiences over the years. Since Heidi's death, I have made CDs that include the music that she and I enjoyed together. Listening to these CDs gives me time to be with her in an emotional and special way. I have included the song that I believe Heidi would have considered for *our* dance. Of course, who knows what time and life would have given us, but I am left with the belief that she would have selected the Righteous Brothers song "Unchained Melody." If you are familiar with the song, you may be asking yourself whether or not Heidi and I had a warped relationship. Special musical moments are created in context, and it's the context that creates the meaning and emotional waves that attend to the music. As my daughters were growing up I took each one of them on dates. When Heidi was in high school the Righteous Brothers came to town. Diane and I had done a good job in "corrupting" our children to appreciate and even like some of our music. So off Heidi and I went to their concert. The time we spent together was priceless. That evening we thoroughly enjoyed the entertainment and each other's company as we talked about life and politics; as we disagreed a bit on some irrelevant issue; and as we made up stories about people that we saw. We smiled, laughed, and I relished in being able to share such an evening with her. Now, when I listen to the Righteous Brothers, I am taken to those feelings of warmth and closeness with her.

All of these experiences are part of the mosaic of my grieving. They are a part of my "time" of grieving. The distinction that is made in the story about my playing "Who Knows Where the Time Goes" to Tara and Kristen is a very important one. We can talk about time as the temporal dimension in experience or we can relegate time to the clock. When we attend to the former dimension, we are talking about how we perceive time in its "flowing" or on-going process of change. We can feel that something unpleasant may seem to drag on forever while a happy moment will last but a fleeting second. When we stop to <u>think</u> about time, however, we judge that it is associated with the clock. This association, however, is a cultural phenomenon that Americans take as the truth about time.

Philosophers, scientists, poets, and others have written about time for millennia, and I cannot do the topic justice in a brief chapter. However, I would like to point out a few salient points that I believe relate to grieving in a very significant way. An analogy that I use to help my students start to recast their vision of the meaning of time relates to how we measure a person's height. I draw a stick figure on the board and ask them: "What are the 3 elements that we need to measure Mortimer's height?" I solicit the following items from them: a measuring device (ruler), a measuring unit (inches and feet), and Mortimer himself. If we compare this analysis to time, we get the following conclusion: the measuring device is the clock, the measuring unit includes seconds, minutes, and hours, and time itself is what we are measuring. We tend to equate the object that we are trying to measure with the measuring tool that we are using. Time on the clock is not the reality of time; it is the measurement that we make of time. So we need to distinguish between the measurement of time (clocks, calendars, etc.) and the reality of temporal experience.

In American culture, we seem to have adopted a philosophy of time that is consistent with what Aristotle and Sir Isaac Newton declared the characteristics of time to be. For Americans time is something that exists independently of anyone or anything that exists. It is an objective medium within which events in the world occur. Each instant of time is just like every other instant; time is homogeneous, can be readily measured or quantified, and progresses at a linear, uniform rate. What changes is not time, but the events that occur within time. So for Americans, an event may last 10 seconds, and we can measure this length. In one case, say in an accident, for example, the 10 seconds may seem to last for hours. In another case, say for a high school student running a sprint, the 10 seconds seems to fly by. For Americans the reality of time is not found in the differing perceptions we have within our experience. Instead, time is that constant "container" into which we pour our experience. Other philosophers have provided us with alternative views of the meaning of time, and other cultures organize their world with different perceptions of what time means to them. My conclusion from all of my studies and writings about time leads me to believe that each culture defines an organizational tool that helps it perceive the world and relate to others within its experience. The reality of temporal experience should be connected to our perceptions and not reduced to the characteristics of measurement that we may use to structure our world.

If we examine our language about time, we can reach an interesting conclusion. Only the present "exists." "Exists" is the present tense of the verb. The past tense relates to that which has existed and the future tense relates to that which will exist. St. Augustine reached the conclusion that there really are three dimensions of time, all of which relate to the present. The present is that which exists. The existence of the future is only our present anticipation or expectation of what will happen at some later moment. The past is what exists in our memory or in recorded events of what has already happened. A French philosopher by the name of Henri Bergson took this idea much further. Time is not what Aristotle or Isaac Newton said, but should be viewed more in the light of what we experience and what this experience means in our life. The temporal dimensions of our experience should not be reduced to some container or some measuring device. I have written a couple of professional articles outlining what I call the "Pulsational-Wave" model of time. Simply stated time should be considered to have both dimensions; each moment is a pulse that contains the energy, the possibilities, the memories, and the context of what's occurring. This pulse, however, should not be thought to be in isolation or as some objective "point." It is flowing with the wave of life, with life's creative consciousness. My model of time seems to be consistent with current ideas about Quantum Theory and the idea of the Zero Point Field. I recommend reading "The Field: The Quest for the Secret Force of the Universe" by Lynne McTaggart for more background and information.

Life's temporal dimensions are awash with meaning, purpose, and the depth of perception that pervades our world. The Context Spheres that I discussed earlier create the landscape of our experience. From a temporal perspective every event in our experience is contextual. This context not only includes all the psychological and sociological influences I've noted before, but also includes our memories, our past experiences, our hopes, our expectations, and our dreams. Thus, it is "pulsing" and alive, not static nor an empty container. In the United States we tend to focus upon the future, maybe in excess. For us the future is some extended "place" in which something is going to happen. We may dread what "lies around the bend" or we may gleefully anticipate some wonderful event in our life. The reality, however, is usually quite different from the anticipation. Americans are planners, and we schedule our lives to make our plans work as efficiently as possible. Some people become obsessive about their plans, and most Americans believe that punctuality is a virtue. Americans are usually task or goal oriented, which means something that we anticipate or plan in the future becomes the meaning or motivation for our thoughts, actions, or decisions. We can extend the future indefinitely and look forward to spending a lot of quality time in the future with those we love, for example. This way of dealing with the future provides us with a sense of control, of hope, and helps us to focus upon efficiency and effectiveness. This view, however, does become problematic for those with terminal ailments or who are very old. Whenever the reality of a foreshortened future hits someone, we feel as if life has been taken away, and we may wait in a state of depression until the worst happens. A truly sad picture that Americans have is the one that has an old person just sitting in a rocking chair waiting for death. The time keeps getting closer and closer which means life is becoming less and less ____. We can fill in the blank with any descriptive word or phrase we chose: important, meaningful, worthwhile, etc.

For me a much healthier and, perhaps, more realistic view of time is one that puts limits on the use of this quantitative perspective. There are times when planning, scheduling, and organizing are essential. However, this view of time should not pervade our entire life nor should it dominate the meaning we give to life. Certainly the experience of grieving redefines one's entire time perspective. This redefinition can lead to a much healthier perspective of what our memory and our sense of hope and possibilities can mean for us. Instead of seeing the future as some extended line into an indefinite future, it is wise to deal with the future as the horizon in our life that is full of possibilities, uncertainty, hope, (maybe fear and anxiety), and blessings. As with any dimension in our life, we tend to talk about the glass being half empty or half full; that is, we can look at life either pessimistically or optimistically. What if we were to expand that perception? Why does the glass have to be considered half one or the other? Why can't the glass be full or overflowing or sometimes just empty? Why can't it be "pulsing" with blessings and possibilities?

My journey of grief has led me to the reality that life is a continuing process of change; time is a continuously evolving pulse/wave. Changes are inevitable. Some are forced upon us while others may evolve through our own choices and efforts. In all cases, the world that continues to evolve and emerge in our life will be different from what it was AND from what we hope and anticipate it will become. We can feel sorry for ourselves, or we can celebrate the outcomes of the changes. The reality, however, again seems to be better conceived as a flowing continuum. Like the color spectrum, the changes are varying hues and shades of what we expected. The death of a loved one may seem to drain all color from life and leave us with a dark, empty hole. How we chose to deal with that reality reflects the health, meaning, and purpose that we have in life.

Each chapter of this book begins with my recollections of events within Heidi's life. If anyone else in my family wrote about the "same" events, the results would be quite different. The differences would result from a variety of contributing factors. My wife, daughters, and I all have different writing skills and styles. The differences would be quite noticeable to anyone who read the passages. The selection of experiences I am sure would differ as well. The important differences that I would like to note here, however, relate to the content each of us would use and the perspective each of us has. In essence, our memories of the events differ. I used the daily journal we kept for Heidi to help me with the details and to get some of the facts straight. The reality, however, is that what these experiences mean varies from person to person. In some cases we were all present, in others we heard about the experience. For example, I was not there when Kristen and Katie took Heidi to Roswell on December 23, 2002. The story of that visit has become part of the family's collective memory. Sometimes the details are the same or at least similar; in other cases collective memory has discrepancies or nuances that alter the contours of the events.

In America we believe that what happened in the past has some type of objective reality and the job of memory is to connect our remembrance to that reality. This presumption is not the only way to look at memory. The reality is that our perceptions create an experience that varies from person to person. Memories always contain a degree of subjectivity no matter how objective we try to be. This distinction is important in any journey of grieving. Some experiences that we have of our loved one will be more important or meaningful to us than to others. It can be painful when we cannot share that experience, even with those we love. For example, Heidi and I listened to a lot of music during our card playing. Two musicals that were a lot of "fun" were "Into the Woods" and "Chicago." In particular "Agony" from "Into the Woods" was a song Heidi and I just giggled at whenever we listened to it. Awhile after she died I remembered playing the song for two of her sisters who were home for a visit. They did not "get it." All of my daughters love musicals, and we have shared so much meaning, laughter, and tears with so many experiences over the years. But there was no collective memory for this song, and my excitement about sharing this "Heidi" moment with them became a sterile disappointment. I smiled to myself as I thought about this inability to share a past moment. I was experiencing what all of us experience when a friend starts showing us pictures of a vacation he had taken. The first few pictures may be interesting, but by picture 150 we often have had enough. This is especially true if we have not been to that place ourselves and have no memory to use as a reference.

Our memories are crucial elements in making our journeys of grieving unique and at times "un-sharable." It is important for everyone who is grieving to accept that there will be some memories that will differ significantly while others just will not produce the type of empathy or response we may need or be seeking. My daughters' responses should not be judged to mean they are insensitive or lack compassion. Their compassion and ability to share what is important and meaningful is boundless. The issue is that there is no shared meaning or collective memory to connect us to each experience in our lives. I know I have responded to some of their stories or experiences with the same type of blank emotive response too. I try to avoid judging others negatively because they cannot share some of my stories or past experiences. I do so because I know that at times I am not capable of sharing other peoples' experiences in the way they may be expecting. On the other hand, when people do listen or do demonstrate interest, then I can cherish the opportunity to give voice to the experience. Sometimes people will listen and understand some of our unique recollections. Other times they may not. Collective memories may or may not agree on substance and/or details. The important element here is the willingness to share and to accept that our recollections may vary. What really is more important in grieving: getting the details correct or sharing a person's feelings of grief?

Another temporal dimension that impacts our lives significantly is anniversaries. In America, age is chronological. We know when we were born and we celebrate our birth date. Family trees and markers at graves note the day someone was born and the date someone died. (Other cultures do not necessarily follow this approach at all.) When someone dies, those who are grieving confront the reality of these anniversaries: birthday and date of death. For Diane and me, we also feel the weight of anniversaries on August 23, the date we were told Heidi had leukemia. Hauntingly, August 24 is both our wedding anniversary and Tara's birthday. After experiencing a number of these anniversaries, we have learned that the anticipation is often more painful than the day itself. We often discuss the impact of anniversaries with the other members of our grief support groups. All of us have come to realize that there are no answers to the question: what should we do? We also have come to learn that others who remember the anniversaries and send us some type of memorial give us such a precious gift. In a very real sense anniversary days are only an enumeration, a marking on a calendar, and yet, they are symbols of a very profound reality. They are markers along the journey. Maybe they are the stops on the subway. These anniversaries are also continuing opportunities for us to grow and heal.

Ultimately, our lives should focus upon integrating the different temporal dimensions we experience. Each day, each moment is a unique gift, never to be repeated. We should cherish it and live it to the fullest; however, each moment is awash with memories and anticipation. If we live just for the moment, we disconnect ourselves from who we are and who we will become. Meaning in life comes from hope, love, and a sense of who we are. Hope is not a future object existing in a place that doesn't exist. It is not some ideal that exists independently in a future state. For me, hope and meaning are integrated; they are the grace that God has given. They are enmeshed in the pulsing dimension of my temporal experience. I am responsible for allowing this grace to permeate my life and allowing it to motivate and sustain my thoughts and actions. "Time heals all wounds" is a phrase that irritates me considerably. Time is <u>not</u> the cause for any healing. Temporal experience, however, does provide a context within which people can do those things that can lead to healing. It is false to assume that after a certain measured period of time, a grieving parent will be healed of her grief. Our temporal flow on the subway follows the shifts and contours of all of those dimensions that I have been discussing in this book. There is a real blessing in realizing that time does not follow the dictates of any clock. The subway ride is full, and it is empty; it is strange, and it is familiar; it has hope, and it has distress; but it only has meaning if we allow grace and love to buoy us through the journey. So instead of assuming that we can be cured of grieving or that we can finish the task after a reasonable amount of time, we would be well advised to resign ourselves to riding the subway and find the meaning, purpose and healthy balance of life that is being made available to us. In essence, integrating all of our temporal dimensions is a healthy response to any death. Expecting that time itself will take care of our healing is a false security blanket.

William of Occam has influenced the way we think in the West. The simplest form of his principle is KISS (Keep It Simple Stupid). Basically, he said that the simplest answer was the most elegant answer. He has influenced thinkers to try to reduce problems to a simple, elegant solution. Einstein died trying to unify all the scientific theories into one grand equation. However, life goes beyond the boundaries of such approaches. We distort too many truths in life when we attempt to find "The" answer or "The" single cause for something. There are multiple dimensions involved in all life. Causation is always multilayered. Thus, understanding the context for any issue or experience is essential for truly understanding what and why something has happened. Wisdom and understanding need to use all the tools we have available to us (intuition, reason, science, logic, perception, etc.) and not just rely on one approach.

Another important dimension with respect to temporal experience is timing or synchronizing with ourselves and others. "Timing is everything" is an American cliché that has an element of truth to it. Grieving parents may be haunted with the awful timing that may have resulted in the death of their child. For those who have experienced a long illness with their child, the time they had with her may be rich with memories and/or filled with the fears and sadness that accompanied the illness. Part of the difficulty for those of us who live on the subway is that now our timing with others seems to be off.

People synchronize their behaviors whether they are conscious of doing so or not. For example, whether you are aware of the behavior or not, two or more people walking together will synchronize their pace. The pace will be comfortable for those who have synchronized in a way that feels natural for the time and place of the walk. Others may feel out of sorts. Their discomfort may be due to the context (they really did not want to walk with these people or someone in the group) or to the synchronization itself (they do not like walking at the pace being set). Experiences may become very memorable because everyone seemed to be synchronized; they were all on the "same page" or everything just seemed to run smoothly. The synchronization and pace of life for anyone who is grieving seems to change. Sometimes the change seems to be imposed from some dark, outside force, while other times it is quite clear that the change is something coming from within one's self. It is rather common for people who are grieving to feel "out of it" in social settings. It is more difficult for them to connect or to feel connected with others. In many cases the underlying difficulty is rhythm, timing, or synchronization. The pace, the pulse, and the wave of life on the subway is different from the rest of the world. It is more difficult to feel comfortable with others or in situations that were so much a part of one's life before the death. This discomfort can lead to anger, fear, depression, or a sense of hopelessness or feelings of abandonment. For some people, it is impossible to return to settings or groups where the asynchrony is too painful. Other people may not be aware of what is going on or may not be attuned to the dynamics of timing and pace. Non-grieving people may tend to dismiss the grieving person, either through pity ("isn't it too bad that she just can't get over ...") or through their own discomfort ("it just isn't the same anymore ...").

American culture does not seem to prepare people for the patience that is required to live a healthy and meaningful life. Americans live in a fast-paced society, and we learn to adjust to the rhythms of varying groups and institutions in our lives. We treat time as a commodity ("be careful, don't waste your time doing ..."). In business or in school, the situation or institution sets the pace, and we adjust to it. We talk about the "rat race" and look for moments to "escape" or "get away." Our lives are cluttered with so much to do and so little time to do it. For me, the core of my grieving beats to a very different drummer than what I experience in the world around me. I may enter the performance or functional spheres and try to accommodate to the rhythms and paces that are set for me there, but I usually do not feel comfortable. Part of the "disconnect" is because I see and feel life so differently, but also because I am now following a different dance. There is very little that can be done to change these dynamics. Society is not going to change its pace. "Life must go on, of course." The grieving parent, for example, is not going to want to dance with the same vigor and vitality that she had before the death. Part of the healing process, I believe, requires the person to accept the different paces and rhythms in life. This acceptance can lead to a greater level of participation, but it does not mean that the grieving person has "fully recovered." Grieving people need to understand what comfort level makes the most sense in their lives, and they need to realize that the pace of life will require a lot of work and readjustments. Just as some friends will come, others will go, so too will the comfort levels in getting back to work, going out with friends, attending social functions, etc. Sometimes the feelings of being out of sync with others is not a function of grieving. Remember, that everyone has experiences of being asynchronous at times. Even with someone you love dearly, some experiences are just not working right. "Timing is everything" relates to everyone. Grieving merely colors the dimensions of this element of human relationships.

IX.

DECEMBER 23, 2002.

The Enigma Is a Paradox

For Heidi, so much was different the second time around. The first year of her battle seemed to be "text book." We followed the doctor's protocol, and even the infections and bumps in the road were expected — by the medical staff that is. For us, it was difficult to see our daughter so vulnerable and so controlled by the disease and the treatments. After her relapse, however, even the medical staff began to feel that Heidi's unique personality was spilling over into her physiological response to treatments. She had medication reactions that did not correlate with any experience the staff had had with anyone else; she reacted atypically to treatments; and her test results were often perplexing.

About a year after her relapse, when we were in the Bone Marrow Transplant unit, Pam shook her head as she looked over Heidi's latest blood counts. "You know what, Heidi, you are just an enigma," she said.

I shrugged my shoulders, "We've known that for years."

Pam smiled at us, and Heidi smiled back with a sly glint in her eyes. "I guess I'm just one of a kind," she said, rather proudly.

Heidi <u>was</u> unique and was always a paradox. In fact, she fostered this enigmatic side even though some of it seemed to be quite natural. As a child she dressed haphazardly and with little care for taste or combinations. As a teen she developed a very classy fashion taste. She was fashion conscious but seemed to avoid being controlled by the marketing gods who determine what teens should wear. She looked as if she could run like a gazelle, but in fact could do no better than a sloth climbing a tree. Her athletic ability was minimal, but she always received high grades in "gym" classes; attitude and attendance were her forte. Her *artsy nature came from her love for the theater, music, and musicals; yet her critical thinking skills were clearly evident with her logical and analytic abilities. High school is a terrible time for dealing with the pangs of belonging or not belonging. Heidi did not seem to be buffeted by the winds of in-group/out-group dynamics. The usual casting of stones and labeling of anyone who was different seemed to be an irrelevancy for her. Heidi's drum beat was slow and rhythmic; she reveled in being seen as paradoxical. She was very clever to keep the same boyfriend throughout high school, especially because he went to another school. Thus, she could easily chat and enjoy male company while making it quite evidently clear what the nature of the relationship would be: let's enjoy each other's company and not get trapped by the physical calls of teen hormones. Heidi realized her charm and power. She wielded it judiciously.*

The context for this particular day, December 23, is essential for understanding what happened. Diane and I had both had childhoods with wonderful traditions for the Christian holidays. We both grew up with the practice of opening presents on Christmas Eve. Both of us were intent upon keeping the religious message a genuine part of our celebrations. With our children we developed very rich and beautiful activities that our daughters still follow. Christmas Eve was a long and event-filled day. Frantic wrapping in the morning; visiting my family when my mom was still alive; going to church; celebrating with Diane's folks, her sister, and her family; then, home to find Santa's visit and opening presents until the early morning hours. That is the barest of outlines and does not capture the little nuances that made the day so special. For example, we bought each one of our daughters a "Susie" doll when she was very young. Santa's elves would take the dolls weeks before Christmas; clean them up; give them new outfits; and Santa would return them with the other presents. We revisited that tradition the year after Heidi's relapse when we found Heidi's Susie doll and had our other daughter's husbands secret the dolls to us. We repaired and dressed them. When we returned from our extended family party, the girls found their Susie's waiting for them. We have a picture that captures the childish glee that our adult daughters had when they were holding their dolls. It's amazing how little things can bring so much emotion to the surface.

For Christmastide 2002 the dynamics were even more accentuated. I'm not sure about anyone else in the family, but I had learned to treat each holiday as if it may be the last our entire family would spend together. I did not live with the constant feeling that Heidi might die, but I made sure that I would squeeze out every ounce of enjoyment I could find in case that nightmare were to ever become realized. Heidi was so looking forward to this particular Christmas (maybe, she too felt that she had to live each holiday celebration as if it might be her last). We had kept memorabilia for all of our girls in file cabinets in our basement: drawings, letters, awards, school activities, and a wide array of papers that reflected moments in each of our girl's lives. The previous September we suggested to Heidi that she could have these files and make scrapbooks for her sisters for Christmas. This idea was one of the best ones we had throughout her entire struggle. She threw herself into the project as if it were a spiritual calling. She planned and organized, using her analytic, left-brain skills. She bought materials, stickers, and borders that followed the creative juices of her artistic, right brain. Each sister received a month of concentrated effort and devotion. The end products were masterpieces, each scrapbook capturing the heart and soul of each sister. Heidi was thrilled with her creations and was excited about giving them. She loved her sisters dearly and felt indebted to them for all of their sacrifices throughout her struggle. The bond of love that we have seen and continue to see in our daughters is a blessing that fills Diane and me with a sense of fulfillment and joy. The three older daughters had taken Heidi away to a resort to celebrate her 21st birthday the previous October. It was a memorable trip for all of them. In Heidi's honor, our daughters still get together each year in October to celebrate Heidi's life; her legacy lives on.

For Heidi, this particular Christmas was so enmeshed in all that had happened to us as a family over the years. Heidi's medical situation at this time was grave. After the second transplant she experienced many terrible and surreal experiences; I've shared some of them in other parts of this book. Her hands were now somewhat purple, possibly due to an onset of Reynard's syndrome, a condition that causes the hands to always feel cold. Her eyes were no longer producing tears, and the constant dryness was painful. Her skeletal system was compromised, and she experienced constant pain in her bones. Her breathing had also become compromised, and she was on oxygen continually. The week before Christmas Heidi began to have a chesty cough and was experiencing even more difficulty breathing. She was getting tired more easily than ever before. The staff told us that only three percent of patients taking the medication for the syndrome experience any shortness of breath, but given Heidi's "enigma" responses, they believed that this might be the cause. On December 19th, as her breathing became more problematic, Heidi announced, "I'm going to be naughty!" and she stopped taking the meds without consulting any of the medical staff. I think it made her feel good to rebel a little. On a number of occasions she lamented the fact that she was so obedient and "good." Her rebellion didn't seem to have any adverse effect, although her breathing difficulties didn't improve.

The other girls started arriving in town and the preparations for Christmas became more intense. On the evening of December 21st Heidi showed her bravery in a very subtle, maybe almost unnoticeable way. Her employer from the Import-Export Company was sponsoring a holiday party at a restaurant. Heidi's breathing difficulties were on-going, and she was fighting genuine fatigue. That evening she dressed in true Heidi fashion and went to that party alone. We drove her, of course, because she was not able to drive a car since her diagnosis. But she did not want us to walk her in or to signal to anyone else at the party that she was having any medical issues whatsoever. We kept the portable oxygen tank in the van and waited in a nearby restaurant until she was finished. She was not going to take the oxygen into the party, even though the staff had seen her with it at work. Heidi loved a party and never wanted anyone to focus on her illness. She never wanted pity; she didn't allow tears.

On the morning of the 23rd Heidi got up with pain and was crying. She refused to call in sick and went to work for her regular four hour shift. Kristen and Katie volunteered to pick her up from work and take her for a quick check up at Roswell. Her doctor and staff were very concerned about her breathing and were hoping that she had a blood clot that would be affecting her heart. It has always amazed me during this entire journey how we could wish and pray for such things as "having a blood clot affecting one's heart" or "hoping that she has an infection." They sent her for a CAT scan that indicated that there was a problem. Dr. Wetzler sat down with her, concern etched on his face. "Heidi, I'm afraid that we are going to admit you today," he said slowly. Daggers flew from her eyes. He quickly added, "But you wouldn't be staying for more than five days." He obviously thought that would soothe the message.

"I'm not going to stay. I'm going to be home with my family." She said adamantly, starting to cry.

Dr. Wetzler tried to reason with her. "I'm sure your family could celebrate when you get home."

Heidi sat up straighter, tears disappearing. "I don't care what you say or what you think. I'm not staying in this place for more than one day and that's final." She had never confronted him like this before.

Dr. Wetzler locked eyes with her for a moment then smiled ruefully. "Okay," he said, "one day." Heidi then handed him the holiday gift she had brought him. "Here's your gift, damn you," she blurted. They both smiled, looked at each other, and began to laugh.

That evening she had more tests. They wanted to do a high resolution CAT scan, which required an IV to move dye through the veins. Heidi refused the test and said that if it was going to have to be done, it would happen after Christmas. The next morning one of the medical team doctors, not Dr. Wetzler, was the attending physician. When she walked into the room, she immediately held up her hands and said, "Yes, I know you're going home today. I'm just here to check on you." We have talked to this doctor since Heidi's death. She has told us how much she admired Heidi's grace, attitude, and courage.

So Heidi made it home, and we celebrated our last Christmas together with the beauty of a family's love. Although other gifts were exchanged, I remember most vividly the scrapbooks. Diane and I saw all the love Heidi poured into them, and all the hardship she endured while creating them. Heidi carefully watched the faces of each of her sisters as they opened the boxes containing the scrapbooks. Her eyes danced with delight and pride and love as her sisters, their own eyes swimming with tears, paged through those masterpieces. The house echoed with their delighted exclamations and laughter. "Remember these dresses Grandma made for us?" "Look at my hair!" "Oh my gosh, listen to this!" "Heid, where did you find all of this?" "How did you do all of this?" "Heid, it's so interesting to see my life through your eyes. What a treasure this is." As Tara, Kristen, and Katie continued to examine their scrapbooks and share with their husbands the stories that accompanied each picture, each memento, each page, Heidi grew quieter. She smiled at the collective memory being explored and continued to watch carefully the expressions on her sisters' faces. I remember wondering what she was thinking, how she must have felt handing over the projects that had consumed her for four months. I thought I saw a flicker of sadness settle into her eyes, but I wonder now if it was my sadness. For a brief time the sounds faded, and I retreated into that quiet place in my soul, the place of care and quiet, the place where I can watch my loved ones as if I am no longer there. Was Heidi's smile and gaze a signal that she too had this spiritual retreat? Was she savoring these sounds of joy and locking them away for future reminiscences?

Christmas for me will forever be defined by the image of my three older daughters, heads bent over the pages Heidi so carefully designed, while Heidi sat nearby on the couch, watching their delight, an enigmatic smile playing on her face.

The Social Dimension of Faith

The connections among death, dying, religion, and grieving are very complex. I cannot do this topic justice here, but there are a few salient points that have particularly touched me in my journey. There are real distinctions among church, religion, religious experience, and spirituality. Churches and the religion associated with them are a social and cultural structure for faith and religious feelings and/or experiences. In this chapter I will use the word "church" to refer to the place people attend (whether it is a mosque, temple, synagogue, store front, cathedral, chapel, etc.). This usage is only for convenience and tries to avoid the cumbersome reference to all the places people may go to worship, pray, or give thanksgiving to God. Each church is associated with a religion, and they provide rules, norms, doctrines, and/or beliefs that members generally may share. The reality, of course, is far more complex than this simplified version. Religions and churches are very much a part of a continuum. Within a given religion there are wide variations of beliefs and a real diversity of denominations or sects. The differences may be due primarily to politics or organizational structures, or they may reflect whether the sacred writings are to be read interpretatively or literally. Subsequent disagreements often become more convoluted over time as the organizations shift and institutionalized doctrines and beliefs become more markedly diverse. Even within particular churches, the members of a congregation may have very widely diverse beliefs. This diversity within religions and within churches relates to contextual, cultural, situational, and personality variations.

Religions and churches become a dimension within everyone's life and usually impact upon someone's grieving journey. Even the atheist or non-affiliated person has had some connection or context that helps define their rejection of God, or churches, or religions. Some people may think of their religion or their church as somehow being immune from the fallibilities of being human. The truth of the matter is that all religions and all churches are influenced by the Contextual Spheres and cultures. It is a mistake to expect perfection from churches or their members. One of the primary motives for people to become or to remain members of any church or of any religion is because of the answers and/or guidance that they may receive during their lives. The meaning of redemption or reformation or salvation, for example, is crucial for people to make sense out of the turmoil and suffering in life. Some people are convinced that their church or their religion does have <u>The</u> Meaning in life or is the repository for <u>The</u> Truth. Such sentiments may bring those people comfort and solace for a period of time. Maybe some people will go through their entire lives believing that they really know The Truth because their religion has provided it to them. I wonder what will happen when they die and discover that Truth was not their exclusive domain. All religions and churches share in the truth/Truth; however, since humans are involved in the organization, continuation, and revelation of the meaning and message of the religion, it is impossible to prevent human fallibilities, ignorance, and prejudices from influencing the rules, doctrines, and beliefs that people experience with the religion. Thus, it is important while grieving to realize that religion and churches may or may not be sources of comfort and guidance.

It is possible that religion and churches may be a combination of both: comfort and pain, insight and ignorance, healing and suffering, fulfillment and rejection. It is possible for people to expect too much from their church or religion; it is also possible that other members of the church may provide too little support or comfort. As with all dimensions within one's grieving journey, the individual must learn to develop a sense of balance, a healthy attitude toward one's self and life, and a meaningful purpose for living. A person's church or religion may or may not support these on-going processes. Religions and churches may be wonderfully supportive and comforting. The caring and compassion that can be found in a church may be a blessing throughout a person's grieving journey. The difficulty comes with the reality that not everyone can depend upon his church or religion to provide this support.

In my *faith journey* I have been involved with different denominations within Christianity and have studied world religions. One conclusion that I would make is that faith is ultimately the relationship a person has with God; this is one's spirituality. How a person expresses this faith (either while communicating or in action) usually involves some type of social context. Religion is so important because it connects individuals to the deepest dimensions in life. When the religion subverts its primary purpose (bringing believers together to thank, honor, petition, and learn about God and the meaning of life and death), it becomes a tremendously destructive force. The most typical way for people to share their faith is through a church and/or their religion. Religions and churches can be very confusing because their rules or social mores may reflect the social stereotypes or beliefs about death and grieving that prevent people from healing or experiencing some sense of balance. It is quite common for people to accept some aspects, beliefs, or teachings of their religion, but reject, ignore, or misunderstand other elements. In essence, belonging to a church or religion should be a lifelong journey always with more to learn. There are unlimited possibilities for growth and meaningful experiences to be shared with others; yet, religions and churches are not immune from shortcomings that we humans embody – such as child abuse, the misappropriations of funds, and the exploitation of the sick and lonely.

One of the primary motivations for belonging to or remaining a part of any church or religion is the message it provides about death and dying. The promise of redemption, salvation, or maybe of experiencing the rapture are strong forces in many people's lives. We live in a world that is dominated by confusion, mixed messages, ambiguity, and events that trouble our hearts, minds, and souls. There is comfort in hearing a message from a church's representative (rabbi, priest, minister, imam, or pastor) that answers the questions: Why did my child die? Where is my child now? What does all of this pain mean? These fundamental questions burn the hearts of each and every parent who has experienced the death of a child, as well as anyone who has dealt with the death of a loved one. They also become real challenges for anyone who is grieving. For some, the church's answers are satisfactory, for others they are not. For some, the answers that were satisfactory begin to lose their comfort over time, and the person may start blaming the church or religion. It is common for grieving parents to blame God for the death of their child. Many people experience profound and troubling doubts about what they believe. They may feel abandoned by their church or religion. Sometimes those who experience this abandonment find themselves in a crisis of faith. What I would like to share is some of my beliefs about the role religion and churches can and cannot have in one's journey of grieving.

Churches can provide a profound support network for members. Churches are organized to help people ask the deepest questions and experience the greatest joys and sorrows of life. Initiations (for example, baptisms), rites of passage (for example, a *bar mitzvah*), and weddings can be times of great celebration and joy. Attending services or prayers regularly establishes abiding relationships that can provide comfort and support. When someone dies there are rituals in a church that can comfort those who are grieving. Some churches provide on-going support, and often church members are visitors to the wakes and attend the funerals or memorial services. Since these people are also members of our society, however, they may treat the person who is grieving in a way that is consistent within our society. For example, men may not wish to show emotions, especially crying, and may not be comfortable when the grieving person wishes to talk at length about her loved one. Some parents sense that others begin to treat them as if they are "those poor people who lost their child." People don't know what to say or try to act as if nothing has changed.

Church members may become uncomfortable after a period of time in making any mention of the child's name. These types of responses do not seem to fit with the grieving parents' need for comfort. We often tend to expect too much from our churches because they are supposed to be the source for all that is good and true.

Problems can become exacerbated when the pastor, rabbi, imam, etc. says or does something that is painful or ignorant. We expect religiously trained people to understand or to be willing to share the grief and pain. Some may be very skilled at attending to the initial pain at the time of death but may not understand the dynamics of a journey of grieving. They may say or do very hurtful things even at the funeral home or during the funeral (for example, some churches condemn suicide and will not allow the deceased to be buried in religiously owned cemeteries). The practices of some churches may be very detrimental to grieving. For example, some churches now no longer permit eulogies to be given. For some leaders it may be an issue that "we can't take too much time for a service" or "we can't risk things being said that we do not want to hear." Some leaders may be more interested in doing the rituals the "right" way according to their interpretation of their religion's rubrics or practices. There are other leaders who are always interested in making any service a show or spectacle. Even within a given church there can be very conflicting attitudes. The people who are grieving may want to have a member of the family give a eulogy, but the pastor or members of the congregation do not. A grieving family usually does not want an impersonal homily or eulogy to be given and usually does not want the service to be rushed or treated as if it was just another routine task to be completed. Unfortunately, terrible things have been said and done during these highly emotional times. Sometimes the stock answers that are used in funerals become a source of pain rather than comfort. For example, the pastor who says that the dead person is in a better place may or may not be helping the grieving loved one or parent. Unfortunately, there are no clear guidelines, especially in those cases where the pastor does not know the person or the family very well.

At my aunt's funeral (the year after Heidi died) the preacher described in vivid detail the rooms that now housed my aunt. I was offended because it seemed to trivialize her death. The context did not help in that situation because I knew the pastor did not know her and so he used vague platitudes, such as, "we know your aunt is in a better place." His words were supposed to be consoling. They were not. Besides, I was still in the depths of my new grief for Heidi. I have heard some priests tell those attending a funeral what the dead person wants the family and friends to do: "Get on with your life." This may be that preacher's pat answer to the sorrow of those attending, but presuming to speak for the dead person is too much for a grieving family to take. How wise is it to tell the parents of a teenager who committed suicide that he no longer will suffer fear and pain in life? Does a pastor really fulfill the needs of mourners when he or she uses a sterile homily that is lifted from a book of generic sermons? It is essential for pastors to spend time with the grieving family before the service in order to have a proper sense of what the people are feeling. Also, pastors should spend time learning how to help people through their grieving, rather than just assume that the teachings of the church are sufficient answers for what they will be feeling.

I do not want to diminish the problems facing clergy, especially in those areas where the supply of trained leaders is far too low to meet the demands. The clergy may not have the time or resources or training to really provide the personalized care that church members may need. Sometimes the clergy member may be facing real trauma within her life too. Conflicts and emotional confusion can emerge for a wide variety of reasons. The situation can become long lasting and create real bitterness. It is sad when expectations are not met and the deep emotional needs for those who are grieving become dismissed or trivialized. My father regularly attended church and served as an usher for many years. He was not a devout man, but he did what he thought was expected of him. He became very ill and had to retire early; he spent the last five years of his life at our home with periodic hospital stays. No priest visited him at home or in the hospital at any of his stays. He became bitter and disenfranchised. My brothers and I provided a service for him at the funeral home before he was buried. My father blamed his church; I did not. Sometimes it is just too much to expect the clergy to satisfy everyone's needs; it is tragic and may become a personal crisis of faith when those needs are not addressed. It is truly tragic when a person's church becomes the source of deep and abiding pain or neglect. Grieving people may feel alienated when no one at the church remembers their loved one's death. As in all things in life, balance and harmony are crucial ingredients in finding meaning and purpose. Pastors need to recognize their limits and not presume to have all the answers. Other members of the church need to provide assistance and minister to the grieving within their parishes. Attitude and presence are far more important than any formulaic response or action.

One important element for any funeral is to share some elements of the dead person's story or celebrate the life of the deceased person. Shortly after Heidi's death I had to lead the funeral service for a church member I had known. I knew his son and former wife, but no other members of his family. I met with them, and they asked me to speak for them. We discussed what they wanted to hear, and I shared a couple of experiences I had that might be meaningful. It was very difficult for me to throw myself into the role of consoler, preacher, and worship leader so soon after Heidi's death. To this day I know that God was giving me the strength to do what was being asked of me, and Heidi was standing near me making sure that I did not turn the service or comments into my grieving or story. This was a funeral for Brian. It is imperative that funerals respect the individual's life. It should never be a show or be centered on the clergy who is leading the service. Expressing the hopes that are embedded within the religion seems to make a lot of sense at funerals, or when sitting Shiva, or when visiting the family. The problem may come with the style, timing, or manner in which these hopes are expressed. Is it wise to tell the mother of a severely deformed baby who dies at seven months that it is better for everyone that the child died; besides, "you are young and can have other children"? Sometimes clergy would be well advised to speak less and show more compassion through listening and silent presence. Some people are very accepting of the impression that all clergy are very busy people, so they may not have time to show very much sympathy or be available to provide comfort. There are others, however, who may expect clergy to be God's perfect messengers. As in all things, it seems best for grieving people to find the reasonable balance in expectations while clergy should really attempt to study, understand, and develop an attitude that demonstrates an awareness of the meaning of real grieving. Sometimes the interpretations of sacred writings or taking a reading out of context are contradictory to healthy grieving.

Another example of creating hurt and confusion in a church relates to memorials. A young pastor in a church we formerly attended had served as a funeral director for 12 years before entering the seminary. The members of the parish mistakenly assumed that that training helped him understand the grieving process. He was adept at ministering to people during wakes and funerals, but quickly began to illustrate his misunderstanding of the needs of those who are grieving. Very early in his tenure as pastor he began preaching about how wrong it was for people to want to place the name of a loved one on a memorial at the church (stained glass windows, or noting names when giving altar flowers for a given Sunday, for example). In his sermon, he was calling grieving people selfish if they wanted their loved one's name included in any memorial. This ignorance can create real confusion or hurt in parishioners; intentionally or not, he was being cruel. Is it wise to call a grieving husband, wife, or parent selfish, if he wants his loved one's name seen? Is it prudent to instill in those who are not grieving an attitude that diminishes the grieving person's opportunity to share in the legacy of her loved one? This pastor went on to display other examples of his misunderstanding of meaningful and healthy grieving. The lesson for me was to realize that churches and religions are social and cultural in their activities. They may or may not provide the grieving person with the comfort that is necessary. It is important not to blame God for the ignorance of His representatives.

One of the consequences for churches is that their rules and doctrines can become very closed to others and to life. Congregations may believe that they are welcoming and friendly, but if you are a visitor, it may not feel that way at all. Some of the practices in churches are designed to be exclusive, for example the Roman Catholic policy of not allowing members from other denominations to receive the Eucharist. Others are unintentionally exclusive (for example, bulletins that are difficult for visitors to follow). Wars have been fought in the name of religion, and terrorists may warp a religion's message in order to serve their own destructive agenda. People and clergy in churches are not exempt from sending mixed, confused, or antagonistic messages to others. Anyone who is grieving should seek solace and comfort in some religious context or in some spiritual dimension. I feel real sorrow for the atheist who does not have this avenue of support during his grieving journey. It is tragic when someone turns away from her religion during her grieving because the church fails to support and comfort her. The real purpose of any genuine religion is to foster meaningfulness, connection with God and others, and personal development.

X.

FEBRUARY 6, 2003.

Her Reflection

On this Thursday afternoon, as I walked in the door from work, I saw Heidi hunched over a sheet of paper, sitting contentedly on the living room couch. A pen dangled from her slender fingers. She was perched upon a pillow to help provide her with some support since our couch, suffering from years of use, created a sagging effect on anyone who dared to invade its space. She had to squint to see because the lack of tearing for so long in her eyes was almost crippling. Her breathing was raspy, and her motions were very slow and labored. The next day Dr. Wetzler would give us the chilling news that would signal that our journey was headed into the subway. Diane was subdued while she stood cooking in the kitchen. Heidi looked up when I walked in. "Hi, Dad," she said. "Do you want to read something?" I smiled to myself; even now she was my little girl, not letting me get in the door before wrapping me into her world.

I took off my coat, put away my briefcase, and sat down to read the piece of paper Heidi shakingly extended toward me. Her chicken-scratch handwriting, made worse by the condition of her eyes and the pain in her hands, was difficult to read. But the message was not. It was Heidi's story of her faith journey: beautiful, personal, and touching. When I finished reading it, I struggled not to show her my tears (not wanting to break her first and most important commandment), but managed to ask her, "Would you like me to type it for you?"

She smiled and replied, "That would be great. But, Dad, I don't want you spreading this all over the place. It's personal."

In her honor I will not reproduce it here nor share with you what she said; however, this personal testimony of faith has been a source of comfort for Diane and me. It is clear that Heidi had found peace with God. She had never blamed God, or anyone, for her leukemia. It happened, and no one knew why. She did not dwell on the cause or the "why," only on how to defeat it and restore herself to health. Her suspension of the quest for an answer to the "why" question has been an inspiration for me to do the same. This story was an affirmation of her deep-seated, personal faith which transcended any connection she ever had with a church or with her religion. God was a real part of her life, and she felt a divine presence protecting her. She had gone through some dark times and did not always feel His presence, but now it was clear that she could feel God in her life and was being comforted.

All of our girls were involved with our church as they grew up. We did not do so to make them remain Lutherans for their whole life; we did so to teach them the importance of connecting their faith to the social dimension of human existence. Heidi used her singing in a wide variety of ways at our church. She sang at a special Mother's Day brunch one year, and sang "Who Knows Where the Time Goes" to the pastor at his retirement party. Heidi had been in choir and in a select chorus at her high school, as well as in the school's musicals. She had spent a number of summers participating in a special summer theater program and had interned at the area's "Shakespeare in the Park" series. She and I participated in a couple of community theater performances, but one of the most satisfying experiences with Heidi and Diane was the year I was the director and they were cast in the play version of "Steel Magnolias." I was always enchanted with her singing and delighted in all of her performances (which I cannot say I did for the dance recitals when she was younger).

Amid all of the memories of Heidi singing in so many different venues, the one most precious for me was her rendition of "Amazing Grace" the Sunday after 9/11. We had celebrated Heidi's "Victory" party the week before, and she had just started attending my Honors course. Diane called us at my office before class and asked if we had heard about the planes crashing into the Twin Towers. Heidi and I rarely turned on the radio when we drove to school. It was a time to parry, argue, and debate about the great issues of our time. We would laugh at each other; we also would goad each other on. We both had learned what buttons to push when we wanted to "intellectually tease" one another. That morning had been no different. So we had not heard any of the news. When we got to class, the students were in varying degrees of shock. A couple had actually seen footage of the crashes on their televisions in their rooms. They shared what they saw with the rest of us. That day was one of a collective sense of disbelief and horror for this country. The following Sunday churches around the United States were filled with a nation in mourning. Heidi had asked us if she could sing "Amazing Grace" at church. When Diane talked to the pastor, he was touched that she would do so.

As close as the church had been for all of us and as supportive as the members had been for Heidi, she had not been to church very often during her illness because most of the time it was too dangerous for her to go due to the risk of infection. People tend to go to church with colds, and children are a constant source of germs. Diane and I had become very conscious of the need to wash our hands and avoid anyone with colds. In fact, Diane and her sister had run a pre-school at our church for 10 years before Heidi was diagnosed. Once we learned she had leukemia, the pre-school was closed; Diane could not risk exposure to the children or bringing home any infections to Heidi. It became a common practice for us to leave church before the end of the service so we could avoid shaking hands or bringing germs home.

But on that Sunday after 9/11 Heidi stood up in the choir loft (in the back of the church's nave and above the congregation) and sang a solo. She sang without the organ or piano. At first her voice sounded weak and distant. The hymn was not noted in the bulletin, and it came at the end of worship. For a brief second people were rustling as they prepared to leave, but like a spreading sunshine Heidi's voice slowly engulfed us all. Her voice became stronger, and the muffled tears of so many became easily detected. My cheeks were soaked with the tears that came from a grief for all of those who had died on that Tuesday morning; that came from an anxiety of what the future held for our country; that came for the joy of hearing my daughter share her inner beauty with people who cared for her; that came from a relief that she was going to survive the leukemia and again pursue her dreams; that came from the worry that my hopes could still be dashed; that came from a life so entwined in the beauty and haunting melody of that very special hymn. Little did I know that 17 months later Diane and I would be in this church and singing that hymn at Heidi's funeral.

After reading Heidi's story, I remember thinking about some of those days at church, and realizing that Heidi's spirituality had grown beyond the limits that a church or a religion place upon a person's faith and intimate relationship with God. On that Thursday afternoon I typed Heidi's spiritual testimony and felt that God was truly present for all of us. After she read the copy that I had typed, she was satisfied. Diane told me that earlier in the day, she had asked Heidi (who was *feverishly writing), "Sweetie, do you need anything?" Heidi, barely raising her eyes, shook her head and quietly said, "Not really. I'm busy. I really need to finish this." Diane and I both know now that Heidi knew she would not be given another opportunity to write this story and it was one that just had to be written and given to her family. It remains a very precious gift for us. She had a great deal of difficulty that day getting up from the couch. She would cradle her elbow in my left hand while my right arm went around her waist. I still vividly recall how light her touch on my arm was; how rigid all of her limbs had become; and how incredibly fragile she seemed. Yet, her smile and eyes showed me that inner strength that had carried her through so many arduous struggles and tortuous moments. She shuffled to her room. We remained silent the whole way, a journey that was much longer than the measured distance. The length was comforting in our embrace, yet painful in the assault upon her body. I sensed a calmness in her that transcended the pain she felt and tried so valiantly to hide. I remember gently turning her so she could take her place on the bed that had become so much a part of the last 2 ½ years of her life. She settled in with a smile and a gleam in her eyes that darted through the arid landscape of those orbs.*

Touching Consciousness

One dimension of living in a Humpty Dumpty society is that we separate our minds and bodies (or soul and body). In Western cultures, the Greek philosophers' writings reflected this view. Socrates and Plato identified the physical world as one of on-going change. It was the intellectual/spiritual world that embodied truth that was unchanging and eternal. Goodness is found in the supernatural realm; sin and corruption are a part of the natural world. This tradition has created the idea that we should control ourselves with our head or with the moral compass that is given to us in our religions or in humanistic secularism. Some people associate evil with the body and goodness with the soul. In response to this split, there have been a number of alternative views (all of which, however, presume that an answer needs to be given to the idea of the soul/body or mind/body split). For example, positivists claim that there really is only one reality and it is physical. The soul or the mind is a by-product of electrical or chemical reactions in our brains. Others claim that we should foster mental or spiritual development and minimize attention to the physical. Other views attempt to find a balance between the two dimensions or parts of being human. Aristotle said that humans are rational animals, that is, a combination of the intellectual/rational and the physical/animal. Humans need to find moderation in all things and develop good habits from their rational thinking.

Within this context of thinking, death is seen as the end of physical existence. The question of what comes afterward has been and will continue to be debated. Those who are grieving no longer can experience their loved one in any physical form. This reality creates the pain of absence and the feelings of separation. My views differ from the western traditions just noted. The soul and body are not two distinct entities brought together at birth. Instead, our birth is the creation of a new consciousness. Its sources are our parents and God. It evolves throughout life and does so in varying forms: some we call physical or material, some we call mental or psychic or spiritual. The source of all these dimensions of life is the energy of consciousness, which should not just be equated to the brain and/or nervous system. While we are alive, the brain and nervous system are necessary for our consciousness to function. However, these physiological and electrical characteristics are not sufficient to explain consciousness fully. When people die, their consciousness is transformed. Because I have not been transformed, I do not know the nature of this eternal, transformed consciousness. What I do believe is that all consciousnesses can communicate, love, and relate to others (both alive and dead).

Everyone has a uniqueness that creates the meaning of that person's individuality. Our uniqueness comes from our individualized past (and memories) and our own perspective. We can share experiences and memories with others, but no two people can ever share the totality of any event and can never completely see through the eyes and memories of another. Identical twins may be the closest to this type of unity, but even they will remain inevitably distinct and unique.

Our culture has moved away from a connectedness with "primordial consciousness." This primordial consciousness is a way human beings can relate to the world and to others without the structures of society intervening and organizing the experience. In essence it is an intuitive connection to life. The Hellenic/Roman influence of our culture has emphasized the analytic and dualistic side of logic and rational thinking. We have minimized the intuitive connectedness that could open us up to the reality and feeling of what the essential meaning of consciousness is. Heidi can touch us through her energy, which continues in her transformed life. Since our intuitive sense has become diminished, it is difficult for us to actually feel her and touch her transformed self. She gives us signs through her energy to reassure us that she is well and has reached a level of fulfillment we can only hope to touch. Because our intuitive powers are lessened, we need more "Heidi" signs; none of the ones we have received are sufficient. We are not connected to Heidi in any on-going physical fashion that we can perceive. The ways we normally communicate and relate to others has been completely transformed, and we struggle to sustain a relationship with her in any familiar way. Our needs for experiencing her are insatiable partly because we miss her so much. Our insatiable feelings are not the result of Heidi's ability to communicate with us; it is in our inability to comprehend this new communication. Transformation does not actually disconnect loved ones, but it does create limits.

Death removes the readily accessible means for sharing experiences with loved ones; however, death does not mean that sharing, or communicating, or relating are forever lost. The ways we connect with our departed loved ones needs to become transformed, and trying to become open to these new ways of communicating or relating is very difficult. Even though I can continue to communicate with Heidi does not mean that I feel confident that I can do so whenever I would like. Also, Heidi's transformed life means that her references to places and times would be quite different from mine. I may expect or want her to be available to share an experience, but that doesn't mean that she always can. People who die do not become God; they are not capable of being in all places at all times. Their individuality has its limits too. Their limits, however, are very different from ours. Frankly, I have no idea what those limits might be, but clearly unlike God they are not omniscient or omnipresent. Their transformation gives them a type of awareness and an understanding that are unfamiliar to us, and they acquire abilities that may just exceed our imaginative powers to discern.

Our culture focuses too much upon the material form of energy. Matter is just another form of energy that moves slower and is denser than, say, light or gravity. We stress what we can see, even though our field of vision is very narrow. Consider the fact that we can't even "see" all the frequencies of light. Once we accept the fact that we are very limited by only having five senses, and each of them has a very narrow band of accessing the world, we can open ourselves to the possibility that we need to expand our understanding beyond the limits of sensation. In like manner, even reason and logic, the bastions of Western thought, are encumbered with inherent limits and boundaries that prevent us from comprehending all that God has made available to us in our world. I am not saying that sensation, reason, and logic should be ignored; rather, they need to be placed within a larger context of understanding. They are not the means for gaining absolute truth or certainty. They are merely tools that are at our disposal to help us on our way. Our cultural views of separating the soul and body and of minimizing intuitive connectedness to life make grieving so much more difficult and painful.

Contemporary American culture glorifies the physical. We have become skeptics, even cynics, of the spiritual dimension of our life. We focus upon what is concrete. We need proof in order to accept or believe anything. We have limited proof to what is determined through logic or empirical forms of thinking. Over the centuries, for example, there have been many "proofs" for God's existence. These proofs are either accepted or rejected based on how one thinks. These proofs really are unnecessary because they cannot achieve their goal. Faith is not something that is the conclusion of a rational argument. Faith really seems to be what Sören Kierkegaard claimed: it is a leap into the absurd. If you need to prove something, then it is not based on faith. Faith requires a suspension of proof and logical reasoning. Freeing faith from the limits of reason and empirical evidence gives it license to search the entirety of existence. This search should not be blind, however. I am not talking about a "blind faith" that totally disregards or rejects reason, logic or empirical evidence. Again, I am referring to a balance. Faith will suspend, not reject, other forms of knowing the world. Ultimately faith, like intuition, needs to be combined with sound reasoning and empirical verification of experiences. Rejecting either our intellect or our intuition diminishes our abilities to comprehend the world and the mysteries of life. Trusting intuition in our culture requires a leap of faith. Trusting someone who shares your intuitive understanding also requires a leap of faith.

It is this trust in God, in my wife, in my family and friends that provides a context wherein Heidi's transformed life makes sense. I can still feel her presence, and I can be reassured that she continues to live with me, with her mother, with her sisters, with their husbands, with their children, etc. Heidi's legacy is not just a set of memories or influences that I and others may experience. It is a living extension of life that is continually wrapping itself around people in ways that we may not even realize. The skeptics may say that this is a nice rationalization and pass it off as the ramblings of a grieving father. For those people, I can only say that I am sorry for their dismissal of what may be the most important dimension within human life: the dimension of spiritual connectedness.

Spirituality necessitates some connection to God. The meaning of God, however, is the real question. Each one of us can develop a meaning of God that relates to our needs and experiences. In this sense, we may tend to create God in our own image and likeness. For me, all of life is creative energy. Energy emerges in a variety of forms and is continually changing. Each moment is new and includes all that has happened before. This energy is a creative consciousness that extends beyond the limits of the electro-chemical synapses in the brain. God is the source and sustainer of the creative consciousness in all of life. We can be connected with God, if we but choose to do so. Faith is this connecting link. The real problem, of course, comes in knowing whether or not our faith is really connecting us to God. There is a very real possibility that what our faith tells us about God is flawed and completely wrong. Faith will always include a dimension of risk-taking. Many people become overwhelmed by the risky nature of faith. They may either turn their faith over to a church or to a group that can reassure them of the truth. Others, however, may just ignore the relationship until there is a real crisis in their lives that makes them confront the issue of life's meaning. A healthy attitude towards faith realizes that belief is risky and that it is possible that what anyone believes may be quite wrong. Isn't this the real meaning of being humble in the face of God? Again, I am very leery of those who have absolutely no doubts that their faith is correct and true. There is a real difference between those who are committed to a faith that they hold firmly in their hearts and those who blindly and arrogantly proclaim that absolute truth is theirs and theirs alone.

I do not believe there is a Divine Plan (meaning everything is predetermined) because I believe that God, the Father, and the Holy Spirit are involved in the changing processes of all life and creation. My beliefs arise out of my Christian heritage. I would hope that they are not overly exclusive of other faiths or religious beliefs. For me, God, the Father, is the "male" dimension and the Holy Spirit is the "female." I always refer to the Holy Spirit as "she," the nourishing dimension of God which bestows grace and blessings to all of life. Many native or sacred religions have a real creative connection to the female source of life. The Judeo-Christian tradition has been more male dominant. God actually transcends gender, and referring to God as "it" seems to create an image that is far too impersonal. Thus, God is the Becoming of all life, the Creator of all that exists. Referring to God as a Being is too limiting because God is not static and is not the result of anyone's thinking. The creative force of life is the vital energy that breathes life into all that exists. I do not believe that there are souls that exist in some pre-existing state that are somehow placed into an embryo at birth. Each birth is a unique creation, a unique forming of energy, a unique beginning of a person who never has existed before and who will continue to exist in some type of transformed life forever. Humans can share in the "power" of creation, a process that is wonderful and blessed, a process that gets its energy from those who are conjoining. It is a microcosm of God's creation of all life. This creative power is precious, and the life that can come from two people's union is blessed indeed. Just as we are distinct from our children, we are also inherently connected to them – in energy, in consciousness, in genetics. God is in us, just as we are in our children. Just as we change with our children's love, life and experience, so does God change with our existence.

As I noted above, there is no Divine Plan that provides an explanation for everything that happens because God bestows meaning and purpose into <u>all of life</u> while not predetermining all of the details. God is not a micromanager who has to be responsible for each detail in existence. If so, there would be no free will, no chance occurrences, no mutations in evolution, and no real responsibility that humans should accept for their actions. God's meaning and purpose includes the laws or parameters that guide and structure life. Gravity and electromagnetism, for example, reflect some of these parameters. Science is a wonderful tool to help us understand how the laws work. Science is not an end-product, but is itself a creative and evolving means for understanding and interpreting what and why things happen the way they do. God has created a world that remains creative. Free will, chance, fate, and chaos are expressions of the creative processes that are inherent in all life. Any religion or science that reduces the majesty of God's creation to static, codified answers has diminished the miracle of life. No one can know the absolute reasons and meaning for life. Because life is creative, new, and continuing to evolve, it is impossible for a Divine Plan to exist or for anyone to know it with absolute certainty. The need for a plan is a creation of people who need a rational explanation for the mysteries in life. The mysteries are only mysteries in the sense that we cannot predict or anticipate or explain all that happens in life. It would be impossible to do so because life is inherently unpredictable or unforeseeable. This "unforeseeability" is the result of the creative and unique dimensions of all life and existence. Science and religion can give us glimpses into the nature of the "what's" and "why's" of life, yet their views and conclusions do have limits. Rather than being antagonistic, science and religion can and should be co-craftsmen in furthering human understanding. The majesty of the universe that astronomy and physics detail actually enhances the awe anyone should have for the source of such wonder.

Heidi's death was not something preordained by God. Many people need the reassurance that God has a purpose for each one of us. Although this is true, we should not take the next step and say that this purpose is preordained and determined by God. One of the graces of being human is our gift of free choice. This gift, like all things human, can be used in blessed and wonderful ways, and it can be used in horrific and destructive ways too. Many grieving parents need the consolation that there is some meaning or purpose to their child's death. God sustains everyone's purposefulness and provides the grace and blessing for each of us to participate in its development. Our life is the journey to try to discover the source from which we can create our meaning and purpose. A real blessing in life occurs when we experience clarity about the true nature of our meaning or purpose. Most people, like me, are not sure if we are fulfilling our purpose completely. There are other people who may hope for a purpose, but may think that life's circumstances have taken them away from this purpose or are preventing it from occurring. Finally, there are those who do not believe in meaning or purpose at all. Free will in humans provides us with the power and opportunity to follow a meaningful life or pursue other options. At least that is what Americans would like to think. The reality is that life has many limits: cultural barriers, language impediments, physiological restraints, natural laws, economic forces, and social influences, to name a few. Thus, free will is enveloped in all of these dimensions in life. The individual's life is a cacophony and/or harmony of all these forces. All of them play a role in one's death: fate, choice, luck, being in the wrong place, laws of nature, social contexts, etc.

People die at different ages and for different reasons. I cannot believe that God has a specific plan that targets the day, cause, and time for each person's death. The creative forces of life are too interwoven into all of life for me to accept that view. God is not responsible for an individual's death. There is no reason to blame God for Heidi's death. The idea of a Good God allowing bad things to happen is a moot question. The forces of life create the conditions within which events happen. Sometimes we may be able to identify particular causes that have led to a person's death. My father had lung cancer and emphysema. He was a long- time, heavy smoker and an alcoholic; he worked at a chemical plant, lived in the Love Canal, and exercised very little in the latter decades of his life. His last five years were painful and increasingly debilitating. In one sense, it was easy to see the causes leading up to his death. In fact, he refused to quit smoking even after they removed part of his lung. As he continued to deteriorate, we expected his death. Yet, when my brother called to tell me to come to the hospital, I was surprised to discover that he had died. Expecting someone to die and knowing the causes leading to the death do not necessarily take away the surprise and grief that comes with a loved one dying. In Heidi's case we do not know what caused the leukemia. We do not really even know why she relapsed nor why the GVHD went to her lungs. Those events were a part of the physiological realities of life. Scientists and researchers continue to provide us with some answers to these physiological happenings. In the end, both my father and daughter are dead. Knowing the causes for one and not knowing the causes for the other does not change the reality that both have been transformed and I cannot see either one of them now. Thus, in a real sense their deaths were not predetermined, but they were inevitable. The forces of nature, choices made, actions taken, etc. all conspired to create the conditions and causes that led to their deaths.

Obviously, there are many other reasons for people dying that are not covered by the example of my father or my daughter. Murders, accidents, overdoses, suicides, famine, wars, etc. provide a wide panorama of possibilities and tragedies that exist within our world. In some cases we may be able to discover reasons why someone was murdered or what may have caused an accident to occur when it did. In other cases, mysteries will continue to be a part of the grieving journey. Underlying all death is the reality that she is no longer alive. Life has changed, and those who continue to live in this world continually face the challenge of trying to learn how to adjust and adapt to the new realities.

Amidst the pain and grief, however, is the belief that Heidi continues to live in ways I cannot even imagine. I have felt her presence and others have seen her continuing impact in their lives. Her legacy is a living, changing presence that has been transformed in some mystical, wonderful way. Spirituality is rooted in the meaningfulness and purposefulness of our connection with God and with each other. This spirituality is not intended to diminish anyone's feeling of pain and grief in death; rather, it is my way of making some sense out of life and death. My spirituality sustains me in my prayers and in my life. It does not take away the pain and does not take me off the subway; it just makes all of it worthwhile. There are times when this faith and these beliefs are not strong enough to motivate me to find joy in what I am doing. I do feel physically and emotionally spent at times. There are days when there is just no energy to tackle a new task, meet new people, or even start another project. Physically I feel worn out and rarely, if ever, feel rested and ready to tackle anything life can throw at me. At all times, however, I do know that Heidi continues to live, and I can find comfort in that knowledge.

XI.

FEBRUARY 10, 2003.

Transforming

Heidi's last weekend alive remains a surreal memory, vivid moments captured in a blinding blur. We were all there: Diane and I, Tara and Joe, Kristen and Bill, Katie and Anthony, our dog, Vragil, and, of course, Heidi. An outsider would say that the events of the weekend appeared rather mundane in their normalcy. We talked and laughed and played games. We joked. We recalled family stories. We baked cookies and ate a scrumptious Saturday night meal that Anthony prepared. We didn't realize then that the lobster and pasta that Heidi so enjoyed would be her last real meal. We poked gentle fun at one another. We listened to music. We watched TV. Those are the things an outsider would have seen: a reunited family enjoying time together. What the outsider would have missed, however, was the depth of feeling cloaking those "normal" activities. The panicked eyes every time Heidi's gaspy breaths grew ragged. The hushed conversations that occurred in the kitchen and bedrooms, away from her earshot. The lumps in the throat every time the doorbell rang and we knew the visitor would be seeing Heidi for the last time. The pain felt as we eavesdropped on Heidi's final conversation with her boyfriend, who was stationed in Afghanistan. What the outsider would have missed was the love we wove into each of those normal, mundane activities.

Heidi's sisters baked two batches of cookies that weekend, following explicitly the recipes she had created in the previous month. Even though Heidi had never lost her dreams of performing on the stage, she had started pursuing other options as well. In the past year, she had watched many cooking shows, inquired into a culinary school, created lavish menus, and, most recently, had created two cookie recipes: *Snow Mountain Caps* and *Chocolate Coconut Decadence*. We laughed heartily when she announced, "I want to enter them into this contest I read about. I want to win third place."

Swallowing my amused chuckle, I asked, "Why third place?"

"Because I want to win the standing mixer. I've always wanted one. That's the third place prize."

"Only you, Heid, would want to win third place!"

After the cookies cooled, we ceremoniously tried them each so we could judge whether they would be winners. "They're delicious!" we declared to a delighted Heidi.

Beneath the surface lightheartedness, however, was the growing realization that Heidi was getting worse more quickly than we had imagined. Going to the bathroom was becoming increasingly difficult for her. For the past few days, I had to lift her onto a portable potty chair. During this last weekend, it became a team effort to help her. I would lift her, then Diane or one of her sisters would pull her pants down and someone would massage her neck while I held her. Her joints and muscles hurt, and it was difficult getting her situated with any comfort. Sometimes she cried in pain; sometimes we just used a bed pan, rather than trying to lift her out of bed and hold her on the portable potty. Two days before she died we thought she may have to be catheterized because she couldn't relieve herself for a long time. Tara, Kristen, and Katie took turns massaging her neck, trying to get her to relax, while she sat on the potty. "Think Niagara Falls," they said. "Running water. Drip. Drop. Drip. Drop." After an hour of this, Heidi's irritation was noticeable. "Just stop it," she said. "No more water talk!" Finally, finally, she urinated. We all shared a collective sigh of relief.

Each of Heidi's sisters had taken turns spending the night with her: Tara slept with her Friday night, Katie Saturday night, and Kristen on Sunday. Early Monday morning, I went downstairs and sat in the rocking chair next to her bed so I could be close. I quietly watched her struggle to breathe as she slept. Kristen lay beside her, eyes shut, but not sleeping. I remember thinking how much closer our family had become since her initial diagnosis. Somehow Heidi's illness had brought out the best in everybody as we all assumed roles we had never anticipated: caretaker, friend, game player, debate contestant, reminiscent partner, trivia tester, TV critic, cooking companion, medication dispenser.

At 6:00 a.m. Monday morning, Heidi awakened the household with her shouts of pain. Katie and Tara came bounding downstairs. We all gathered in her room, dreading the worst, but, suddenly, the pain subsided and Heidi sat back on the bed. I went to shave, preparing for our scheduled trip to Roswell, while her mother and sisters stayed with her. While I was upstairs, Heidi looked at Katie, who was sitting next to her. "Am I going to die?" she asked, saying those dreaded words for the first time.

"Yes, honey. You are."

The girls told me that Heidi looked a little surprised before saying, "Do I at least have a few days?"

"Yes, there's some time."

"Is it okay to be scared?" she asked.

"Yes," her sisters replied.

"Well, then, I'm a little scared." Heidi paused. "I'm a lot scared."

"We all love you,"

A frank discussion then ensued between all of the women. Even though the conversation has been relayed to me, I don't remember who said what, but the gist was clear: Heidi finally realized that no measures existed that would cure her. A respirator may prolong her life, but she would still die. At the end of the discussion, Heidi made it clear that she no longer wanted the option of a respirator. Then one of her sisters asked, "Heid, have you given any thought about how we're going to get you to the hospital today? It's so painful for you to move."

"We could just call Meir and tell him you're not coming in. We could have nurses come to the house. They could bring a wet oxygen mask."

"We can do that?"

"Heid, we can do anything you want."

"They won't be mad?"

"No, we promise."

"This isn't giving up?"

"No, honey."

"Okay, you can all cry now."

When Diane informed me that we wouldn't be going to the hospital that day, I was genuinely puzzled. "Why?" I asked

"It would just be too tough for Heidi," she said, quietly. I nodded. I understood.

From that moment on, we began an unspoken vigil. We read; we talked; we stayed with her. Even Vragil spent the day snuggled under Heidi's legs, as she bridged them for some comfort. Heidi's breathing was getting worse and her congestion was irritating her all day. I talked to her physician a couple of times, and we increased her Ativan and called in Hospice. During one conversation with Dr. Wetzler, I said, "She has really deteriorated over the weekend. I don't know whether she will last for days or weeks in this condition."

"It won't be weeks," said Dr. Wetzler, a slight catch in his normally calm voice. I knew then that he would never see her alive again.

We sent two of our sons-in-law to do some preliminary work at the funeral home and the cemetery for us, making our final arrangements after her death more bearable. Years before, Heidi had told Diane she hoped to be buried underneath a tree so that family and friends could visit her and sit and read. "I want people to enjoy visiting me, even when I'm gone," she had said. Throughout her illness, her mantra had consistently been to relieve all of us of any guilt or pain and have us enjoy being with her. Bill and Anthony found a spot with a large Eastern White Pine. We were so thankful.

Throughout the day, Heidi slipped in and out of coherence. At one point she asked her sisters to be sure to enter her recipes in the contests. When someone suggested that we tell some jokes Heidi replied, "Don't bother, we're not a very funny family." She would settle into a sort of stupor, and then, suddenly, shout something out. "Skaneateles!" she shouted once. Her sisters looked startled, tears creeping into their eyes. "Yes, Heid, we took you there for your 21st birthday. Didn't we have a great time?" Her sisters reminisced a bit about the trip before realizing Heidi was no longer tracking their conversation.

As the day wore on, Heidi became more and more fixated with her clogged nose. We would ask her if she needed something, and she'd cry out, "A decongestant. All I want is a decongestant!" She didn't seem to understand that a decongestant would not help her any longer. Katie suggested that she take the nose piece from her breathing machine and place it in her mouth, since she wasn't really capable of breathing through her nose anyhow. There were times when her gasping for breath was very frightening. By the afternoon Hospice had succeeded in sending us a mask for her breathing. It helped for a little while, but it was not going to provide the breath of life for very long.

For the last couple hours of Heidi's life, Diane was lying in bed with her, stroking her hair and placing a comforting arm around her shoulders. "Find the light, Heid," she kept whispering. "Find the light." I was standing next to Heidi. "It's okay to relax, sweetie," I repeatedly said. "Find peace. You don't have to fight any longer." Toward the end I, too, stroked her hair and patted her head. I just needed to touch my little girl, keep her close to me. The other girls and their husbands also crowded into her room, alternately joining Diane and Heidi on the bed, or crouching on the floor. She kept struggling to breathe and straining to stay awake. Just as she would start to doze, she would snap her head up and open her eyes, as if she were arousing herself to continue her struggle. "Relax, Sweetie. It's okay to go to sleep," I would say. Sometimes she would respond with a soft, sweet "Okay" that was almost melodious. I had heard that same "okay" so often in the past few years as she faced so many difficult situations. I can still hear it echo today.

Although we knew Heidi was going to die, I did not believe it was going to be that night. I had hoped Heidi would go to sleep and have another day with us. But, I also had the conflicted feeling that by telling her to relax I was giving her permission to die, to find the peace that would come after struggling for so long and so hard. Was her last "okay" her way of telling us that she was through; she was going to find the light; and she was no longer going to fight the losing battle? I remember praying. "Either give my baby peace or miraculously start repairing her lungs and give her the life she should have." God seemed to pick the wrong option.

Heidi's eyelids were getting heavier and heavier and were staying closed for longer periods of time. We would think she was asleep and then her eyelids would flutter and she'd look blankly around. There were choruses of "We love you," and "We're all here," and "You're such a good girl." Finally, Heidi looked around, made eye contact with us, and said, "Good night." She looked at me again. "Good night," she repeated and finally fell into sleep. Her sisters and husbands went into the kitchen to make some coffee, knowing it was going to be a long night. Diane and I continued cradling her. Slowly her breathing changed from staccato and strained to regular and peaceful. "Girls!" Diane shouted. "Come quick!" My other three daughters vaulted into the room. Kris and Katie threw themselves on the bed, while Tara hovered by Heidi's side. The gaps between Heidi's breaths got longer. Then, in the flash of a moment that has implanted itself indelibly in my consciousness, Heidi stopped breathing.

There are no words to describe the next couple of hours. Family and some close friends came to see her and say "Good night." Heidi's sisters and cousins cleaned her body; Katie dug the clots out of her nose; they dressed her in her pink silk rose pajamas. We prayed. We started to share some Heidi stories. We cried. We even laughed a little. When the funeral director carried her out of the house for the last time, we all unconsciously formed a line from her room, through the living room, and out the door. We surrounded her with our presence, our love. We watched her leave.

Numbness settled over me. My journey of grieving had begun.

Death's Singularity

Death is singular. Each one of us will die, and it will be unique. No matter how many people we may see die and no matter what the experiences may be, our own death will be our own. Although we may realize this fact when we stop to think about death, I think Americans are often affected by the social forces in our culture that tend to categorize and label death in particular ways. Many people are uncomfortable with the topic. In fact, many people do not even want to use the word "death." Death is the Ultimate Negative – the End. Americans want progress, change, and new beginnings. We are driven by life and want to avoid being uncomfortable or confused. When a loved one dies, the word can become horrific and tied to the pain and suffering of our grief. So we talk about crossing over or passing on or passing away, rather than utter the horrid word that means the end. Sometimes we whisper the word so as not to give it too much reality. Death is the ultimate loss, and Americans don't want to lose anything. Death is painful and Americans strive to avoid pain as much as possible. Self-imposed pain (exercise, for example) makes sense, but inflicted pain needs to be eliminated as quickly as possible. Advertising plays to this feeling by promising instant relief. We use drugs, whether over the counter, prescribed, or illegal, in a constant dance designed to keep us pain free and capable of doing whatever we wish to pursue.

Grieving is experiencing separation, and, if you listen to people carefully, you will hear them talk about "losing" a loved one (or will refer to someone else's loss). Frankly, I do not believe that I have "lost" Heidi. This difference is not just semantic, but reflects a core of belief that guides the way I now live. Referring to a loved one who has died as "lost" is a subtle way of objectifying a person. In American culture we objectify everything in our world. Words become associated with objects. Basically, our language is made up of sentences which have a subject doing something to an object. The verb is the action that connects the subject to objects in some form. Businesses objectify their clientele; the medical profession objectifies its patients; etc. In many jobs people work at depersonalizing their actions, words, and behaviors in order to protect themselves. Despite this depersonalization, businesses, schools, government, hospitals and, in fact, all institutions have to work consciously to treat their "objects" in a personal fashion. Advertising works very hard at proving how the company, school, etc. provides "personal" service. We constantly have to reassure our customers (even our friends and our family) that we care about them as people who are individuals. The reason we do so is because we live in a culture that structures the world as if it is made up of objects that interact with one another. We live daily with the contradiction of depersonalizing the world while wanting to be treated personally. We treat space as if it is an empty container that is filled with objects, and we treat time as if it is an empty container into which events occur. This type of world view easily leads to the idea that when an object is no longer in our space, it is lost. Thus, when someone dies, we have lost a loved one.

Another factor that seems to reinforce this idea of "losing" a loved one stems from the belief that we own one another. We usually don't consciously want to admit this belief, but, again, I believe it is a subtle way we think about relationships and is embedded in the way we talk. "My" wife, "my" friend, "my" loved one are all subtle forms of saying that somehow and in some fashion they belong to me. We usually have to backtrack when someone takes objection to this view. How many arguments revolve around the complaint that "I am my own person"; you "don't own me"; etc. We have a strong sense of ownership when it comes to our family, our friends, and our loved ones. Americans are truly driven by a territorial imperative, a drive for ownership. This sense of ownership may be one of the root causes for jealousy and envy. Thus, when we no longer possess someone we love we feel that she is lost. When a child or friend or loved one walks out of our life, we feel empty; we have "lost" a part of our life that had meaning and purpose. In this context, some divorces are a form of grieving.

There is a subtle distinction between the idea of losing a loved one and the feelings of loss that we may experience. Usually we focus upon the object – the person who was lost. That idea is the one that concerns me. I have a problem with treating Heidi as a lost object. I am uncomfortable when people refer to my loss or even to their loss of a loved one. This sense of loss is driven by our need to have a simple concept to express our confused and complex feelings. It is easy to say and brings a quick response from others whenever we talk about our "loss." Besides, it is the common way Americans refer to the relationship that now exists between the one who still lives and the one who has died. The survivor has lost a loved one. This phrase is subconsciously ingrained into our language and our culture. However, as I have examined my heart and my feelings, I have come to realize that Heidi is not lost; she is not a misplaced object. In fact, she is not someone I can find. The reality is that she and I are now separated in the physical world. As I indicated in the last chapter, Heidi is truly still present in my life in very spiritual ways. The reality is not that she is lost, but that I do not have the capacity to bridge the divide between my living self and her eternal consciousness. I am feeling a sense of "absence" which is in fact not based on reality. The reality is that Heidi's consciousness remains alive and her legacy continues to touch my life and so many others' as well. She remains real. My feelings are related to my inability to describe her transformed life adequately and to my diminished capacity to touch her intuitively. Thus, instead of talking about losing a child, it is healthier and more accurate to refer to our feelings as those related to separation or absence. I have not lost Heidi; rather, my relationship has become transformed. Unfortunately there is no easy, one word expression to grasp this concept.

Many people are uncomfortable using the word "death" in association with a loved one, and it is too cumbersome to say "my child who is now physically absent from my life forever" or "my child who has a transformed existence." I know that even if people agree that referring to our dead child as lost is an erroneous expression, there will be no change in what they will say. What I do hope is that people will realize that the feelings of "loss" that they are talking about really refer to the inadequate ways we have of describing the sense of separation that we may feel. The problem is for those who are alive, not for those who have died. Their transformed life can and should still be an integral part of our lives. We just need to learn how to understand what this means and develop ways to feel and talk about the transformed relationship we now have with those who have died.

I have buried both of my parents, some good friends, uncles and aunts, grandparents, and I was present when we had to have our dog "put to sleep." In each of those deaths of family and friends I felt a very strong sense of "loss" and emptiness. Someone important to me was no longer with me. Each one of those "losses" gave me a real sense of loneliness and sadness. I now realize, however, that I did not truly grieve in any of those situations. My journey of grieving for my daughter has changed the way I live, think, and feel. Despite feelings of absence or separation, I still do have times when I can still feel Heidi's presence. Her consciousness — her living energy — still continues to exist in some other way. I may still have feelings of loss, but those feelings are tied to my inadequate ways of connecting to Heidi's new way of existing. She is not "lost," even though I may feel that way.

These feelings are just a part of the confusing puzzle of death. So many movies, poems, songs, and books are dedicated to death and dying. We have been bombarded with too many contradictory and paradoxical ways to view death. Our society is a cauldron of mixed messages, confused values, and conflicting perspectives. Death is not an easy topic for us to discuss. Not only do we refer to death as a type of loss, but we also tend to generalize the meaning of death. Even though we realize that death is singular, we still tend to treat death in general terms and in vague references.

I would hope that each one of us can respect the importance of each person who dies. When we hear how many died in a plane crash or how many casualties occurred in a particular tragedy, we tend to lose sight of the singularity of each one of the victims. Of course, it is necessary to protect ourselves from being overwhelmed when we think of the collective tragedy in such circumstances. Every American can recall the profound impact that 9/11 had on our consciousness. It was horrific because we saw the pictures of the tragedy and of the loved ones frantically seeking to find out whether their son or daughter, wife or husband, friend or neighbor had survived. Unfortunately, however, I believe that we, as a nation, did not seize the moment of our collective grief to address a healthy attitude toward death and grieving. For the most part, the American attitude toward death and grieving is unhealthy. Our language blinds us from a balanced journey of grieving. This book is not an attempt to change the language that Americans use; rather, it is a reflection of how my life has been transformed during my journey on the subway with Heidi.

XII.

FEBRUARY 15, 2003.

Saying Good Night

On the day of Heidi's funeral, the icy cold outside mirrored the icy numbness in my heart. Before going from the funeral home to the church, we held a private, family ceremony to say good night to Heidi's body. Our extended family was present, along with our two friends who had come from the Netherlands.

We prayed and told Heidi stories. We laughed and cried just as we had done the night she died. While we were talking, I stood up and opened a small journal we had discovered in Heidi's nightstand shortly following her death. We all knew that she had written advice on coping with cancer to submit to the people at Roswell. What we did not know was that she had written a final section that she had kept from us. When we found the passage in her journal, we all cried at the sight of its title: On Death. I knew I needed to share her thoughts with those who loved her best. I struggled to read it. I remember that I was never ashamed of my tears and was intent on completing the reading, even if it was punctuated with my choking and long pauses. The force of feeling as if I had failed her by not protecting or curing her required that I, at least, be able to read her message to those sharing our sorrow. I wanted my helplessness to reach a state of relativity rather than one of absolute dominance. Here is what she wrote:

On Death

It's okay if you can't read this section right now. You are going through these treatments to live. The focus of all of this is life, not death. It is important to deal with these fears in your own time and in your own way.

Everyone dies.
>   You may die from cancer.
>   You could also get run over by a bus.
>   The important thing is that you are living now.
>   Sometimes friends die.
>   You are still alive.
>   Your friend is still with you.
>   He wants you to live.
>   Keep fighting.
>   Cry, then find your smile.
>   It's a good idea to take care of the legal stuff (health care proxy, will, advanced directive, etc.)
>   It's not fair to leave that to loved ones.
>   It's okay to be scared.
>   Life goes on, though.
>   Keep living.

A friend of ours had given us paper hearts to hand out to everyone, so that we could all write one last message to Heidi. For a while, the only sound was sniffling and the scratching of pencils on those paper hearts. I don't remember what I wrote; I just remember how much it meant to give her something. When we had finished sharing our thoughts and feelings, we each walked past Heidi's body, gave her our note, and paused (to say good-bye, good night, sweet dreams, I'll miss you, we love you, etc.). To know that I would only see her face in pictures ever again was heart wrenching. To realize that I would never see her smile light up a room or feel her eyes change my mood was crushing. To sense the loss of her touch was devastating.

I don't really remember the ride from the funeral home to the church. The funeral service itself is somewhat blurry, although a few vivid moments stand out: Diane and I singing "Amazing Grace"; people touching my shoulder on the way back from communion; the casket sitting so lonely in the aisle. Tara delivered the eulogy wonderfully. Her sisters worked with her as she wrote it, and her husband stood behind her in case she could not finish what she had written. Afterward she told us how she felt as if she had become two people – one giving the eulogy and another watching herself do it. It was that sense of separating from her feelings for that period of time that got her through the experience. I had a similar experience 16 years earlier when I delivered the eulogy at my mother's memorial service. As difficult as my task had been, Tara had a much more difficult assignment. Of course, Tara also knew that Heidi would not permit a poor delivery of the eulogy; the "show must go on." The following is a portion of what Tara said:

"... I know I am up here to somehow, in some way share the story of Heidi. However, words, images, songs – none of that can capture her life story. But I <u>can</u> share with you some thoughts. And I can share with you some moments. You must continue to add to those moments and those thoughts, though – share them with others. Pass on the story of Heidi. ...

"Heidi's life was way too short, but, wow, wasn't it rich? And beautiful? If full can be described by how many lives are changed, how many hearts are touched, how many dreams are dreamt, then Heidi's life was fuller than any I know.

"Heidi changed the lives of so many people, partly by what she did, but mostly by who she was. She led by example. People wanted to be like her. She had style – not just in clothes or hair styles or makeup, but in attitude and presence. One conversation with her and your life was changed – you wanted to be a better person. She taught all of us that there are no limits to joy and no challenge too difficult to tackle. ...

"One of Heidi's and my favorite quotes is from Anne of Green Gables: "It's not what the world holds for you; it's what you bring to it." The world <u>didn't</u> hold much for her, but, oh, the things Heidi brought to the world. Heidi touched people's hearts. From the minute she was born, one glance into her eyes and you were hooked. Her eyes were light and dance and joy and hope and sarcasm and intelligence and sly wit and song. ...

"And boy, could Heidi smile – not just with her eyes or her mouth or her face, but with her whole being. She sparkled with light. I remember the first time I saw her after she was diagnosed – I was terrified of what to say, what to do. I walked into her hospital room, expecting tears and anger and despair. Instead, her whole face just lit up, "Tar," she exclaimed. "Happy birthday! I'm so glad you're here!" She put everyone at ease who walked into that hospital room. We all thought we were there to help her; I think it was the other way around. She made our role easy. We got our strength from her. ...

"Heidi defies definition. She was one of the most creative people I ever met, yet she also possessed an incisive, logical perception that thrived on organization. Her favorite movie stars, from the time she was a child, were from an era gone by: Audrey Hepburn, Walter Matthau, Gene Kelly, yet she was completely up-to-date on the contemporary Hollywood scene. She loved music, especially musical scores, but scorned the commercialized music business. She contemptuously dismissed poor acting on TV, on movies, in theaters, but she loved <u>The Golden Girls</u> and <u>Lois and Clark</u>. She was consumed with the arts, but she had so many other interests as well: She loved to argue politics and had very definite opinions on all issues. She loved the Food Network, Trading Spaces, and HGTV. She loved to read.

"In fact, one of the special connections Heidi and I had was books and reading. When she was a little girl, I read to her all the time. ... Even when she was old enough to read to herself, she would still want me to read to her. "You do all the voices right," she said. ... And then came the "Anne of Green Gables" books. Neither of us knew the impact that reading those books would be. .... One of the last real conversations Heidi and I had was about Anne and her ability to make friends. In Anne of Avonlea, Anne says "I'd like to add some beauty to life. I don't exactly want to make people know more – though I know that is the noblest ambition – but I'd love to make them have a pleasanter time because of me ... to have some little joy or happy thought that would never have existed if I hadn't been born." Heidi fulfilled that goal every day.

"One of Heidi's greatest gifts was her performing talent. Those of you who saw her perform know of what I'm speaking. When she appeared on stage, everyone else seemed muted, flat, not-quite-charismatic enough. She had presence ... she proved that the stage was her calling and her domain.

"Heidi faced battles that no 19, 20, 21 year old should ever have to face. She faced them with bravery, with dignity, with grace, and with so much love. She was always concerned about how her illness was affecting others. She told me early on that she thought that if she could be strong and positive, then other people would follow suit. She was so right. Even as she was struggling, she taught us how to live. No one knew the extent of Heidi's suffering, fear, and loneliness; she was an actress and convincing the world that she was and would be fine was her greatest role, a role she played to perfection for 2 ½ years. She made it easy to forget that she was in misery. The show went on.

"Heidi had dreams. Since Heidi will never achieve the Technicolor dreams she had for herself – the Oscar, the Tony, the world recognition of her acting talent – we all need to help her dreams, goals, and beliefs live on, not just this week or through the next few months but for all time. Kristen, Katie and I have compiled a list of things you can do, not just to remember Heidi, but to enrich the meaning of Heidi's life and carry on her legacy:

- *Dye your hair purple, just for the fun of it*
- *Leave generous tips*
- *Always have a project brewing*
- *Absorb every Audrey Hepburn movie, picture, memoir, glance, and gesture*
- *Decorate at least one of the rooms in your house with bright, funky colors*
- *Critique movies harshly, except for the ones you love*
- *Every time you experience a setback, throw a party to celebrate life*
- *Plan extravagant theme parties*
- *Read the Anne of Green Gables books and watch the movies so often you can recite them by heart*
- *Vote*
- *Know that leather boots will make any outfit look good*
- *Turn off lights and water when not in use*
- *Sing in the shower. Sing out of the shower. Sing anytime.*
- *Support local theater*
- *Go see a Broadway show*
- *Follow all the rules*
- *Play games. Many games.*
- *Dress with style*
- *Accessorize!*
- *Order something you've never tried before when you go to a restaurant*
- *Listen to music. It heals the soul.*
- *Create and experiment with recipes and food*
- *Eat a lot of popcorn*
- *Give of yourself fully*
- *Smile at everyone – especially people you don't know*
- *Dream big*
- *Never give up*

"And as you do these things, know that Heidi is a part of you and your life. Somewhere she is dancing now, probably with Gene Kelly, and watching over all of us with her loving grace. ...

"There are so many memories, so many moments I would love to share with you today, but as the cliché goes, there just aren't enough words and there isn't enough time. I know each of you has your own memories, your own private recollection of her. And that, I think, is part of Heidi's legacy — she gave us beautiful moments. The last image I'm going to leave you with is one of my favorites. Heidi had just been rediagnosed, and I was spending the night in the hospital with her. It was four in the morning. I was looking out the window at the supposed meteor shower, trying to glimpse some shooting stars, but the small, double ply windows at Roswell created a glare and provided a tiny field of vision. Heidi got up to go the bathroom. On the way back to bed, she said, "See any?" When I said no, she said "Maybe if I sit with you and we both look they'll be easier to see." So she perched on my chair-turned-bed, IV pole and all, looked out the window, and immediately the meteors started flashing. "I've always thought," she said, "that shooting stars are not just about wishes but about dreams. There's a difference you know." We talked that night for about an hour, mostly about dreams; I don't remember all that was said, but I knew then that I would remember that moment, that feeling of complete peace and beauty forever.

"Please take a minute now and think of *your* beautiful Heidi moment. I guarantee it will make you smile."

Hopefully Tara's eloquence will give you a view into Heidi's heart and into the blessings she gave and still gives to us. After the funeral service a long procession of cars with family and friends wound its way to the cemetery. The sun was shining, but the air was bitter cold. I remember the awful crunch of the snow as we walked from the car to the site we have visited so often since that horrid day. The Pastor said a few prayers, and people filed by the casket. They placed roses on it while many embraced us or touched our shoulders. In a little while we all would be eating, drinking, and laughing at the reception. Our sons-in-law had made all the arrangements, and we had a party – exactly what Heidi wanted us to do. The Yin and Yang of life were so evident that day: the laughter and tears, the embracing and the letting go, the silence and the music, the cold and the warmth. The truth of Ecclesiastes resounded in my heart and in my mind: Yes, for absolutely everything there is a time and place under heaven.

Attitude's Power

The ultimate paradox in a journey of grieving is the gift of a more meaningful, balanced, and healthy life that is available to us. The gift and blessings that our loved ones bestow upon us may often go unrecognized or undetected. In the midst of the overwhelming grief that I experienced with Heidi, she began to take my heart, mind, and soul to a depth I had merely conceptualized before. Now I was experiencing it. In my studies and teaching I have focused upon living an integrated life (psychologically, temporally, physically, emotionally, spiritually, etc.). The key is learning how to integrate all the dimensions of life (putting our pieces back together in this Humpty Dumpty world of ours). During my journey of grieving, I have felt and "gone" to places that I only intellectually considered before. This learning process is really the journey of living and, now, is the journey of grieving; they have become interchangeable. In the United States, grief is only seen or discussed as a tragic "part" of someone's life. Our cultural norms allow for a period of time for us to "go through" the pain; then, we are expected to move on. As I have indicated throughout this book, this attitude is unhealthy and does not lead to the transformation that grieving can provide. Therapists and professionals who foster this agenda have a misplaced approach to healthy, meaningful grief. Another image that is part of American culture is the idea that those who have "lost" a child will always feel the loss, but they must re-engage in life and return to their normal ways of living. The attitude that is expected for those who grieve is one that places grief into some type of psychological compartment so that normal activities may resume. Again, I no longer accept those attitudes as relevant to my journey of grieving. We need to integrate our lives and learn to resign ourselves to our grief without letting it overcome us. It really is a journey that is defined by attitude and a reaffirmation of the values of love, care, health, and balance that should be guidelines for our lives. Grieving is much more like riding the waves than going through stages or phases that can mark the completion of some task.

Wave imagery is far more meaningful for me than the static ideas of stages or of a linear notion of "going through" steps. When we are "in" or "on" the waves we can drift in the sea aimlessly; or crash onto the boulders at the shore; or gently ride the tide; or become submerged in the turbulence around us; or tread the waters struggling for answers, peace, or the presence of our loved one on the beach. Wave imagery keeps the reality of the ever changing contours of our sadness; we can never be far from the sight, sound, smell, or breeze that wafts our sadness back into focus and consciousness. To find closure may be good for criminal proceedings; it is disastrous for relationships that need to be nurtured and cherished. To "move on" signals a turning of one's back to the person or situation; that may be true for jobs or sales, but not for loved ones. And although we may have feelings of loss, let's not think that we have lost our children; they are not objects that are misplaced. They remain in some transformed way that is beyond our comprehension, so let's not project our ignorance upon their transformed way of being. Riding the waves is noble, frightening, and precious. It is the strange blessing that comes with dying and it can empower or destroy us. Watching people in the water illustrates the uniqueness of grieving: some wade, some swim proficiently, some float, some sink, some splash, some drown, some laugh – yet everyone is in the water. Grieving has so many styles and ways to swim, yet we all share something terribly in common: we get wet.

One of the challenges I have discussed above relates to receiving "permission" to experience joy again in my life. There are two types of joy: there is joy in a given moment or experience, and there is the joy that pervades or even defines a person's life. The latter is a type of carefree attitude toward life. It doesn't mean that the person has no cares in life; rather, it means that the cares and worries of life can easily be set aside at any given moment. This type of joy hasn't come like a bolt from heaven to wipe away my sadness and restore me to wholeness. That image is great for television or the movies, but for the vast majority of us who grieve, it is a silly way to look at our new life. Receiving permission to have a joyous type of life will take a long time. In fact, it is quite possible that a grieving parent may never feel as if he will ever receive permission to leave the subway and throw all cares to the wind. In grief, joy becomes fundamentally redefined just like every other important dimension in life. I can experience moments of joy, and I can adopt an attitude toward life that is positive and based upon looking for and experiencing the blessings that are given. The idea of a carefree joy or a life that is joyous through and through just does not seem reasonable any more. The more I contemplate this idea, the more I firmly believe that the truth we all know captures reality: there is a time for joy and a time for sadness; a time to laugh and a time to cry. To pursue a life that only has joy is to pursue a dream that cannot exist. However, to surrender to sorrow and live in self-pity and constant sadness is a tragic waste of the grace and gift of life that each one of us has received. Experiencing joyous moments is crucial for restoring balance and health to any ride on the subway.

The signs that we continue to receive from Heidi are a reminder of how important she is for us. They are a way to stay connected to her. She is woven into our hearts and minds. The signs are her way of telling us that we do have permission to experience joyous moments again. The cliché that our loved one wants us to be happy and would not want us to live in constant sorrow begins to point in the direction I feel. It is not a comfort for someone to say this to me, however. It is a feeling that I have inside and I need affirmation of my permission from Heidi and from my own conscience and sense of separation. Intellectually I can readily reach this conclusion: joy should be an integral dimension in my life; otherwise, I cannot be a good father, husband, friend, teacher or neighbor. Emotionally, the currents of life and experience bring opportunities for mirth and laughter, and I have learned to ride these waves with relish and "enjoyment."

As I think about the journey of grieving as riding on a subway, I now realize that the subway is not a trap, a prison, or a place of constant sorrow and sadness; it is a way of living. The reality of grieving depends upon the attitude that I have about myself, about my grief, about life, and about the ultimate values that permeate my journey. The tragedy that I see is for those who cannot live within this journey by finding the grace, gifts, and blessings that will continue to be made available. These positive dimensions are not the only characteristics we will experience. Other injustices, tragedies, and painful experiences will continue to be a part of our journey's landscape; they are all inevitable. Thus, the only real measure for our journey, if we must measure anything, should be directed at our attitude toward life, ourselves, and our loved ones (dead or alive). Attitude ought to shape who we are. Heidi's advice for coping with cancer is a very good roadmap for how to live. Attitude seems to be the most common denominator in all that she says, and even more importantly, in all that she was in her life and throughout her entire illness. Her positive attitude lifted all of us up during those long months and years of her struggle, and it has become a beacon of hope and resolve for my journey with her on the subway.

Pythagoras, the Greek mathematician and philosopher, once said, "Man is the measure of all things." This idea has become translated into a variety of different schools of thought. With respect to attitude, there is a common belief that a person's attitude can somehow create his life: a positive attitude always leads to good things; a negative one leads to bad. Although this view is very appealing, it contains a fundamental flaw. Humans are not the measure of everything; we are not the sole creators of our experience; we are not capable of altering and bending the social and biological realities of the world. Heidi was a prime example of how important, yet limited, attitude plays in life. Her positive approach to her illness and her ability to find blessings amid horrid circumstances are a testimony to the power of attitude. This power enriched her life and gave her meaning and purpose. It also enriched the lives of those she has touched, both during her illness and even now after her death. Her death cannot be attributed to an insufficient capacity for positive thinking. The physiological realities of her leukemia outstripped her ability to impose the positive upon life. Finding empowerment in a positive attitude is absolutely essential for living a meaningful and fulfilling life. It can transform life in dramatic and wonderful ways. On the other hand, it is folly to presume that we alone can determine the course of life and what will and what won't happen to us and those we love. As I have illustrated throughout this book, our entire family adopted Heidi's style and approach; we found blessings, and we looked for the positive. We believed she would survive and flourish. She certainly flourished for her brief life, but her death was not the result of an inadequacy in her will or her attitude or in ours. Such an idea misses the elemental truth that life is a complex set of interdependent forces. Humans are only one of these forces. We have our limits and we have our abilities. Discovering and recognizing the balance among them is our life's challenge.

Certainly a person's attitude is an important characteristic in how we judge whether or not we want to spend time with this person. For people we love and for family members who have negative attitudes towards life or events, we may wish that they would change their perspective or not ruin the mood or moment that we may be sharing. It seems to be a cliché to talk about the importance of attitude because we all experience its importance and impact each and every day. During my journey of grieving, however, I have thought about its meaning and significance in ways that are different than before Heidi died. One of the real challenges toward a positive attitude comes from the expectations that others have about us. Once we have gone through a "reasonable" grief "period," others expect us to return to some type of normalcy. Those who are compassionate will understand that our lives are changed forever and will try to understand and relate to us in ways that continue to be loving and nurturing. Others will not understand the dynamics of grief and will either become impatient and disengage if they can or will try to minimize contact for fear that they may "catch" something.

Most of us spend a great deal of our working and vacationing time around strangers, fleeting acquaintances, and colleagues or companions. These people will relate to us within the context of our encounters. For example, at work we have roles to fulfill, and people relate to one another according to the norms of those roles as prescribed within the context of the work place. We have to adapt our behaviors and attitudes to the context and the people with whom we are working. We may develop friendships or we may not. We may feel in sync with some and not with others. The more skilled a person is at adapting and changing with the varying roles in work and life, the more successful the person becomes. "Games people play" may define the rules that govern how we are to be successful. Grieving, however, is a process of redefining our life and attitude. Thus, one area of real difficulty comes with coping with the games, the rules, the norms, and the context of work or of other social settings. How we adjust and cope with these settings will go a long way in defining how well we adapt or redefine our attitude about life in general. In work and social settings the context may not be affirming or necessarily supportive of our grieving journey. Some settings or work places may have a number of sympathetic colleagues or friends, who will try to be understanding. It is probably unreasonable, however, to assume that these contexts will become environments that completely provide the guidance, support, and assistance that we need while we are grieving. The person who is grieving will also have to deal with developing an attitude within these contexts that permits him to complete tasks and fulfill the expectations of the roles that exist. These roles are part of the functional sphere that surrounds life. Most of our work activity will not be about grief and will not be conducive for healing. Our challenge, then, is to adjust our attitude to take these roles and contexts into account while not succumbing to the temptation of placing our grief into some psychological container. To do so may spare us some of the pain that comes with grieving, but it just may not be the most meaningful way to deal with our journey. In essence, grief calls us to transform our life. Attempting to transform grief may be unwise.

Once the journey brings the grieving person to the awareness of the absolute nature of death, she will confront a real crossroads with respect to the attitude that she presents to others and to herself. This realization does not need to occur with a singular epiphany. Like so many dimensions within the grieving journey, this awareness evolves and takes on different depths of meaning. It is normal to want to awaken from this nightmare and expect to see your child or loved one walking through the door years after her death. Those fleeting whimsies do not mean that a person is unaware of the absolute nature of the experience of death; rather, it illustrates how deeply we miss our child, husband, wife, friend, etc. Trying to integrate all the dimensions, feelings, thoughts, hopes, dreams, fears, etc. of a person's life is an on-going task. A fundamentally important aspect of this task is to recognize that there is a different type of reality for those who have died. Heidi continues to live in a transformed reality that is beyond my intellectual abilities. Intuitively I remain connected to her spirit and living energy, and I am reminded of this reality through signs and through the beautiful experiences I have with others when we share her legacy. This belief is an essential ingredient into creating a healthy attitude in my grieving journey.

Our attitude needs to attend to the contextuality of our grief. Anniversaries (death date, birth date, diagnosis, etc.) become landmarks that rearrange our calendars and experience. Sub-consciously our attitude may shift as we approach the dates, and we will need to remind ourselves of these factors influencing our mood and challenging our well-being. If we can grasp the paradoxes of grief, we can begin to develop a healthy, balanced attitude toward living. A few of these paradoxes include: 1. Answers to why our child died and the necessity to accept that no satisfactory answer will ever be found. 2. The absolute nature of death and the unyielding sense that we will wake up from this bad dream. 3. Our sorrow is so deep that we sometimes feel as if it is impossible to breath, yet we have responsibilities to ourselves, to others, and to our loved one to engage in the blessings of each day. 4. Other people think they are causing us pain by talking about our loved one, yet the real pain comes when they fail to mention her name or hesitate in listening to our stories.

American culture tends to minimize the importance of myths or stories that help unravel the mysteries of life. This tendency creates barriers for achieving intuitive connectedness. Other cultures have an active and integrated attitude that positively incorporates myths, fables, and parables into life. All humans and all societies need myths and fables to help us navigate the unknown and the unknowable. In America we tend to think of myth as some type of fantasy that is not grounded in reality and does not carry the weight of "truth." This is an unfortunate belief. Myths provide us with stories that have meaning and transcendent values that touch the very essence of what it means to be human. I remember my graduate school mentor (who, by the way, was a Logician) once telling me that education in the United States lost its grounding in values and turned away from teaching students about the most important truths in life when Aesop's Fables were removed from the curriculum. His point was that humans need stories; we require myths to help us piece together the most important lessons in life. We need to enhance our connectedness to stories and the truths that fables and parables can provide us. I have become acutely aware of this truth as I have read stories to my grandchildren. These stories are geared toward children, but many of them touch on the simple awareness about what connects each of us to those values we should espouse in our lives: caring, love, honor, respect, wonder, and believing in the possibility that the world can become what it ought to be. We really do not have to succumb to the negativity of the skeptic in all that we do. Just as we need to learn our limits, so also should we recognize what life can teach us and how a positive attitude can enrich our lives and provide us with a sense of meaning that we may otherwise lose without it.

In many ways the paradoxical gift that our child provides us is a life in which we can develop an attitude that resigns ourselves to a healthy, balanced, and meaningful journey. In this sense, we are "born" again only if we choose to recognize and embrace it. We shall need to learn how to live on the subway because it is a different road from the one we were experiencing before. How we live this rebirth is one way of referring to the personality development we ought to experience. There really isn't a simple textbook to give us all the answers; there is no simple roadmap, and there are no prescribed stages with tasks that need to be completed. This book is intended to share a part of the first stepping stones that are a part of my journey. One of the realities that relates to the attitude that may emerge through anyone's rebirth is that a person's attitude is not a permanent state of mind. It will ebb and flow with life. At times it may feel very fragile as other traumatic experiences invade our life. Other times it may feel more secure or even more fully developed than it was earlier in our life or even within our grieving journey. Our attitude can lift our hearts and can help us to reach out to others in our life. If it becomes destructive, confused, or turns very pessimistic, then the health and meaning in our life will come into question. We really will confront the existential question of whether or not life has any meaning at all.

In one sense our attitude may be related to the condition of someone who is an addict (an alcoholic, for example). For the alcoholic the problem appears to be drinking, but the source of the problem is not alcoholic consumption. In order to start on the road to recovery the addict must first admit that he has the problem (drinking). That admission, however, is only the first staggering step to recovery. Without it the journey does not begin, but without so much more work, the journey can never become successful. Addicts require a great deal of support and assistance. Support groups, professional counseling, loving friends and family are just a few of the people necessary to succeed in getting the addiction under control. The addict is never cured. The possibility of relapse is real, and on-going vigilance and effort are needed to keep the addict's life in balance and harmony. The attitude that should emerge throughout our grieving is very comparable.

I have learned to resign myself to my grief and the fact that grief remains at the core of my existence. I will forever be on the subway with Heidi. This admission frees me to begin working on my life and my grief in ways that will lead to a meaningful and balanced life. I need the loving support of family and friends, and I would be foolish to believe that I no longer need any professional group or assistance. Grieving is not a problem to solve, and the journey of grieving has no final destination point. As with the addict, someone who is grieving must assume responsibility for his life and his attitude. For me this first step is the one that resigns me to the reality of Heidi's death and assumes that what I do for the rest of my life matters. Sometimes it feels so much easier to just surrender to nothingness and indifference. That attitude, however, destroys the gift of life that our dead loved one has given to us, as well as denies the grace that God makes available to us throughout our life. We may ignore or reject those gifts, but doing so seems to be an insult to the legacy and will of our dead loved one. How could I feel so sorry for myself that I refuse to live in a way that gives dignity to Heidi's life and message? She could find blessings in the days during her illness; how can I possibly turn my back on the blessings that continue to manifest themselves in my own life? If I do not look for the blessings, of course, I will not see them. It takes effort and a will to do so. It is not easy. This journey is not for the weak or the impatient. It is for those who believe or hope their dead loved one has transformed. For the nihilist, he must ask the question of whether or not his attitude is really only an excuse to feel miserable or to justify moving on without having to work at the never-ending struggle of grieving. The gift of a new life sets an entirely different context for us. We need to relearn how to live; how to feel; how to behave; and how we are to adjust our attitude to ourselves, others, and the world around us. This idea that we are on a journey illustrates the basic reality that meaning, purpose, and our health will continually be changing. Sometimes the changes will be imposed; other times we will be able to mold and shape them. The most important characteristic is the need to remain open to the inevitability of change and the need for continually growing in heart, mind, and spirit.

One of the major barriers for developing a healthy, balanced, and meaningful attitude in life is indifference. It is even more destructive than any cynicism could cause. The cynic may start from a skeptical view of life and then become jaded because of his experiences.

Indifference is a truly destructive force in life and in grieving. Indifference destroys possibilities and blinds people to life and grief. Someone who says something that offends me gives me the capacity (whether intentionally or not) to disagree, to challenge or to try and change that person's mind. Indifference stops everything. I am more disturbed with those who do not care about my grief or about my daughter than I am with the well-intentioned person who just does not understand. I am not sure whether any discussion of attitude is relevant to those who are indifferent. A real tragedy is to go through life without caring for anyone or for anything. An indifferent life really does reject meaningfulness and purpose.

On the third anniversary of Heidi's death, I was at a conference in Indianapolis. I spent a lot of my alone time thinking about this book and what I should write. I have felt compelled to write, being driven by some source that I cannot identify. One evening I was having a lonely dinner. I had taken some paper with me because I always want to have the ability to write or make notes when I am sitting alone. I knew that the book had to include a section on attitude. It struck me that evening that I had a problem with this chapter. What good would it be to merely say that "it all starts with attitude" without indicating **how** we should go about changing or adopting or sustaining a healthy, balanced, and meaningful attitude. I felt stuck because I had no clue what I should write, and I did not want to research the topic. I decided at the outset that this would be a personal reflection of my journey, not a scholarly work or one that relies on what others have written before. What was I going to do? I remember turning my inner voice to Heidi and saying: "OK, sweetie, what have you got for me to say on this question?" The following suggestions come from the inner "voice" that guided my hand that evening. I hope some of them are meaningful for you.

1. **Start a blessings book.** As often as possible take a few moments to consider the blessings that have been given to you on that day. Learning to see the blessings and taking the time to focus upon them AND write them into some type of journal will help adjust your view about the world.
2. **Make a SFGTD (Something For God To Do) container.** Feel free to write anything you feel you may need to say to God; then, turn the issue over to God. There are some issues and instances in life that are just too much for us to handle. Turning them over to God relieves us of the burden

and can free our attitude about the other people or experiences in our life. If you do not believe in God, then just turn the troubles over to the cosmos.

3. **Journals are an excellent way to share your fears, anxieties, joys and frustrations.** You can write in a journal those thoughts, words, and feelings that you rarely, if ever, share with others. You can write to your loved one and you can say anything you feel needs to be expressed. There is a real freedom that a private journal can provide. There are no rules for a personal journal – just opportunities.

4. **Attitude is connected to a person's willingness to listen.** Listening can be a huge challenge, but learning how to listen and to do so actively and with a genuine level of interest in the other person is a tremendous asset in developing a person's attitude. You don't actually have to develop an interest in everything someone else has to say. I can't imagine anyone who is actually interested in any and everything that interests other people. The reality is that we need to learn to listen to what others are saying. We need to learn to listen to our hearts, our inner feelings, and listen to our dead child's messages. In this area especially indifference becomes incredibly destructive. How well would someone listen if he does not care? Feigning interest is not indifference. There are many topics which do not interest me in the least. I have found myself straining to listen in these discussions; but if I care about the person in any way, I will corral my feelings and try to focus to the best of my abilities.

5. **In a related sense we can improve our attitude by working on our communication styles with others.** I have been trying to speak with less of a professorial tone and with a greater sense of what my feelings are trying to say. Personalizing ideas, beliefs, and values does not come naturally to me. I do not believe that I am alone in this regard. Just listen to talk radio or TV, or read through the "op ed" pages of any newspaper or magazine, or log onto any blog, and the message will become clear: people love to speak their mind and will tend to do so in a generalized fashion. All too often comments become judgments, and a person's particular ideas become statements that are intended to be universalized. This tendency is most clearly evident in the very controversial issues. Learning to say what you mean

without reducing the statement to a universal judgment is a constructive way to improve communication. I have learned that sharing my feelings is crucial for sustained health and has had a positive impact on my attitude.

6. **It is healthy and meaningful to attend grief support meetings.** This activity will provide gifts and opportunities to address your attitude.

7. **Reading is a wonderful venue for helping your mind, heart, and soul.** Find inspiring stories to read. Diane has read a lot of the books related to grieving and has found some of them to be helpful for her journey. We have read books aloud to each other for a long time. We continue to do so and have read some grief books that inspired us, touched our journey, and comforted us. The reading, however, needs to go beyond just those materials that deal with grief. When I was growing up I read very little. In college I began to read, but still most of it was for coursework. In graduate school I had so much reading for my program that there was little time for extra reading, so Diane and I started reading to one another to get me beyond just my required books and articles. After graduate school and as our daughters were born, I started reading a wide variety of books so Diane and I could provide an environment that encouraged reading for our daughters. I have come to realize that reading expands my horizons and is a real source of enjoyment and enlightenment (sometimes a good book can be both). Of course the content of what you read can have profound impact on your view of the world and your attitude about life. It is important to recognize the interplay that your reading has upon your attitude.

8. **Somewhere during a person's journey, forgiveness needs to emerge.** For people who go through the feelings of anger and direct their wrath on the dead child, spouse, etc., they will need to find a way to forgive their loved one and not remain in the clutches of indignation. I have had a great deal of anger through the beginning of my journey, but none of it was directed at Heidi. I found other deserving sources for my anger. In some cases I came to realize the folly of this projection, while in other instances the anger arose from very troubling circumstances that would solicit anger in any person whether he was grieving or not. The process of working through the anger and adjusting my

attitude toward the person, group, or institution remains a healthy way to learn how to improve my attitude. In fact, learning to forgive is a primary example of developing an improved attitude. Being "mad as hell" should be a fleeting, emotional response; it is unhealthy when it becomes a way of living or a permanent political position.

9. **In Heidi's advice on coping with cancer she says that we should embrace those friends who stay and release those who do not.** As I thought about her attitude about friends, I realized that this advice could be taken even one step further. We need to realize that we may have some poisonous relationships in our lives. We need to release them because they are wearing away our strength. People who are grieving are vulnerable. Our psychological defense systems are compromised. Identifying groups who are destructive or people who abuse us or individuals who deceive or harm our loved ones (or us) need to be released from our lives. Taking this step can be very difficult. I mentioned that Diane and I left our church after 30 years because the Pastor and some of the people became a source of on-going pain. The relationships were poisoned by the lies, slander, and cruelty that were directed at me. Instead of fighting for justice and what I thought was right, I believe that we made the wisest decision to leave that church. This decision was difficult and sad. It took a long time to reach this conclusion. We left good friends and people who cared for us and people for whom we cared, but sometimes it is better to do what is good and healthy, rather than fight for justice or what we think should be done. Unfortunately there are no clear guidelines or instruction book that helps us know when to fight and when to walk away (or as Kenny Rogers sings: "You've got to know when to hold 'em and when to fold 'em").

10. **Prayer sustains the connection with spirituality and is a medium for touching your loved one.** In a real sense anyone who talks to her loved one is praying. The idea that prayer is only about making requests, giving thanks, or praising God seems too limited. Intuitive connection to spiritual consciousness allows us to commune with those who are dead. Learning how to listen and understanding the responses to our prayers will be difficult tasks on our journey. In the past few years I have found that I spend

more time trying to listen while I'm praying, rather than articulating my hopes, thanks, dreams, requests, etc. Do I hear voices? No, although I wish I could really hear Heidi singing or talking with me. Do I believe I am connecting with Heidi and sharing my fears and thoughts? Yes. Heidi's attitude toward her illness and toward life is slowly mingling with my own attitudes. I feel enriched and nourished by her spirit. These feelings are driven by grace, a gift always available to us. Grace can sustain the balance and meaningfulness that are so essential for healthy grieving and living.

11. **Love is the most powerful bond we can experience.** Love affects who I am and who I am becoming. My attitude is a reflection of how I interact with other people in the world. Being open to the gifts of love that family and friends provide and reciprocating this love may be the most important ingredient in finding health, balance, and a meaningful life. Anyone's attitude is enriched and will gain in positive, creative ways whenever she sustains or develops the beauty and depth of loving relationships. The best context for love is often a person's family. Resolving long-standing conflicts or accepting the dynamics of such conflicts is one key for removing barriers for sharing love. Again, the theme is one of work; life requires work and effort.

12. **Patience is very difficult for most Americans.** We are a culture of instantaneity. One of our primary criteria for judging the value of a product or of an activity is whether or not it makes things or life easier quickly. Often when people are trying to convince themselves or others of the value of a course of action, the notion that it will make the task easier is appealing. In America only the fool would select the more difficult path when an easier one would accomplish a similar goal. Our focus on ease is one of the contributing factors for creating our collective and individual sense of impatience. We hate to wait and disdain wasting time. Success is usually measured by accomplishments, and patience is often disregarded because it does not create an attitude that promotes ease and success. Grieving is a different journey; its time is not one of schedules or hurried activity. The feelings of being overwhelmed and helpless, as well as the constant sense of separation and sorrow, shift the landscape of our lives and alter the tempo of our

experiences. Part of the process of resigning to grief (without being trapped in a vortex of despair) is learning how to become patient with our self and with the inevitable changes that continue to jar our lives and our experiences. There will be times when the best means for improving our attitude about life is to stop and do nothing. Sometimes we need to give ourselves permission to cry and to succumb to the waves of tiredness and exhaustion that we feel. It's okay to turn away from being driven by the "shoulds" of our lives and just live within the natural flow of life itself. My life's rhythms are very different from those of society. The natural demands of life are now synchronized very differently than the way our family or other groups organize their ways of living.

13. **Everyone is fallible; we are imperfect beings.** Too many of us remain ignorant of our own weaknesses and have blind spots. My journey of grieving has demanded that I become more tolerant of others and of myself. I should not expect others to feel and see life the way I do. They can't possibly know the depths of my pain or the gift of life Heidi has given to me. In fact, I am only starting to understand these dynamics myself. Tolerance, however, is essential in developing an attitude that accepts the fallibility of others and the wide array of limitations in my life. When Socrates was asked about the Oracle of Delphi's claim that Socrates was the wisest of men, he said that he knew he was the most ignorant of men. Wisdom and understanding start with an awareness of ignorance. It is impossible to learn and develop yourself if you believe that you know everything or have all the answers. We should be tolerant of humanity's condition of ignorance – both in ourselves and in others.

14. **Sometimes it seems impossible to connect with other people.** Our grief can overcome all reasonable assessments and we feel alone, isolated, and the only one who is going through this pain. Of course, reason and common sense tell us that there are others who experience their own pain and have their own grieving journeys. Our attitude can shift when we realize the truth of the all too pervasive experience of grief in people's lives. Our attitude can further develop as we begin to recognize these people and try to become open to sharing their pain. The capacity for

sharing will shift daily and will depend on the time and context for each person. Developing a willingness to share the pain others experience will deepen the ability to develop a healthy attitude toward life, yourself and your grief.

15. **Fear and anxiety are inevitable constituents within all of human experience.** At times when we are grieving the helplessness and sorrow become so powerful that we can no longer identify the source of our fears. We may become blind to the pervasive *angst* that we feel. We should recognize that both our fears and our anxieties may be rooted in our grief and the frustration and helplessness that arise with the death of our child or loved one. This recognition will not necessarily lessen the feelings. In fact, recognition may not even alleviate the fears or anxiety that we are experiencing. Becoming healthy and developing a meaningful life does not include the elimination of (maybe not even the diminishment of) these crippling feelings. Recognition allows us to name our fears and to accept the fact that anxiety will forever be a part of our lives. This recognition will provide us with a type of empowerment that will resurface whenever we are submerged in the waves of dread that will buffet us. This empowerment converts itself into our attitude. We may not feel strong; we may not believe that we can continue to live with this pain; yet there is a source of hope and energy that is beyond us. If we are open to this source of love (God and our loved one), we will be able to continue to heal.

16. **Unresolved issues with dead loved ones play a significant role in the development of a person's attitude.** I have unresolved issues with both my father and with my mother. A friend of mine suggested that I picture them sitting in a chair and have a conversation with them. I have not had as many conversations with my parents as I probably need to have in order to reach some type of resolution that is healthy and balanced. The process of dealing with unresolved issues with a loved one can be a very important part of the healing process. Simply ignoring these concerns will not help anyone heal. Sometimes we try to brush away the unpleasantness that may be a part of our relationship with a loved one. I feel blessed that I do not have these feelings with respect to Heidi, but I am fully aware of the

burden they continue to have when I grieve for my parents.

17. **Not only do we need to work toward a permission to have joyous feelings and experiences, but we also need to give ourselves permission to expand our lives and the horizons of our lives.** In a sense Heidi has given me real freedom in a number of ways. I no longer fear my own death. Also, I feel freer to invest my time and talents in those activities that are meaningful to me. Writing this book is in response to some feeling or call that I have. Doing so meant that I had to put aside the projects I had wanted to pursue. Our attitude can cause us to shift our priorities. In fact, this is probably inevitable as we grieve. But we can take this attitude one step further. We can use this freedom to become the person we have always wanted to become. As we become more thoughtful and experience our inner feelings more fully, we have the opportunity to unearth hidden or neglected talents. This life is our only opportunity to do those things we really wish to do or have hoped we would do. It really is the time to seize the day. In life people and continuing obligations may get in our way; but, maybe, it is more important to immerse ourselves in a hobby, project, or some such activity than it is to follow the dictates of others. Poems, songs, and literary figures all teach us that it is the journey that is most important. Do not hesitate to seek professional assistance to help identify and release these inner talents or desires. Our loved one surely gives us permission to become all that we can become, if for no other reason than to honor her memory.

18. **In American culture we seem to use the word "real" as if it means the negative, cynical, or skeptical perspective.** Being realistic usually means that we should stop being optimistic and look at the difficulties and impediments in our life. Western education promotes skepticism as the doorway to knowledge. This skepticism and this knowledge is not the whole picture. The intuitive and the spiritual are real and may actually be more important than the concrete and observable. It is so easy to be swept along with the negative, the cynical, and the skeptical. Oftentimes our humor is predicated on any one of these attitudes. Too often people judge others and belittle them in order to feel superior or more important. Jealousy, envy, and feelings of inadequacy can override our attitude and

give us a warped sense of ourselves and of others. It might be difficult, maybe impossible, for most of us to expunge these attitudes from our life; however, recognizing the force that they play in our world is an important step in placing them in a reasonable balance in our life. A balanced life would find ways to counter the effects of cynicism, to keep skepticism as a useful tool in certain situations, and to lessen the hold that negativism may have on our consciousness and attitude toward life, ourselves, and others.

19. **Participating in sports is one way that people can learn how to recognize and cope with adversity.** I love sports, both as a participant and as a fan. Some of my coaches taught me how character-building these adversities may be. This point may seem trivial because "overcoming adversity" is a cliché. In this case, however, we would be wise to realize the power it reflects. Grieving is ultimately about adversity. All of the skills we have gained in our lives in dealing with adversity should be mustered during our journey. How foolish we would be to ignore the knowledge and wisdom we have gained before our grieving began. It may be easy to feel overwhelmed and to throw ourselves into a tailspin of despair and dread; yet, everyone has had to deal with adversity before. While we are grieving, we need to develop those former strategies or coping mechanisms that we used in other areas of our life. The difficult work of grieving should include all of our talents and all of our skills.

XIII.

JANUARY, 1989.

The Show Must Go On

By the age of seven Heidi had already learned to love the theater. After being in our district high school's production of "Hello Dolly" when she was six, Heidi decided to audition for the next year's production of <u>South Pacific.</u> The director wanted two elementary school children to play the roles of the plantation owner's children. Diane took Heidi to the audition, and all of us were concerned about Heidi's response to being rejected. She had not yet become fashion conscious. As she got older, Heidi became tastefully stylish – dressing well and establishing a reputation for "accessorizing." Family and friends still hear Heidi's admonitions concerning the value of tastefully doing so. For this audition, however, she wore old yellow sweat pants and sweat shirt. The audition consisted of each child singing in a room alone with the director. On the way home from the audition, Diane tried to prepare Heidi, "Did you see all those other kids trying out?" and "You're so blond and fair; they're looking for somebody who looks Polynesian." Heidi just smiled. "What did you sing," Diane asked? "Oh, just something" was all Heidi mumbled. Sensing Heidi wasn't going to provide any more details, Diane asked, "Wasn't it fun to just audition?" Heidi just sat in the car and nodded with a satisfied smile on her face.

When they arrived home, a message from the director awaited them: Heidi had the part, if she wanted it. Diane immediately called the director. "Are you sure you have the correct girl?" she asked. The director laughed. "Heidi had perfect pitch. We can easily remedy her blonde hair and fair complexion with temporary dye and make-up." Heidi was thrilled, but not overly surprised. She enjoyed the rehearsals, something she did throughout her life. Performing was great, but rehearsing was also special. For Heidi the whole experience (reading, rehearsing, make-up, blocking, miscues, props, etc.) of theater was a true joy. Rehearsals put her in contact with a deep seated love for performing and experiencing the magic of being someone else.

Heidi was sick the day before the dress rehearsal with chicken pox. The pox marks were beginning to show, and Heidi had a fever. When we tried to console her about missing the opportunity to perform, she looked at us as if we were from another planet. "What are you talking about?" she said with her wide-eyed intensity. "The show must go on!" There was no question in her mind that she was going to be on that stage and be the best Polynesian girl she could be. The director agreed to let her perform. Heidi not only made it to the dress rehearsal, but also to each performance. She never complained and never missed a line or a note. Most people did not even know that she was sick. She looked for no sympathy. She relished in her performance. "The show must go on," became her trademark theme. We now have that phrase on her grave marker and the bench next to her plot.

Whenever I feel sorry for myself or wish to crawl under the covers of the bed and stay there, I am inspired by Heidi's theme. I could never feel so sorry for myself that I would miss a "performance." Heidi's will and determination pushed me to return to the class the next day classes were in session after her funeral. I even smile at the irony of that first class session. As I stood at the podium just before beginning my teaching I looked out the window and saw a funeral procession driving into the cemetery that is across the street from the college's main campus. Was Heidi involved in the timing in some mischievous way? We had the type of relationship that makes me wonder about such things. "Dad, the show must go on. Don't be so distracted. Don't think about yourself, now. Teach well, and enjoy the blessings that you can find in teaching others." Yes, Heidi, I got the message.

Signs

The following passage is taken from a daily prayer guide that Diane and her mother read. The date: Tuesday, February 11, 2003 – The day after Heidi died.

Psalm 30: A new day
You have turned my mourning into dancing (v. 11)
"To hear these words in the midst of grief is no easy

thing. Mourning rather than dancing, weeping rather than laughing, is a way of honoring those we love. It reminds us of what we have lost. The move to laughter and dancing feels like a betrayal. Not only have we lost someone, but we have started to heal. The sting of death has started to subside. And this can make the loss even more acute, more complete.

"When God turns our mourning into dancing, the pain of loss is not erased. We dance because we know that even greater blessings, more abundant life, lay on the other side of death. We mourn our loss, but we celebrate the new life that has begun for those we love."

Some people may consider the timing of this passage to be a coincidence; we do not. The whole image of dancing is so meaningful to us. One of Diane's childhood friends (Donna) was struggling with her own cancer while Heidi was on her journey. Donna and her partner lived in Minnesota. They stopped to see us a couple of times as they traveled to Vermont for skiing, and we visited them after Heidi died. Donna continued to engage in life with as much intensity as she ever had. Her laugh was infectious and her jovial spirit connected with Heidi on a very special level. Both of them displayed a remarkable attitude toward life and their cancer. Their attitudes proved to be so powerful and inspirational for anyone who knew either one of them. Donna loved Lee Ann Womack's song "I Hope You Dance" and shared it with Heidi and Diane. It was a song of hope for all of them. When we hear it today, it always brings back Donna's infectious laugh and *joie de vivre*, while also connecting us with Heidi's smile and courage. Thus, the prayer we were given for Heidi's death was one of hope and joy. We knew that at the time, but the pain we were experiencing far over shadowed any form of consolation the prayer could initially provide. In a way, this feeling may be at the very heart of any signs we experience. In each case, the signs connect us directly to Heidi; they reaffirm her continued existence, but in the end no sign is ever completely sufficient to remove the core of grief that remains at the center of our lives. Just recently Diane found a reflections calendar that someone had given Heidi. It was opened to February 10 (the day she died). The thought for the day was: "Don't fear tomorrow. God is already there." Another coincidence?

Signs are essential in grieving. I never really encountered them or took them too seriously until they became a fabric of our current grieving journey. Until Heidi's death, I never really grieved in a way that was healthy or deeply meaningful. Now signs are an integral part of our grieving process. There are times, however, when we encounter some of them and don't even recognize what is happening until afterward: "Oh. That was Heidi." Sometimes they are quite vivid and clear while we are experiencing them. When I perform my character of Sancho Panza, he asks, "Why do people follow the bible of the cynics and skeptics?" This question is central to understanding the meaning of signs. For those who have not experienced the death of a child or someone for whom you deeply cared this chapter on signs may be read according to the "bible" in Sancho's monologue. They may see the stories as mere coincidences or the desperate delusions of grieving parents. For those who are riding on the subway, hopefully you will see from the "inside" and find real peace and meaning in the following pages. In essence, this book is an attempt to go beyond the limits and distortions caused by cynics or skeptics. For those who dismiss signs, I can only say that, hopefully, they will open themselves up to all the vistas for connecting to life that are available to us. I would also recommend reading *Messages: Signs, Visits, and Premonitions from Loved Ones Lost on 9/11* by Bonnie McEneaney. It contains powerful testimony to the meaning and depth of signs for those open to this real dimension in life.

Some of the people we know who have experienced the death of a child have gone to a medium or psychic to try and receive a message from their loved one. Some of them believe that a connection with their loved one was made; others have been disappointed. Psychic experience is just like all human enterprises. There are some who are genuine; others are charlatans. Some are skilled at reading body language and have adopted a philosophy consistent with "psychic" existence; others just use a person's grief and try to minister to them by telling them what they want to hear. Sometimes a psychic who really does have the "gift" can experience miscommunication and not understand what is being conveyed to him or her. Messages can always be distorted; doesn't everyone learn that lesson with the childhood game of sending a whispered message around a circle? Why do we have to dismiss the abilities of all psychics just because some are frauds, some are well-intentioned but not gifted, and miscommunication or misunderstandings do occur?

Life continues after death in a form of consciousness that is beyond my ability to describe. Consciousness is energy; it is life. Many of the signs we have experienced are connected to electricity – energy. Heidi remains connected to us in so many ways. **The key component in any sign is the context within which it occurs and the meaningfulness that the recipients feel.** Heidi selected the rosebud as her symbol of hope. We have incorporated roses as a symbol in many of the things that we write or cherish about her. Family and friends have given us roses on the anniversary of her death. I would like to use a rose to illustrate the varying, yet legitimate, perspectives people can have of life. The botanist can study the science of what makes a rose grow and bloom. The florist can picture the beauty of using roses in displays or in marketing their products (especially for St. Valentine's Day). The gardener may learn the techniques for enhancing the growth and beauty of the rose, while studying the aesthetics for placing them for maximum effectiveness in gardens. A lover may send a message with a bouquet. A passerby can look at the roses, or maybe even stop to smell them. For my family the rose is connected with Heidi, irrevocably. Whose meaning is genuine? Correct? Or complete? Doesn't the meaning shift from context to context?

I have decided to group the signs Diane and I have experienced into six categories. The first relates chance occurrences associated with finding pennies. The second relates to those signs that can readily be dismissed as coincidences by others who do not share the context or meaning of the sign. The third relates to those signs that a cynic or skeptic could dismiss because there just has to be a better explanation than our experience of a sign. The fourth group relates to experiences with animals (especially birds and butterflies). The fifth relates to dreams and the visits we have of our loved one while asleep. The sixth belongs to those experiences that just defy any reasonable explanation on any grounds other than these experiences were "authentic" signs. Most importantly, however, each sign, regardless of the category, is real and genuine for us. Sometimes we may doubt them at first, but the reality remains that we have had a meaningful encounter and experience with our daughter. These moments are precious and continually help us affirm our belief in her continued life. I have found that wanting a sign to occur is not necessarily a prelude to one being given. Any parent can relate to this experience with her child while she is living. Children do NOT always behave according to parental expectations. Why, then, wouldn't that attitude also carry over after death? Heidi has not lost her sense of humor or the basic components of her personality. Sometimes the sign occurs without us paying attention or even recognizing it as such at first. I wonder how many signs have been given that I never did realize were signs.

Our grief group has a saying that a sign to one is a sign given to everyone. Each sign affirms the continuation of life after death. That reality is a central focus for anyone who is grieving. For those of you who are grieving and accept the meaningfulness of signs, the following stories are intended to affirm your faith and belief. For those of you who remain skeptics, these stories are not intended to change your mind; they are given for you to ponder and consider the possibility of the continuing nature of interconnectedness with a person's loved one.

(1) Pennies from heaven.

Finding pennies that Heidi "sends" to us occurs often, especially for Diane. She will ask for pennies and inevitably one will be given to her. For example, just the other day she was shopping and had been missing Heidi badly. As she entered the supermarket she told Heidi that she expected to find a penny. It didn't appear until she unexpectedly returned to the frozen meat section. A penny was waiting for her on the floor. As she smiled to herself, she went one step further and told Heidi that if she really wanted to make her mother happy the penny should be dated 1981 (Heidi's birth year). When she picked it up her request was honored; the date was 1981. Diane has come to believe that since she expects to find pennies, she will. Heidi isn't going to disappoint her. We have a "Pennies from Heaven" jar that was given to us sitting on the bookshelves in the living room. Diane's first encounter with finding pennies came one month after Heidi's funeral (March 15, the Ides of March, 2003) when all of her sisters returned home to be together and share our collective grief. We were all walking to the Original Pancake House (Heidi had worked as a hostess at another location prior to her diagnosis) when she found four pennies, one for each of our daughters. Later that day, she and I were walking and she found two more pennies; so we started with six pennies that represented our nuclear family.

On February 10, 2004, the first anniversary of Heidi's death, we decided to go to breakfast at the Original Pancake House. Good friends (Bart and Jody) who were consistently present during Heidi's illness and who have shared her death and our grief in very beautiful ways joined us. They brought a rose for us to take to the cemetery. While we were eating, a couple of songs were playing in the background that touched us very much. One was "I Hope You Dance" (the song we relate to Diane's friend, Donna). The other was "It's a Wonderful World," the song that Heidi loved so much and the one that has deeply touched me at weddings. As we were leaving, we saw a penny. As soon as Diane bent over to pick it up, the Righteous Brothers' song, "Unchained Melody" (the song that I believe Heidi and I would have danced to at her wedding), started playing. This was the third song that directly connected us with Heidi. Yes, Heidi was with us. We went shopping for roses to take to the grave and found a penny at that store. The grave site felt exactly as it had the previous year: cold, snowy, and unforgiving. We went to see the movie "Phantom of the Opera" because of the musical's meaning for our family. I found a penny while I was waiting for Diane. Finally, we went to a favorite ice cream parlor for some comfort food and because Heidi loved going there. While we ate our ice cream, "Unchained Melody" came on again. Coincidences? Maybe for the skeptic, but for us, these signs were clear messages from Heidi that she was still with us and understood our sadness on that anniversary.

A few weeks later I was at a conference in Richmond. Even though I had been extremely active in this organization since the 1980s, I felt quite out of place. My friends and colleagues hadn't changed; I had. One evening I went for a long walk. It was late and I felt very lonely. I was thinking how the penny sign is more for Diane than for me, when lo and behold there was one lying on the sidewalk. The following year I was in Indianapolis for the conference. I had spent a lot of time alone and thinking about this book. I realized that I hadn't found a penny and was a bit disappointed. The last evening, when I was feeling rather distant from everyone, including close colleagues, I was walking through the city's dome walkway back to the hotel. Sitting on a table was a penny for me. The table had a white cloth and the penny was the only object sitting on it. I picked it up and immediately ran into a man I have known for years. He stopped me, gave me a hug, and asked whether we could meet the next morning. When we did he asked me if I would be willing to perform Sancho Panza at another organization's national convention. I was stunned and excited to bring Heidi's spirit alive, even though I didn't expect academics to feel the emotional elements of the performance. I was pleasantly surprised when I received a standing ovation and many warm comments afterward. Were these just coincidences???

In March 2005 the grief support group held a "Men's Only" get together at one of our houses. During the meeting the issue of signs emerged, and we talked about their meaning, how they are never quite enough, and how to deal with the inherent skepticism that we feel. When the sessions were done, we stood around chatting a bit before leaving. Jim, the host, turned on the radio for some quiet background music. The first song was "Unchained Melody." As I was leaving I found a nickel on the street next to my car.

In May 2005 I was teaching and Diane was attending a grief group session. The group was discussing the issue of signs, and a great deal of skepticism was being shared. Interestingly enough, the lights in the room flickered while the doubts were being raised. Even Diane and I have doubts about signs sometimes, despite the rich history we have already experienced. We have been so trained analytically with a skeptical attitude that we even find ourselves in the trap of not always believing. Diane was in that mood on this day. That afternoon we were going to watch one of our nephews play a soccer game at another local college campus. We had never done so before. Diane rode over with her sister and her husband, and I drove from my campus after classes were over. I was having trouble finding a spot, then saw two open up. Instead of taking the nearest one, "I decided" (or maybe someone else was guiding me) to pull into the further space. I met Diane, and we watched the game. As we were walking to the car, we were talking about being on a campus together. One of the difficulties I experience while teaching is coping with the fact that I am constantly dealing with Heidi's peers. Instead of completing college she spent most of her "college life" fighting leukemia. She died when she was 21, and her last years will always be etched in my consciousness as her college years. I taught her peers until I retired and felt a strong sense of sadness in all of my classes. On that day Diane and I both felt that we needed to feel Heidi. In her mind, Diane asked Heidi to give her a penny to make her feel better. Before reaching the car Diane told me about the session at the support meeting in the morning and the flickering lights. I have a habit of opening the door for Diane. When I was unlocking the door on her side, she proclaimed, "My gosh. There's a penny. No, there's more." We got on our knees and collected the pennies that were spilled all around our car and the now vacant space next to it. In all, we collected 76 pennies (7 + 6 = 13; Heidi's birthday is 10-3). There were no other coins, just pennies. It was clear to us that Heidi was emphatically telling us to stop being so skeptical. How could we possibly doubt the validity of signs and how could her mother share in the skepticism in the group? It was obviously something that Heidi would do because there were times when she would forgo subtlety to get a message across. The message that day was abundantly clear to us.

One evening Diane and I attended a performance of *Camelot*. It was a musical that had no connection for us with Heidi. The theater was full, but there was one empty seat next to me. We thought nothing of it. At the intermission both Diane and I had had the same feeling that Heidi would have loved this musical. The woman who was playing the role of Guinevere was portraying the character in a way we thought would be similar to Heidi's interpretation. We both could see our daughter in the woman's performance. When the show was over, I felt as if Heidi might have been with us. As we started to leave, Diane bent over and picked up a penny that was on the floor in front of the seat next to me. We looked at each other and realized that, in fact, Heidi had been with us and had enjoyed the performance also.

Another example occurred in the summer of 2003. We went to Tuscany, Italy, with our friends from the Netherlands who became our tour guides and made the decisions about where to go and what to do. Diane and I were quite incapable of making decisions then. We cherished their friendship, and the gift of taking care of us for a few weeks that summer was very special. They had planned to visit Heidi in January, but Peter's mother became critically ill (and died shortly thereafter), so they postponed their visit. When they heard that Heidi had died, they decided that they needed to come. They arrived at the funeral home on Friday night and attended the funeral and the Sunday morning get together at our home. They drove to Toronto and flew back to Holland on Sunday evening. The fact that they flew all the way from the Netherlands to share our grief and attend Heidi's funeral is a testimony to our friendship. While in Italy, we stayed at a villa in a remote area away from other tourists. The villa had a grassy court yard. Each evening we sat out there and had wine, bread, and fruit as we played cards. Every morning I would go there to do my Tai Chi. We had been at the villa a couple of days. The third night we were there we had had a difficult night and Diane had a "prescient" dream. As we were sitting there, Diane saw a penny under my chair — an American penny. No one else was staying in the villa while we were there. I had left all of my American money back in the Netherlands, so it could not have dropped out of my pockets. Yet there it was, sitting quietly under my chair waiting for Diane to find it. Why hadn't we found it on previous nights? Why had I not seen it on other mornings? Why did we find it when we really needed to do so? Coincidence?

The last example I'll share involves editing this section of the book. One Saturday I was editing this section for the "last" time before submitting it to prospective publishers. Diane also read another chapter from the book on "Messages" or signs that I noted above. That night I spent a lot of time rethinking my feelings about signs. The next morning I was going to drive about 25 miles and lead worship at a small church in a rural area. I had been there once a few months earlier. I awoke much earlier than needed and stayed in bed for another hour praying and thinking about and talking to Heidi. I was wondering if there would ever be any more signs; were they all used up? As I was showering I decided to wear a different pair of shoes (loafers rather than the tie shoes I usually wear when I lead worship services). At the time I didn't understand why I would do that. When I arrived at the church and got out of the car I felt a "stone" in my shoe. When I had the chance before the worship service, I pulled off my loafer and found a penny. Of course, I smiled, said hi to Heidi and felt a warm comfortable ease descend over me. Earlier when I was looking for the church, I had turned off our radio (it was tuned into the Broadway station we often listen to). When I got into the car after the worship service I turned the radio back on. The first thing I heard was a young woman's voice saying: "Did you find a penny?" Startled I listened intently to the short dialogue that begins "We're in the Money" from 42nd Street. Heidi had had the lead in this musical in her senior year of high school; it was one of her grandest roles. It obviously means a lot to me (and to her). This song has been connected to more than just this sign (see below for details). Yes, Heidi had been listening and had provided me with a wonderful example to close this section on pennies from heaven.

(2) Random incidents

There were a number of incidents that occurred just after Heidi died. They all had an impact on us:

- The day after her death an out of town acquaintance had sent Heidi a postcard that informed her that she would be receiving a subscription to "Angels on Earth."
- Two nights after Heidi died *Breakfast at Tiffany's* was on TV. It was one of Heidi's favorite Audrey Hepburn movies. Also that night Diane was having trouble sleeping and was flipping stations. She landed in the middle of a Disney program about a traveling family that had a minor accident near the yard of a farm family. The story was about how the girl in the accident was a perfect bone marrow transplant donor for the girl living on the farm who had leukemia. This is what Diane wrote in

our "Heidi Moments Journal": "At one point an angel takes the donor 'into the light' where she sees the farm girl sitting in a white robe, bald. It could have been Heidi sitting there. The resemblance was so amazing. It took my breath away." Diane had been telling Heidi to find the light the night she died.
- The night of Heidi's funeral "My Fair Lady" was airing.
- Tara belongs to a book club. The book for the monthly meeting when Heidi died was about characters who had secrets. The secret near the end of the book was about a man who had a 21 year old sister who died of leukemia.
- When Katie returned to work after the funeral she went into the cafeteria and the old fashioned popcorn sign said, "We use Sunflower Oil." That was Heidi's favorite. I have always loved popcorn and have passed this passion on to all of my daughters. For Christmas 2001 there was a gift under the tree for Heidi and me. That was an unusual combination until we opened the present. Kristen had purchased a popcorn maker that had a handle for turning the kernels. Included in the package was a wide assortment of brands of popcorn along with evaluation sheets. Kristen had created the "Magnificent Popcorn Taste Off" for Heidi and me to complete. The rating sheets had five rankings: revolting, mildly revolting, adequate, quite nice, and incredible. The categories for these rankings were: overall appearance, butter hue, popcorn to kernel ratio, texture, flavor, chewiness, salt factor, aroma, and overall rating. There was a comments section at the bottom. Heidi and I had a great deal of fun filling out these forms for the wide variety of brands that we had been given. Of course we also made popcorn for everyone at different times when they visited. We ritually made popcorn when we watched some favorite television shows or whenever the Buffalo Bills were playing. Our rankings varied from brand to brand, but the difference between Heidi's score and mine were never more than one number apart. One brand called Pop Secret produced the following comment: "The secret is what did they do with the flavor?" Theater Popcorn had "a natural taste that was better than the buttery taste of the microwave brand." Back to Basics with Caramel proved to be "a delightful surprise that produced a nice change of pace." Pop Secret with White Cheddar seasoning: "The white cheddar flavoring transformed a mildly revolting popcorn to a good tasting popcorn."

Katie has made popcorn for me and does so because of all that it means AND because we love it. Thus, she was taken aback when she saw that the cafeteria was using Heidi's favorite type of oil.

- After the funeral Diane and I made a list of some of the things Heidi wanted to do and see. Two weeks after the funeral we did the first one; we went to see the Harry Potter movie that had been released over the previous Christmas. After the movie Diane went to the rest room. We had not been to this movie house before, and I drifted down the darkened hallway. I stopped to wait and nonchalantly leaned against the wall. I bumped into something that was hanging. When I turned around I saw "the" picture of Audrey Hepburn that is the classic pose taken from "Breakfast at Tiffany's." So I decided to discuss the movie with Heidi until Diane was finished.

- Outside of Heidi's bedroom window was a Clematis that I had helped to climb over an archway leading from our patio to a path we have. This Clematis was spectacular. It had white, tiny blossoms. The previous summer there were thousands of these blossoms, and the fullness of the plant was amazing. It too died that winter with Heidi. Just like her it had had a short, but brilliant life.

- Another beautiful experience occurred the summer after her death when we were with our friends in Italy. One day we were visiting Florence. We wanted to see the statue of David, but our friends were more interested in some architecture that Tiny had been studying. We had arranged a time and place to meet. When we got together they said they had found the perfect restaurant for us to eat; it was located across the street from the Philosophy Department at the university. We were a bit stunned when we saw the name *"Trattoria Teatro"* ("Theater Restaurant"). The timing was unnerving because we had been given money from Heidi's godfather to use on the trip to treat the four of us to dinner. Diane and I had decided earlier in the day that this would be the meal to celebrate Heidi's life. On one wall was a pair of long armed gloves; something Heidi wore when she was a lead in 42nd Street during her senior year in high school.

(3) Music and electricity

I have shared a few examples of how meaningful music has come to us at significant times. Timing really is so important in giving real depth and impact to signs. At Christmas time 2005, Diane and I drove to the cemetery, listening to the endless stream of holiday music on a radio station dedicated to playing Christmas carols all day. Since the holiday season is so rich for our family, we were struggling even more than usual. When we got out of the car, the cold, damp air struck us as somehow appropriate. At the grave, Diane said, "Heid, we need a sign." When we got back into the car, we heard the beginning of "It's A Wonderful World" by Louis Armstrong. The incongruity of that song being played at the exact time that we wanted to hear from Heidi was incredibly moving. We both smiled, then cried.

Earlier in this book, I discussed how consciousness, as a form of energy, continues to live after death. The Chinese talk about *chi* which is the energy that flows throughout our bodies. Chinese acupuncture is predicated upon a different geography of the body. *Chi* moves throughout the body in different meridians which have no correlation to the nervous system used in Western medicine. The needles are used to help stimulate the flow of energy, *chi,* to restore a person to balance and harmony. Einstein's famous equation, $E = MC^2$ is all about energy. In fact, energy is a basic ingredient in all life. Now for us, energy becomes a source of our continuing connection with Heidi.

We have had some significant signs come to us by Heidi's use of electricity. On April 3, 2003, just months after Heidi died, we were at our friends (those who were with us when we received those horrible phone calls from her doctor that started this journey) to try and comfort them. They had just returned from California where their only son had died of a strange and undiagnosed ailment. We were there to listen to their story of his dying and share a mutual bond that we never want to have with anyone. For Diane, the week had been a very difficult one. We were now recognizing the absoluteness of death and discovering that the pain of grief does not lessen; it just keeps evolving. I had decided earlier that day that I would try to give Diane a "pep" talk about some of the signs we had already had that were meant to reassure us that Heidi is okay and continues to live. On the way home from our friends' house, just as I started my feeble attempt to reassure her, the street lights on one side of the street went out. When we stopped at the sign at the corner, they came back on. We looked around to see if there were any power outages in the homes or other street lights, but could see nothing out of the ordinary. We thought that was strange, but proceeded down a busier street. I returned to my "pep" talk and a section of lights went out as we approached. They went back on when we stopped at the sign at the end of that street. So we began to wonder. As we pulled into our driveway, the street light on our lawn and the one on the yard of Diane's good friend across the street went out. Diane got out of the car and said, "Heidi?" Both lights began to flicker, then came on very brightly. No other lights on the street were affected. We began to talk about Heidi, and then thought maybe our friend's son was joining Heidi in this display. As we started to walk up our porch both lights flickered again. Both of us said in unison, "Heidi, is that you? Are you okay?" We went inside and knelt on the love seat at our living room window. The lights flashed out for a brief moment, then flashed back to life. For us Heidi was telling us that she was okay. I checked the lights for the next few nights when I took our dog out, and they never flickered.

The following December another series of episodes touched us. At the time, Diane loved a television series entitled *Joan of Arcadia*. On a December evening we were going to watch an episode about a young boy with a terminal, respiratory disease. Heidi died of respiratory complications; my father and a close uncle of mine died of emphysema; and I am an asthmatic. Watching this show was going to be difficult for us. Before we started I took our dog out for his nightly ritual. The light across the street in front of our friend's house began to flicker. I noticed this and asked Heidi if she was trying to get my attention. The light flickered again, and I told her how much we missed her. The light briefly flickered, then came on and stayed on. I smiled and told Diane what had happened. While we were watching the show Vragil needed to go out again. The light was on and shining as usual. I was a bit disappointed because I wanted the light to flicker "hello" to me. I looked down at my feet and thought how insatiable Diane and I are with signs. I looked up at the dog and the light went out completely. "Heidi, is that really you? Are you using light again?" It flashed back to life. The dog and I, then, went back into the house and upstairs to watch the show with Diane. While we were watching the taped show, we interrupted it to talk for a while because in it there was a reference to life as energy. I was telling her about the Chinese idea of *chi* and my belief that electricity is a perfect medium for those who have died to use in order to reconnect with loved ones. I recalled the conversation and wondered about the light going out and flashing back to life when I was out with the dog. I thanked Heidi for talking to me and went to bed.

The next night when I took the dog out the light was shining as usual. As I was waiting for the dog, I looked up at the moon and thought about the Moon Party. The moon that night was full and beautiful; it was a bittersweet moment for me. When I looked away from the moon the light went out. I started to talk to Heidi. I ended by saying that I missed her. Immediately the light began to flicker in a staccato fashion that was very different from any of the other times. I really felt as if Heidi was using that light to "talk" to me. I answered, "I love you too, Buv (my nickname for her)". As I said these words, the light seemed to pause and when I had finished it instantly became brighter than ever. At five the next morning Diane got up and looked out the window. The light was out. Diane said, "Okay Heidi" and the light came on and stayed lit. The following night when we went out the light was on. When we got home and got out of the car the light flickered so we "talked" to Heidi again. When we finished, the light came back on and remained on. Later when I took the dog out the light went out immediately when we got on the porch, flickered while I talked to Heidi, then stayed on when I was finished. We have never had such an encounter with that light ever again.

Another electrical experience happened with Kristen. On Mother's Day 2006 she gave birth to twins. We believe that Heidi has been with each one of her sisters during their pregnancies and deliveries in very special ways. On this particular day Kristen and her husband, Bill, felt and "saw" her presence. After the deliveries and after the staff had taken care of the initial needs of the twins, Kristen and Bill went down to the unit to see their babies. Kristen and Bill were thrilled, excited, tired, etc. When they returned to the hospital room, the lights began to flicker quite rapidly. Bill immediately said hello to Heidi, and Kristen knew Heidi was there. A nurse came into the room and asked what was going on because she had never seen the lights act in that way before.

The most profound electrical experience that I had came at Christmas 2004. During high school Heidi wanted to build a Christmas village. Her boyfriend had a wonderful set up and Heidi wanted to do something similar, but distinctly different. I had an old mirror panel that she used for her pond and an upside down bowl became her mountain. Over the years she became a bit more sophisticated with her village and the number of buildings increased to ten and finally she had a train for an added effect. She would meticulously place cotton on the table for her snow and bury all the electrical cords under it. When she was fighting her leukemia, building the village became more important for her. The last time she built one was her last Christmas. It was almost painful to watch her carefully work on the snow and the placement of the people, buildings, trees, train, etc. I helped her a little, but the creative part of the design was always hers. She changed the village design each year despite using the same materials. After she died, I decided that I would continue her tradition; Diane found it too painful to do. The first year I put it on an extended portion of the computer table that stands in our Van Gogh room. In 2004 I decided to spend a little more time and do it "right." It was the Monday before Christmas. Kristen was wrapping presents in the room, and I decided that this year I would use the oak table that we had bought for Heidi's sewing machine (which she was never able to use). I started putting the village together and decided that I would not have the train go in a circle; instead, it was going to cut through the town and run "endlessly" in either direction, my way of having the display touch eternity. I kept changing buildings around because I just could not feel comfortable with their placement. Finally, I was finished. I turned on the lights and felt satisfied but incomplete. Two days later we had Diane's family coming over to celebrate Christmas at our house. Just before everyone arrived Diane and I went into the Van Gogh room to listen to a particular song she had discovered in her grieving. We turned off the lights, stood near the door, hugged each other, and looked at the village. In an instant we saw what no one had noticed before. Above the village on the wall was a large "H" – just hanging there like the star over Bethlehem. There were no other reflections from the village on that wall. I wrote the following in "Heidi's Moments Journal" on Christmas day.

> "I am sitting at the computer chair and staring at the village in the darkness. There was a bright light in the church, so I decided to pray. 'Guide me; help me see what it is that I am to do.' My gaze went back to the blessed "H" and I remembered Monday night in a new light. I had set up the table and eventually went to bed with a heavy heart. We had set up the Christmas tree that day and I had set up the village. Heidi was around but not really. While I was in bed I had an overpowering feeling of my need to see and talk to Heidi. I missed her so much. I felt a tap on my shoulder as I lied in bed and felt a surge of Heidi's presence. I got up and felt sure I would receive a sign that night. I went around the house and even looked out the window at the street lights, hoping. I "knew" I

had to go to the Van Gogh room; she would be there. I turned on the village but doubt hit me quickly. "What am I doing? She's never coming back. Death is absolute." I saw nothing that night. The next morning Diane and I went to a grief support session, and we were talking about hope – signs – our loved one's presence. Heidi had given us a sign, the "H", but I did not see it. I knew she was present because I had really felt that tap on my shoulder. I was sure I would receive a sign that night, but I was blind. I didn't see the 'H' until Wednesday night. Was this experience to show me that my doubting is only blinding me to her real existence – even her real presence for us?

"How was the 'H' created? By Heidi's hand in the creation of her village? I will discover the electronics of this positioning when I take the village down. For now, it is a gift from her. The village was set up differently from any time before. I kept changing the positions: the track, the road, the buildings. I had no design in mind; I just placed the items in places until it felt 'right.' Why couldn't that feeling have been Heidi being with me so she could leave her mark on the wall for all to share? Maybe this village isn't just for Christmas, just as Christ's presence and grace is not really just for Christmas. It's for everyone. When Christ said 'I want you' years ago, maybe the answer is to spread the grace that comes with loving someone in life and in death. Earlier today Diane asked if I believed in the signs really coming from Heidi. Was I sure she was okay and that she's really reassuring us? Diane wondered how those who believe got to that point. I said that I wasn't absolutely certain (but almost so); she said she was 70 percent convinced. Can I allow this experience to be my epiphany, the moment and days of Christmas that give me a real spiritual birth or rebirth? Can they give me a sense of grace in Heidi's resurrection and new life? Can I remain open to grace and these blessings? Last Tuesday at 'group' I told others they should be open to the grace and blessings of signs. Can I follow my own beliefs? Is this a road to joy that remains always wrapped in sadness. I love you, Buv."

We have never taken that village down. It remains just as I made it that Monday. How could we ever think to remove the "H" that guides our life?

(4) Encounter with animals

Animals have an instinctive connection to life; it is the basis for their ability to survive. Our dog certainly sensed something with Heidi when he spent the night before her diagnosis on her bed and when he spent the entire last day of her life on her bed. I have listened to other parents talk about the signs they have received via butterflies and birds. I listened with an open mind, but deep down I did not feel that they were authentic signs. Thankfully, I am learning to be less dismissive and less skeptical myself. Last summer I had an encounter with a hummingbird that opened my mind to the possibility that connections with animals are an authentic source for signs.

I was watering one of our garden areas that includes a statue of a girl with her arms raised upward; one of our grandsons has named her "Star Bright." Behind the statue are some tall Sneezewoods and next to them is a Rose of Sharon. While I was watering the other flowers, a hummingbird flew to the Rose of Sharon. I watched with keen interest when the bird began to hover near the Sneezewoods about five feet from where I was standing. It did not touch them nor even get that close; it just hovered for well over a minute. I thought it was looking at me; so I smiled and asked, "Heid, are you flying with this beauty?" I continued watering the garden and even moved the spray toward the bird to see if it would fly away. It didn't. The bird continued in that position for awhile longer then flew to the Crab Apple tree about ten feet away. We planted that tree the summer after my mom died in her honor. The bird stayed in the tree area and seemed to be waiting. I watered the garden under the tree then proceeded to another area along our back fence. I kept glancing to make sure the hummingbird was still in the tree; it seemed patiently waiting for me. The portion I was turning to water next has two Clematis flowers climbing up the sides of a decorative set of shelves – there are also a variety of annuals, a white rose bush a friend had given us to remember Heidi and a Scarlet O'Hara bush. ("Gone With the Wind" has a very special meaning for Diane and me.) Again, I looked up to see the hummingbird still waiting and watching me. After I watered one of the Clematis, it flew down about six feet from where I was standing and began to hover by the plant. Again, I asked Heidi if she were with the bird. It stayed for awhile then went to the clematis and began to clean herself; it looked as if it was taking a shower. It rubbed its head, then wings and body along the wet leaves of the plant. I continued watering around and beneath the bird and started to talk to it as if Heidi were with me. After it finished its "shower," it hovered for a few more minutes while I continued to talk to Heidi, then flew up to the tree and stayed there. I decided that the bird wanted me to get Diane so she could say hello. When Diane came back, the bird was waiting for her. It flew over to another Clematis that is climbing the remains of Heidi's swing set. It hovered, then flew to the Trumpet Vine, took some nourishment, and flew back to the Crab Apple. It hovered around the tree and seemed to be waiting for something else to happen. I ran inside, retrieved our camera, and took a picture. After I did so, the bird swooped down and across our yard; it reminded me of pilots who fly their jets in a salute to those on the ground.

We have had hummingbirds in our gardens before, usually at our Butterfly Bush or at our Trumpet Vine. I have also watched them in other locations. This was the first real encounter that I have ever had where the hummingbird seemed to be "connecting" with me. Connecting is the only word that seems to describe what I felt about the experience. The bird spent time with me, looked at me, and continued to connect with me far longer than I had ever imagined for a hummingbird. I felt a closeness with Heidi and a sense that she was appreciating the view of the garden and enjoying spending a little time with me. Since she no longer has any physical form, and she knows that I am too limited to directly experience her new conscious life, I have chosen to believe that she connected with this hummingbird and influenced its behavior so that I would know that she continues to share in our life. I know I never would have written these paragraphs before Heidi was diagnosed. I never would have considered this experience as anything other than a strange event. Now, I firmly believe that Heidi was present and was giving me another sign that would help me grow in my understanding of my ride on the subway with her.

Butterflies have become another source of connection with Heidi. Over the past couple of years we have had experiences with butterflies that have the characteristics of signs. Turtle doves and butterflies are common visitors in our backyard when I'm doing my morning Tai Chi. We also have many butterflies throughout the summer in different garden areas. One day when I was exercising a butterfly hovered around me then went to the butterfly bush. I stopped for a second and said "Hi, Heidi. Won't you hang around for awhile so I can take your picture for mom?" I finished about 10 minutes later and the butterfly was dutifully waiting for me. I went in, got the camera, and took a number of pictures that Diane was able to use for making greeting cards. Recently in Hawaii we had a few "meetings" with butterflies which lasted longer than the usual "fly by."

(5) Visits in our dreams

In American culture we believe that dreams are not a part of reality. Reality is correlated with what we experience while we are awake. There are other cultures that do not make this distinction; they believe that whatever someone experiences is part of reality. Most Americans realize that there is some connection between dreams and a person's life. The nature of that connection varies from person to person, and the frequency or relevancy of dreams varies considerably. Dreams can become a significant part of anyone's grieving journey. They have definitely been a part of Diane's and mine. We both feel as though Heidi has actually visited us in them. These dreams have felt different in many ways from other dreams. I have a very active dream life, yet I do not readily recall all the details within them. Usually I may think about them for a fleeting moment and then let them pass into an obscure recess of my memory that I know I will never try to tap. This is not so with my Heidi dreams/visits.

My first Heidi dream/visit came in April 2003. In the dream I was riding in some type of cart and moving around an airport that really looked like a hotel. Diane was walking nearby and looking for the gate for Heidi's arrival. We were both confused because the gate number was at an area that was under construction. A friendly supervisor came by and told us not to worry; people would be arriving soon. Very shortly a group of people started coming through a tunnel and Heidi was behind the first small cluster. She was taller than the others and was wearing her black hat that changed into a blue bandana. Hats and bandanas were signatures of hers. She wore hats well throughout her life. Especially as a child she wore all kinds of different colors and types of hats. As she got older she wore ones that reflected her mood and the image she was projecting. When she first lost her hair, we got a wig from the hospital. Heidi quickly decided that she was going to wear her baldness proudly. She never wore a wig but would often wear a bandana that matched her clothes. I now use some of those bandanas as a handkerchief with my characters that I portray in class or in other performing venues.

In the dream Heidi was dressed exactly as she was the first time she flew home from college her freshman year. Diane waved and ran down the tunnel to greet her. Diane was so relieved because she was very worried that Heidi wasn't going to make it home. I got out of the cart, and Heidi had a big smile for me. I could feel her hug. She was so thin and her hands were clenched behind my back. She was so terribly cold. I told her that I would warm her up. When I woke up I could still feel the hug, and, in fact, the memory is so vivid that I can still feel that hug when I recall this dream. Heidi's coldness was a clear message to me. Diane and all of my daughters have a different thermostat than my sons-in-law and I have. Heidi was no exception. Dealing with the coldness that the women in my life feel has been a constant part of my consciousness. Another very painful feeling that I have of Heidi's funeral and burial is the reality of how cold her body had become and how cold the cemetery was that day. In those first few days after her death, the pain of Heidi's coldness was haunting and troubling. Whenever we visit her grave during winter all of these terrible feelings swell back into my consciousness. The feeling of being helpless to warm my little girl is a deep and abiding pain. I do not believe this sense of failure will ever leave me. I am sure that psychologists and others can readily interpret the symbolism in my dream; however, the meaning of my dream is special to me. I was able to "touch" my daughter again, and that touch was reassuring and remains significant and powerful.

The first dream/visit Diane had was while we were in Italy on July 21, 2003. Both of us were feeling rather out of sorts that night. We could not sleep, mosquitoes were bothering us, we were far from home, and we were not feeling Heidi's presence. We talked about our pain and tried to find some consolation in the signs and other "Heidi moments" we had experienced since her death. Diane has always needed more reassurance than I have. That night she was saying that she really needed something definitive so she could feel that Heidi was okay. The following is her verbatim description of her dream that night: "Heidi was bald in our basement by the wash machine when I went down the stairs. She rushed up to me, all smiles. She had a plastic cast on each arm and she 'sort of' released them. She said, 'Mom, Mom, I'm all better; I'm fine', as she released the casts to the floor. I threw my arms around her and we hugged. This was on February 8, so I knew what was coming. As I hugged her, she assured me she was fine. I saw Jody who visited Heidi frequently during her illness standing behind her. I kept mouthing to my friend as I hugged Heidi, 'Why? Why?' It felt so good to hug her." Diane shared the dream with me while we were in the cathedral in Pisa the next day.

That evening we found the penny underneath my chair while we were sipping our wine and enjoying the time with our dear friends.

One dream that I had in Italy after Diane's dream was a very short one. Diane and I were somewhere and the phone rang. I could see and hear Heidi clearly saying to me, "I'm okay." She said so four or five times. I tried talking to her, but I could not get through. When she finished saying, "I'm okay," I woke up. When I went back to sleep I dreamt that I was telling Diane and Tara about the dream I had had and how I wanted to remember all of the details.

(6) Defies reasonable explanation

The following signs have been very powerful experiences for us. Two days after Heidi died, our dog walked into Heidi's darkened room. It was clear that he was looking for her. He didn't seem to know what to do. Diane picked him up and held him while she sat on the bed. Suddenly a buzzing noise came from the nightstand next to the bed. Diane had no idea what it could be. She screamed. Katie ran into the room and looked through the drawers until she found the source of the noise. It was an electronic massager. Heidi never used it while she was alive. Our daughters and their cousins love to give one another massages. In fact, there have been times when they have formed a line while sitting on the floor giving the person in front of them a neck and shoulder massage. The massager was an excellent choice for Heidi to use: it was clearly connected to her; it illustrated something she loved to do; and it reflected health. She was okay. The massager has never gone off again, and it sits in the same drawer that it had before.

The next sign needs some explanation to understand. Heidi and I have bad habits of fidgeting with our hands. While she was sick, she received a number of electronic, hand held toys/games to use. She would play with one while she was in the hospital and while she was in bed at home when we watched TV. I also bought her a laptop to have in the hospital when she was first diagnosed. We loaded some games into it, and she would play them while watching shows. Heidi and I played games constantly at home, in the hospital rooms, at the chemo or medicine clinic, even while in waiting rooms. One hand game that she had was a poker game. I actually used it far more than she did. She teased me about stealing her game. It was a draw poker game with three variations. I **always** played straight up and Heidi **always** played Jokers Wild. I still play the game once in awhile when

I am sitting and watching a sporting event. The game was and continues to be a constant way for me to touch something that Heidi and I shared. About one month after she died, I was supposed to go out with my brother-in-law, who continues to be a source of support and comfort. I had had a terrible day. The night before Diane had cried herself to sleep, and I woke up in the morning feeling as if I had lost a heavyweight boxing match. Before going to teach, I read Tara's eulogy for the first time since the funeral and reread Heidi's spiritual story for the first time since the day she wrote it. I cried long and hard. I felt my teaching that day was rather uninspired.

On the way home I kept saying how much I did not want to go out. Diane wasn't home when I arrived. I went up to the bedroom and was thinking of excuses I could use so I could just stay home and feel sorry for myself. As I started walking to the closet, the poker game started playing a jingle. I thought this was very odd, since it was closed and I hadn't used it since the Wednesday before Heidi died. I had put it on my dresser weeks earlier. I was the last to use it and I never had the sound on, so I was perplexed: how could a jingle be playing? It required too many buttons to get to that point. I slowly picked up the game and opened the lid. The jingle was indicating that a Jokers Wild hand had just won. I hummed the tune so I would remember it because I couldn't recall the name and knew Diane would be able to identify it. I sat down on the bed and realized that Heidi was talking to me. I later found out that the jingle was "We're in the Money" from *42nd Street*. As I sat there I realized how amazing this really was. How could all of the buttons have been pressed for this to occur? First, one button had to be pressed to turn it on; then more buttons needed to be pressed to change the game from draw poker to Jokers Wild; another button had to be pressed to deal the cards; more buttons had to be pressed to hold the desired cards; another button had to be pressed to receive the selected cards; and another button would have to be pressed to turn the sound on so I could hear the jingle. Heidi selected a whimsical way to get me out of my "funk." By the way, the winning hand was three tens (her birthday is 10/3). "Dad, stop feeling sorry for yourself. Enjoy life and go out." I could hear her chiding and smiling at me so I did go out.

A similar occurrence happened when Diane and I were in Maui. We had been gone for a couple of weeks and felt out of touch with our family (and with Heidi). Although Diane had found some pennies, we had not really felt Heidi's presence. While Diane was getting ready for bed, I picked up the poker game. Although I had used it after the preceding experience, I had not used it in over a month. Thus it had been reset to straight, draw poker. When I turned it on, a jingle began to play and the winning hand was Joker's Wild with three 10s. (By the way, in all the times before and after this experience, when I've turned the game on to use, it always reverts back to the setting I had when I last used it.)

The last sign I'm going to share is related to the Subway Chapter. Recall that I was invited to share Heidi's story at a Remembrance Service. I had written my comments long before the event, but finished editing them only a few days before the service. When I printed out the pages, I was astounded at what I saw. One word and one word only did not appear. The word was "relapse." Heidi's leukemia relapse was crushing for her. She embraced the initial diagnosis, but the relapse was a different story. Our printer has never before and has never since failed to print only one word in the middle of a text. In fact, it only fails to print when there is no ink. A couple of days later (after the service) I printed another copy so I would have a clean, hard copy and the word "relapse" printed. It was a clear message to me that Heidi liked the Subway analogy, but I was NOT to use the word relapse when I spoke. I did not.

Open yourself to signs. Embrace the stories that others tell you. Whether you believe their experience was an authentic sign or not is unimportant. The meaning and purpose of signs is that our loved ones can still contact with us and are trying to share their continuing love. Hearing other people's stories is a gift for us because a sign for one is a sign for all who are grieving. Remember that you are not in control of the timing and nature of these signs. Some people may consider them to be self-induced, but those of us who have experienced "genuine" signs know that we did not create the experience. It is important to be open to the possibility of signs. If your mind is closed, you may miss the message.

XIV.

FEBRUARY 6, 2004.

Celebrating Her Life

What an evening of emotions! One year, almost to the day, after Heidi's death, Diane and I sponsored a dinner theater at our church. The dinner was a pot luck affair that family, friends, and neighbors attended. After the meal, I performed a monologue as one of my characters. For the past 25 years, I have been writing monologues from the point of view of differing characters and performing the pieces in a variety of settings: in my school courses, at our church, and at neighboring churches. The three characters that I have routinely represented are "old men" who are sharing reminiscences of their life: Raoul, from The Phantom of the Opera, Marius, from Les Miserables, and John Newton, the author of "Amazing Grace." On this evening I was introducing a new character: Sancho Panza from Man of La Mancha. The evening was dedicated to Heidi, and I could feel her presence as I shared my adventures with Don Quixote.

The road to this evening was a trail of grief, comfort, tears, laughter and was sprinkled with a creative spark that connected me to Heidi's spirit.

During Heidi's illness, she often sang the song "The Impossible Dream" from Man of La Mancha. Heidi's spirit is so wrapped up in the song's lyrics and in the very character of one who lived for how life ought to be, not how it is. She had adopted the rosebud as her symbol of hope and promise, and her attitude was always focused upon her dreams. She lived each day coping with the vicissitudes that leukemia created in her life. She went beyond just coping, however. She looked for the blessings in the day and did not fall prey to the trap of living ONLY for her dreams.

She relished the way – the life – the process that was entailed in pursuing any dream. For her, the ultimate dream was Broadway. She loved attending plays and musicals; our life at home was full of listening to music, attending theatrical shows, talking about the performance, and, for Heidi, reading *Playbill* religiously. My wife loves musicals and introduced all of our daughters to the genre when they were young. For Heidi, this love became a passion. One of her favorite musical theatre performers was Brian Stokes Mitchell. She saw him in both *Ragtime* and *Kiss Me Kate*. During Heidi's final months of life, he was starring in the reprise of *Man of LaMancha* on Broadway. Heidi so wanted to see him in that show. Not only did she admire his singing and acting ability, but she felt that he was someone special. Additionally, Heidi always saw herself as being quixotic. She was idealistic and would argue passionately about causes she believed were just and would criticize discrimination, injustice, and unethical behavior of any kind. Most of all, however, she never lost sight of her dreams – the impossible dream.

While Heidi was sick, Diane had the idea of writing to different people Heidi admired, hoping they would send pictures, letters, cards, etc. In fact Heidi did receive letters from Fred Rogers and Madeline L'Engle and a signed picture from Mandy Patinkin and James Earl Jones. After Heidi died, Diane and I decided to do many of the things Heidi wanted to do. At the top of our list was going to see Brian Stokes Mitchell in *Man of La Mancha.* Diane wrote to him and explained why we were going to see him and the date we had tickets. He wrote back, saying that he would be honored to meet with us after the show, and he would dedicate that evening to Heidi. We met with him after a very moving and emotionally packed performance for us. Walking down Broadway to the theater felt like a pilgrimage, bringing Heidi's spirit home to her Mecca. As we sat in the theater while the orchestra was warming up, I remember talking to Heidi and saying, "Well, Sweetie, we're here; hope you enjoy the show." I felt butterflies, as if I was going on stage and performing. As the curtain rose, the butterflies morphed into chills which quickly subsided as I was swept into the lives of the characters. Each song took me to a different emotional setting. Listening to "The Impossible Dream" shifted me into a realm of hope and sadness. "Of course, Heidi, your dreams can be fulfilled in a much different way. But, my little Buv, I miss you so much." At the end I felt spent and Diane's face was flush with the residue of crying. We made our way to the stage door and showed our letter to the burly man protecting the actors from unwanted visitors.

Mitchell was very gracious and talked to us for quite awhile. We laughed, gave him Heidi's picture and a copy of her advice for cancer, had our picture taken with him, and hugged him for Heidi. Because his performance inspired me so much, I decided to read Cervantes' novel, upon which the musical is based, and develop a character in Heidi's honor. Thus, I created Sancho Panza's character as an older man who taught himself how to read and write. His arthritis now hobbles him somewhat, but his spirit is intact. He uses music from the Broadway score to tell his tale of the adventures he had with Don Quixote. His story is sprinkled with the wisdom that he learned from his master and is dedicated to the belief that all of us can look at life as full of possibilities and wonder. He focuses on the transformation of his own view of "Dulcinea." In this area, I have used the theme of the musical more than the characters developed in Cervantes. Sancho first sees the girl as she views herself, but later learns to see her through Don Quixote's eyes. The underlying theme of love and the transformation it brings to relationships and life is central to this world of dreams and hopes. I took some poetic license and have Sancho refer to a girl in his village that he knows. This is how he introduces the singing of "The Impossible Dream":

> *In my life I knew a young woman. She had a terrible disease which eventually killed her. But throughout her struggle with her disease, she looked for the blessings in life. She sang about dreams and kept striving to achieve these dreams. She could not ignore the pain she experienced; she wasn't one to ignore the basic realities in her life. Yet regardless of the negatives and onslaughts that her cancer gave her, she kept her dreams alive. Those who knew her admired her; she became a hero to so many. She dared to dream when others would have felt self-pity. She was a living example of Don Quixote's quest: the impossible dream.*

Sancho ends his story by sharing the following before I play the "Finale":

> *We all will die. How we die is quite another matter. Was it not better for my master to die as Don Quixote? Was it not better that he return to his quest and continue to strive for his impossible dream? ... In the end, truth, goodness, and beauty were served. Don Quixote died and showed all of us that the impossible dream is a most cherished gift in life. Will you dare to honor this man of dreams as you return to your life's journey? Will you dare to seek the impossible dream along with all the fools who try to do so? Will you*

take your unbearable sorrow and dare to go where even the brave dare not go? How far will you go for a dream?

As I was in front of the audience that evening in our church, speaking Sancho's words, expressing his emotions, I felt Heidi standing next to me giving me encouragement – and pointers. Afterwards I went into the sacristy and broke down sobbing. The tears were cleansing. Her presence was real.

So You Have Cancer

At the conclusion of each semester I share Heidi's story with my students in each of my classes. I alter the story's narrative by assessing the chemistry of the class. In some cases I have gone into many details, others much less so. In every case I talk about the significance of Heidi's life to her family and how her friends slowly removed themselves from her life. My message is direct and clear: When (not if) a member of your family or a friend has to deal with a struggle, such as cancer, or experiences the death of a loved one, you will not have the perfect words to say; you may not have any idea what to do; and you may feel awkward, inadequate and/or helpless. It does not matter because the grief, loss, or struggle is "not about you." I tell the students to get over their own feelings and reach out to the other person. Their presence is what is important, not what they say nor even what they may do. At first I felt awkward about ending the semester in this fashion, but I have come to realize that it may be the most important lesson in the whole semester. Colleges rarely attend to such important issues as death or severe illness. Often when these topics are addressed, they are done so in a scholarly or academic way. My approach is personal, sometimes emotional. The responses that I have encountered each semester indicate how much need there is for this type of educational opportunity.

In addition to telling the students portions of Heidi's story and telling them some of the lessons we have learned from her life, I give them handouts. The handouts vary from class to class (again depending on the context and feel I have for the students in the group). The one constant element is that I hand out Heidi's advice. Usually I distill it into those items that deal with "how to live." Heidi's life is a testimony to how one ought to live whether or not that person is dealing with cancer, a disabling condition, or other tragedies in life. Her advice provides a wonderful insight into a positive way of living.

Her advice is being used in a variety of different ways. Not only do we distribute it with Heidi's Hats at Roswell, but the Institute has also posted it on their website. We have heard of one group of clergy who have used it for meditation and discussion. The college where I taught has sponsored annual retreats through Campus Ministry for those who are dealing with cancer in their lives (themselves or loved ones). At those retreats Heidi's advice was used as a contemplation/discussion piece. I attended the second retreat and one of the participants has been lobbying for a grief support group to begin at the college. We will continue to expand the distribution of her advice in a variety of ways.

Heidi's story is not about royalty or fame or the life of a nationally recognized personality. It is not a great drama with surprising plot twists. At the time of her death there was no national story or AP byline saying that she had died. The President did not declare a day of mourning. The world continued on its merry way with no cessation to its rhythms of life. The story I tell my students, however, is about my daughter. This book is my reflections and feelings about how one person affects and transforms another person's life. Heidi has given me meaning and has become my teacher. I hope you can learn from her life and strive to bring health, meaning, and balance to yourself and others. My hope and prayer is that you may come to feel as I have: there are blessings given to us each and every day; life is a beautiful gift imbued with power; and we can seize each day with a beauty and grandeur that will inspire others.

"So You Have Cancer"
By Heidi Schmditke
Heidi's advice for dealing with cancer/leukemia

So you have cancer. Here are some ways to combat the difficulties that you will invariably face.

As an Inpatient:

1. Walk! (It helps nausea and it gives you something to do!)
2. Question EVERYTHING that you don't understand.
3. Know ALL your meds and why you're taking them.
4. Smile! (You'll get a good reputation and you'll be surprised how much better you'll feel!)
5. Bring in food. (Hospital food may be better than airplane food, but yuck!)

6. Be nice to the nurses. (You spend the most time with them!)
7. Be nice to everybody else.
8. Do crossword puzzles.
9. Remember ... you will feel better.
10. Make good use of physical therapy.
11. Make good use of the psychologists.
12. Make good use of occupational therapy.
13. Make good use of pastoral care.
14. Make good use of the social workers.
15. Play Yahtzee.
16. Bring in your own pillow.
17. Accept the fact that you will be interrupted every time you try to sleep.
18. Your skin will get dry – Moisturize!
19. Bring your own toilet paper (much softer).
20. Bring your own tissues (ditto).
21. Decorate your room with comforting pictures.
22. Thank those that help you.
23. Remember —- you will get to go home.
24. Ask for sedation with painful procedures (i.e. bone marrow biopsy, line placement, intrathecal, etc.).
25. If it still hurts ... ask for more!
26. It's okay to be frightened and scared.
27. Surround yourself with those you love and those who love you.
28. Accept thoughts and prayers from anyone and any religion.
29. The doctors and nurses are there to help you.
30. Make a list of the things you want to do after the hospital: no matter how bizarre.
31. Get to know fellow patients – they know what you're going through.
32. Follow the rules and restrictions – they are there for a reason.
33. Laugh as often as you can. (Endorphins are great medicine!)
34. Get socks with treads, so you can walk without slipping.
35. Wear your own nightgown/pajamas – preferably newly bought.
36. Find out how many laps around the nurses' station is a mile and aim for that.

Surviving Chemotherapy (Outpatient)

37. Do as much independently as you can.
38. Ask for help if you need it. (It's okay to be a little dependent.)
39. Eat as much as you can.
40. You will be tired – nap when you need to.
41. Come to terms with losing your hair. You are still beautiful.
42. Get a wig, if that makes you more comfortable.
43. Make use of the hospitality room at the hospital.
44. For women: put on makeup, dress up and feel as pretty as you can. (When you look better, you feel better.)
45. Have a date with your significant other. (This does not mean you have to go out, but it's nice to feel loved.)
46. Show your appreciation for the things people do.
47. It's okay to need to cry.
48. The chemo/infusion lab is moving as efficiently as possible – try to be patient.
49. Take your meds.
50. Keep the nurse practitioner and the doctor informed with how you're really feeling.
51. Keep laughing.
52. The less you see a doctor, the fewer your problems generally are.
53. You will probably need blood or platelets. Appreciate the donors.
54. If you can afford it, buy a treadmill and a headphone.
55. If not, walk around the block, walk the stairs, walk someplace. Keep active.
56. Drink, drink, drink fluids.
57. Don't drink alcohol.
58. Don't smoke.
59. Have visitors that make you happy.
60. Do your mouth care.
61. It's okay to have a bad day.
62. Shots can hurt – Sorry!
63. Mouth sores can hurt – Sorry!
64. Hemorrhoids can hurt – Sorry!
65. Vomiting and diarrhea may occur. Remember, it will stop.
66. Play games ... have fun.
67. Tell those you love that you love them.
68. Take nausea medication – it helps.

69. Chemo is difficult – it ends.
70. You will feel better when your counts come back: I promise.
71. Take care of your line or port, if you have one.
72. It's okay to veg out and watch TV.
73. Know your blood counts.
74. You are stronger than you think.
75. Some friends will go, let them.
76. Some friends will stay, embrace them.

Surviving Radiation

77. Nap when you get tired.
78. When you feel badly, let someone know.
79. When you feel good, enjoy it.
80. Radiation is much easier than chemotherapy. Appreciate the change.
81. Be nice to the technicians. You're going to see them every day.
82. Become friendly with the patients in the waiting room. It will give you something to look forward to every day.
83. Go out to lunch.
84. Go see a movie.
85. Be careful around crowds. Avoid them when possible.
86. It's still okay to have a bad day.
87. Relax and pamper yourself.
88. Keep walking and exercising.
89. Read, if it makes you happy.
90. Write, if it makes you happy.
91. Sing, if it makes you happy.
92. Don't do these things, if they don't.
93. Anything can be fun: Find the fun in radiation.
94. Enjoy your weekend off.
95. Radiation will end.
96. If you have a mass or lump, enjoy watching it diminish in size.
97. Laughter is still the best medicine.
98. You are strong enough to do this.

Surviving setbacks:
#1 – Infections

99. Sometimes infections just happen, even if you do everything properly.
100. It's more difficult to fight infections when your body is suppressed.
101. Fight hard.
102. Wash your hands often.
103. Make those around you wash their hands.
104. Take the antibiotics.
105. Tell somebody at the first sign of infection.
106. It's okay to be sad.
107. Take your temperature.
108. Rest up and sleep.
109. You can make it through this.
110. This will not be fun.

#2 – The Cancer has come back

111. Have a party before you're readmitted. (One last hurrah before you go through it all again.)
112. This time will be much harder.
113. It's really okay to cry this time.
114. This will be tough on your loved ones.
115. You are stronger than you think. You can do this.
116. Once you've cried, it's time to smile.
117. It is no one's fault that the cancer came back.
118. The doctors and nurses really do care.
119. Trust in the things you've learned and the things you know.
120. Prayers really can help.
121. Make sure to keep walking.
122. Make sure to keep eating.
123. Make sure to keep laughing.
124. Do what you need to survive.
125. It's okay to scream.
126. You can learn a lot, if you want to.
127. Tell people how much you appreciate them. (They in turn may reciprocate.)
128. You <u>know</u> how to fight this, so do it.
129. Tests are always scary. (They sometimes **do** have positive results!)

130. This is a very frightening time.
131. Rent your favorite movie.
132. Have your favorite meal.
133. Go back to your childhood. (Stuffed animals and children's books or comic books can be a great comfort.)
134. It's okay for other people to cry.
135. It's okay for you not to want them to cry in front of you.
136. Find a hobby. (Days will seem longer the second time around.)
137. There are always people who care.
138. You can be a hero.

Some last minute thoughts.

139. If you decide to just go bald, wear a hat in winter. (You lose the most heat from your head!)
140. If you decide to just go bald, people at the hospital and loved ones will compliment you.
141. If you decide to just go bald, you may get strange looks from other people.
142. Let it go. Being bald can be original!
143. You're still alive – that's a blessing.
144. No one can ever take away your experiences.
145. Your life will be forever changed from your struggle.
146. Make your life better than it was before.
147. Take the lessons you've learned and teach someone else.
148. Keep smiling and laughing!!!
149. Congratulations on being a strong person.

Recovery and going through GVHD

150. Your liver enzymes may go up.
151. A rash can cover your body.
152. Rashes itch!
153. The doctors may be very happy that you feel like crap.
154. Initially, it's a good thing.
155. If you have tears, appreciate a good cry – it's cleansing.
156. If you don't, I'm sorry.
157. Steroids suck.
158. Try to keep smiling.
159. You may get poufy.
160. You may get weak.

161. If you can, go back to work.
162. Maybe just part time.
163. Take time for yourself.
164. Your joints may suffer.
165. Take all your meds.
166. The hospital staff really does want to help.
167. Being poked is no fun.
168. You are getting better.
169. Find people who will support you through good and bad.
170. You will have both.
171. Pay attention to the good stuff.
172. Find a hobby.
173. If you love it, do it.
174. If you don't, find a new hobby.
175. Some suggestions: writing, painting, drawing, cooking, knitting, cross-stitching, wood-working, reading, scrap-booking, follow sports you love, shopping.
176. Exercise the best you can.
177. Take help when you need it.
178. You will probably need it.
179. Take a day to be miserable.
180. Then snap out of it.
181. Eat the foods you love.
182. If you can't eat the foods you love, find new foods.
183. Life is different now.
184. Adapt.
185. It won't be easy.
186. But it may be better.
187. Try and give back a bit to those who were there for you.
188. The doctors are not trying to torture you.
189. You always have the right to question!
190. Relearn why you're on what med.
191. Drink a lot before blood draws.
192. Moisturize.
193. Do something that you always wanted to do, but never got around to.
194. It's hard to still be dependent.
195. It's very hard if you can't drive.
196. Eyes are wonderful things – enjoy being able to see.
197. If you can't see, enjoy music.
198. Life is truly beautiful.
199. Travel, if you can.

200. It's still okay to feel yucky.
201. It's still okay to be tired.
202. Catnaps are a good thing.
203. Being poufy can be embarrassing.
204. Try to get over it.
205. Listen to a child's laughter.
206. Listen to your favorite music, often. (It will heal your soul.)
207. Your skin may get taut.
208. Your eyes may burn.
209. Your mouth may get dry.
210. Your mouth may get sores.
211. It'll heal.
212. Don't just read self-help books.
213. Self-help.
214. This may be the hardest time.
215. But maybe not.
216. Do not forget all that you have been through.
217. Don't dwell, either.
218. Play lots of games.
219. Keep active.
220. Thank people more.
221. Thank your God more.
222. Thank yourself more.
223. Your joints may swell.
224. Your muscles may cramp.
225. You'll pull through.
226. Smile.

On Death

It's okay if you can't read this section right now. You are going through these treatments to live. The focus of all of this is life, not death. It is important to deal with these fears in your own time and in your own way.

227. Everyone dies.
228. You may die from cancer.
229. You could also get run over by a bus.
230. The important thing is that you are living now.
231. Sometimes friends die.
232. You are still alive.
233. Your friend is still with you.

234. He wants you to live.
235. Keep fighting.
236. Cry, then find your smile.
237. It's a good idea to take care of the legal stuff (health care proxy, will, advanced directive, etc.).
238. It's not fair to leave that to loved ones.
239. It's okay to be scared.
240. Life goes on, though.
241. Keep living.

CPSIA information can be obtained at www.ICGtesting.com
Printed in the USA
BVOW081418120113

310463BV00011B/209/P

9 781457 516221